Please renew/return items by last date shown

So that your telephone call is charged at local rate,
please call the numbers as set out below:

	From Area codes 01923 or 020:	From the rest of Hertfordshire:
Renewals:	01923 471373	01438 737373
Enquiries:	01923 471333	01438 737333
Textphone:	01923 471599	01438 737599

L32   www.hertsdirect.org/librarycatalogue

DARKNESS SHALL COVER ME

DARKNESS SHALL COVER ME

Night Bombing over the Western Front 1918

Humphrey Wynn

Airlife
England

Dedicated to the gallant memory of all those who
flew on the Western Front in the First World War,
and especially to that of my dear friend Leslie
Reed Blacking and those who served with him on
No 207 Squadron at Ligescourt in 1918.

Title page illustration: The badge of No 207 Squadron — 'the first British
squadron used solely for long-range night bombing and the first to operate
Handley Page bombers' (*Bomber Squadrons of the RAF and their Aircraft*,
Philip Moyes, Macdonald, 1964) — whose Western Front operations are
described in this book. The black winged lion is the heraldic version of the
felt black cat badge worn on their helmets by the Handley Page 0/400
aircrew flying nightly from Ligescourt in the summer and autumn months
of 1918.

Copyright © Humphrey Wynn, 1989

British Library Cataloguing in Publication Data

Wynn, Humphrey
Darkness shall cover me
1.   World War 1. Air operations by Great Britain.
Royal Air Force. — Biographies
I.   Title
940.4'4941'0924

ISBN 1 85310 065 X

First published in 1989
by Airlife Publishing Ltd.

Airlife Publishing Ltd.

101 Longden Road, Shrewsbury SY3 9EB, England.

Contents

If I say, Peradventure the darkness shall cover me:
then shall my night be turned to day

Psalm 139 verse 10

Acknowledgements

My thanks are due to the following, who in the course of the writing of this book have helped with information or assistance of various kinds: J M Bruce, the authority on British First World War aircraft and formerly deputy head of the RAF Museum (where Leslie Blacking's flying helmet and jacket now reside), for information on the Handley Page 0/400; Mrs Sheila Walton of the Department of Photographs at the University of Keele, for producing a photograph of Ligescourt airfield, which became a V-1 launching site in the Second World War; the staff of the Ministry of Defence library in Adastral House for their endless patience in looking up reference material to answer my queries; and staff of the RAF Museum for information on First World War flying clothing. Finally I salute the professional skill and determination of Mrs Moreen Knight for so ably deciphering and typing my manuscript.

Introduction

Not often does a friendship span the generations in the way that mine did with Leslie Blacking. I first met him at RAF Clyffe Pypard, Wiltshire, in September 1953. We were both serving in the RAFVR, the difference in our ages notwithstanding: he had been in the RFC/RAF in the First World War, flying heavy bombers; I had served with the RAF, also as a pilot, in the Second World War. Although he was attached to Movements at Lyneham for his annual reserve training, and I went off on a flying trip to Kenya, we struck up a friendship which was resumed when we met again and which lasted until his death in 1981. During those years we met many times and corresponded frequently: he was an excellent talker, with a fund of stories in the Somerset Maugham vein about his banking days in the Far East during the inter-war years and his experiences as a bank manager in New York during the Second World War. He was also a very good letter-writer, with absolute clarity of expression and a very articulate memory, particularly of his service with No 207 Squadron on Handley Page 0/400 operations at Ligescourt in 1918.

Gradually I formed the idea of writing a book about his RAF experiences, and this book is the result. Leslie read much of it before he died; unfortunately it was not possible to finish it in time for him to see it all, but so strong was our rapport that I have often felt his presence at my elbow and I wrote — could even hear his voice — and had his marvellous letters and notes to guide me.

Although the form of the book is that of a novel, with speaking characters, the facts on which it is based are those which Leslie Blacking gave me: the descriptions of squadron life, and his operations, are derived entirely from his information. As the central character he is the only one to be given his real name; the others all have fictitious ones, although the squadron was a real one. I have used the novel form — as has often been done before — to recreate the atmosphere of a bomber squadron on the Western Front, with all its attendant perils, apprehensions, friendships and acts of heroism.

All his life, Leslie Blacking had the spirit which characterized the airmen of the First World War: he was always keen to 'get up and go' — even at the age of eighty he realized a lifelong ambition when he hitch-hiked to Dawson City in the Yukon. He attended our annual

RAF reunion dinners — there was nothing he enjoyed more — and when I visited him in hospital in Alderney in his last days and took his wife Monica out for lunch he asked eagerly, 'Can't I come with you?' — the spirit was always willing. At his funeral service in St Anne's parish church I quoted from Chapter 40 of Isaiah:

They shall mount up with wings as eagles; they shall run, and not be weary, and they shall walk, and not faint.

Leslie always wanted to run, and to his undaunted spirit I dedicate the following pages, about his days as a nineteen-year-old pilot in the RAF. 'Please don't make a hero of me,' he once wrote. 'I was just a young fellow doing his best to perform what he was ordered to do. The lives of two others, neither of whom could fly a plane, were in my hands, in addition to a ton of bombs. With no parachutes, although scared stiff, one had to keep calm.'

Humphrey Wynn
May, 1989

1
The Squadron

The sunlight woke me, striking in through the open flap of the brown bell tent. I wondered where I was. Yesterday (or was it the day before?) I'd been in England. I remembered getting on the train at Victoria and meeting an old friend with whom I'd served in the London Rifle Brigade; now an observer on a DH4 squadron, he was returning from leave. We'd crossed from Folkestone together, and in Boulogne his pals were waiting for him; I'd been invited to join their reunion at the Officers' Club, but we'd barely finished dinner when there was an air raid and we had to take shelter in the cellar. Around midnight they'd taken me to the railway station and poured me into the train for — where was it? — Hesdin, in the Pas de Calais. When I got out there was a Crossley tender waiting, and in the early darkness of a summer morning we bumped along to our destination. On the way the driver said something about 'the big bombers — only operate by night,' and when we slowed down to pass a sentry and before turning left into a tented area, I'd remembered seeing the shapes of what looked like hangars along the tree-lined road.

As the sun lit up the inside of the tent, I took in my surroundings. There were two greatcoats and a flying suit hanging from hooks on the tent pole, which descended into a boarded floor that was about three feet below ground level, while all around the inside of the tent the ground formed a shelf on which various odd objects had been deposited. These belonged to the only other occupant, the top of whose brown-haired head was the sole part of his anatomy visible on his camp bed, though his snoring was audible enough. Outside, everything was still, and I closed my eyes again and reflected. Only last week I'd been sent on convalescent leave from Stonehenge, where I'd trained as a night bomber pilot. Then came a telegram: 'Report to Air Ministry immediately for service overseas,' and here I was in France.

The recollection of 'big bombers — by night' brought me back to consciousness with a jerk. This must be Ligescourt airfield, if the tender had brought me to the right place; I'd dropped down into the tent by the light of a torch, and fumbled my way into bed. If so, this was the home of No 207 Squadron with its Handley Page 0/400s, the type I'd flown at Stonehenge with an instructor in the seat beside me. At the realization that I'd only done ten hours' flying on Handleys I shut my eyes again quickly, as if to hide myself from reality a little longer, and I must have dozed off. The next thing I knew I was being shaken by the shoulder, and a voice saying, 'Tea, sir — seven-fifteen.'

I turned on to my elbow with a 'thank you' to the batman and took the cup; as I did so a voice said, 'You must be Blacking — we've been expecting you.' It came from the other camp bed, whose occupant was now more visible — a dark-haired, cheerful-faced fellow of about twenty-four. 'I'm George Harrison,' he said. 'We're to fly together, I think.' I mumbled, 'How do you do,' and gulped my tea to hide my embarrassment. Was this what I'd volunteered for? Still, there seemed to be a reasonable degree of comfort. But what about the big bombers; how was I going to cope with them at night?

George took me over to the large marquee which was the Officers' Mess, where we had a bacon-and-egg breakfast, sitting on benches at trestle tables. There didn't seem to be many people about, and nobody appeared to be in any hurry. On a night-bomber squadron, things started to happen in the afternoon, I supposed. My new acquaintance told me he'd been in the infantry before becoming an observer. He was twenty-four, and I noticed he was wearing a couple of wound stripes. As we drank our tea he said, 'I think I'd better take you to the Adjutant, so you can book in, then perhaps you'd like to look at the aircraft. How many hours did you say you'd done on them?' I hadn't, but I said it now, very quietly, 'Ten.' He appeared not to hear, or was too polite to evince any reaction apart from a well-controlled wince, at the idea of such a novice flying him over enemy territory.

The Adjutant, an older man and clearly a non-flyer, was polite but indifferent. He seemed unimpressed at this brand-new addition to the squadron's operational strength. Harrison and I left him to his

paperwork and wandered past the tents towards the road, which had
been closed off by a gate, where a sentry was posted. I could see the
backs of the hangars on the other side. 'Where does the road lead to?'
I asked. I wanted to try to get my bearings. 'Well, that way,' said
Harrison, pointing to the left, 'goes to Ligescourt and the other way to
Creçy. There's an evocative name for you. Remember when the
English were over here before?' I fumbled in my memory, though I
wasn't feeling very bright after yesterday's long journey; indeed, I was
rather disorientated and apprehensive in my new surroundings. Was
it Henry V's campaign? No, that was Agincourt. Perhaps the Black
Prince. Anyway, it must have been around the thirteenth or fourteenth
centuries. I just nodded, indicating that I knew the answer to his
question.

As we crossed the road, the weapons of our war came into view —
I'd never seen so many of the Handley Page heavy bombers before. At
Stonehenge there were only four, and two of those were the earlier less
powerful 0/100s. Here was a line of ten 0/400s, the biggest aircraft on
the Allied side, nearly sixty-three feet long with a hundred-foot upper
wing span twenty-two feet above the ground, painted olive-green but
looking as black as the night in which they flew. Down the line, various
maintenance jobs were going on, following the previous night's operations. I noticed under one aircraft a tray of oil in which pieces of the
gun from the front cockpit were lying; another had one propeller off.
Pieces of fabric were being repaired and bracing wires tightened; one
tail was jacked-up for adjustment to the skid. Several of the 0/400s had
their outer wings folded back, for easier access to the engine — some
had Rolls-Royces of 375 hp, others the considerably less powerful 275
hp Sunbeams.

'Let's find one where they're not doing anything,' said Harrison.
'You wouldn't normally see a full line-up like this until just before the
night's raid,' he added. 'It's just happened they're still where they are
when they came back last night.' Down the line we spotted an 0/400
which no-one was working on and from which nothing had been
removed. 'After you,' said Harrison, and I climbed up the ladder into
the front, then crawled through the tunnel into the cockpit. It didn't
seem much different from those of the aircraft in which we flew at
Stonehenge. The same two seats, for the pilot on the right and the
observer on the left, the wheel on top of the control column for the
pilot, the rudder pedals in front of it and the compass down on the
floor to the right.

I eased myself into the seat and pulled back on the control column. It felt very heavy and flapped forward like a dead weight when I let it go. Beyond it was the familiar instrument panel — a simple array with another compass, an airspeed indicator, a bubble turn-and-bank indicator, an altimeter and a clock. On the right were the throttle levers with their mushroom-shaped tops, which you twisted to control either engine, then pushed forward together when they were synchronized. I rested my right elbow on the padded cockpit coaming, pushed my back into the seat and glanced ahead through the clear Pyralin windshield. Immediately ahead was the front gunner's cockpit with its rotatable Scarff ring on which the twin 0.303 inch Lewis guns were mounted, and now pointed skywards. Following the line of their barrels, I looked across the airfield, which didn't seem very large for such a big, heavy aeroplane. But at the far edge of it the ground seemed to fall away — which could be an advantage on occasion, as I was to discover.

'Satisfied?' Harrison's voice came up from down below, and I looked over the side to see his upturned face. 'I think they want to work on this one now,' he added. I climbed down, somewhat pensive. It had been one thing flying Handleys in training, just taking off and landing (though that could be ordeal enough for a run-of-the-mill pilot like me) and making mock attacks on Eastleigh, Southampton or Weymouth. But this was to be the real thing, taking off with a war load of bombs and bullets and fuel, battling along against the weather and the cold, the searchlights, ack-ack and Hun fighters.

'You'd better come and meet the CO,' Harrison said as we walked back along the line of bombers, interrupting my dark thoughts. 'Though I should warn you — he may not be the type of chap you expect.'

'Why?' I queried.

'Well,' answered Harrison, 'what you probably had in mind as the CO of the 0/400 squadron you are joining is a warrior-leader, an ace pilot who's there by reason of his success. But that doesn't happen with our kind of unit, which is still pretty new, so there aren't the aces about. What's wanted is more an administrator, used to handling large numbers of men — we've three crew per aircraft and have more groundcrew than the scout squadrons. You'll find that the CO exercises leadership on the ground, but the leaders in the air are the two flight commanders.'

We'd got to the end of the 0/400s by now and turned left to cross the road into the headquarters area, where there seemed to be considerably more activity than there had been half-an-hour ago. There were a few wooden huts and some Nissen huts. Harrison took me to one of the former and knocked on a door marked 'Adjutant'. A voice inside bellowed, 'Come in!'

'Hello, George,' it added in more friendly fashion when Harrison entered with me at his tail. 'Ah, is this the new pilot we've been expecting?'

'Second Lieutenant Blacking, Charles,' said Harrison. 'We've just been to look over the aircraft and I thought he ought to see the CO.'

'Excellent idea,' said the Adjutant, standing up and extending a hand in my direction. 'How d'you do, Blacking. How much experience have you got?' As the Adjutant wasn't a flying man, I could see that what he really wanted was some information he could pass on to the CO, so I replied confidently:

'Only ten hours on H-Ps, sir, but I've done quite a lot on Fees. I told the RTO that but he said there was a shortage of multi-engined pilots.'

'We're short here,' said the Adjutant. 'Either they're all going to the Independent Force squadrons, around Nancy, because those have the priority, or the training units are too busy turning out scout pilots to replace the losses. I'll tell the CO you're here.'

When I was ushered in and saluted smartly, the first thing I noticed was a pair of cavalry boots under the table the CO used as a desk. They were highly polished and somehow seemed out of keeping with their surroundings — as did the CO, for although he wore RFC wings, he had no medal ribbons nor wound stripes, thus looking rather non-operational. But he greeted me in a kindly manner, in rather clipped tones which sorted with his well-trimmed moustache.

'Welcome to No 207, Blacking. I suppose you know what we do?'

I started to say something about strategic bombing when he interrupted sharply.

'Yes, that's true. But we're not part of Independent Force, you know. We're on our own here — a GHQ squadron; we get our orders from them via the Wing at Monteuil, and we work in co-operation with a day bomber squadron, 208. Who's Blacking down to fly with, Adj?'

'Harrison, sir.'

'Well, you've got a good man there, Blacking — a bit older than the other aircrew and a very reliable character. I think you'd better sit in on the briefing tonight, then watch the aircraft go off, and tomorrow you can fly on the raid as a gunner, to get your first experience of going over the lines. By the way, you'll be in 'B' Flight. Good luck.'

The interview was over. The CO was already looking down at his papers again. I saluted and walked out.

'How did it go?' said Harrison cheerfully.

'Well, he wished me luck,' I replied, 'and said I was flying with you.'

'The other way round,' corrected Harrison. 'The captain of the aircraft is always in charge, whatever his rank.'

Ignoring this, as I felt a bit self-conscious at being a Second Lieutenant, I responded quickly, 'The CO says I'm to sit in on tonight's briefing, then watch the take-off, and tomorrow night fly as a gunner.'

'Well, that's fairly normal,' said Harrison. 'I hope you pick a good trip for your first one over the lines. It's quite an experience.'

These words went through my mind as we walked towards the Mess tent. Just what would it be like?

'Which flight did the CO say you were in?' asked Harrison.

As before, his question brought me back to earth. 'B Flight,' I replied, glad to have something mundane on which to concentrate my mind.

'Good,' said Harrison as we ducked under the entrance to the Mess tent and made our way to the bar. 'I'll introduce you to some of them. Semple!' He called out to a youngish-looking pilot with tousled hair. 'Come and meet Blacking who's just joined us. Texas!' This to a real character who was leaning up against a tent pole. 'Come and meet . . .'

Three or four of my new colleagues came up. I noticed they were only drinking lemonade or ginger beer.

'Where did you train, Blacking?' asked Semple, who I noticed had an intense look, his eyes staring very directly when he put the question.

There was quite a haze of tobacco smoke, for cigarettes were cheap and the aircrew had no inhibitions about them as they had about drinking. I peered through it and replied, 'At Stonehenge — mainly on Fees.' I thought I'd better be honest about that.

He's got ten hours on Handleys,' chipped in Harrison, helping to make a case for the new recruit to the squadron.

A cynical cheer went up from the little group. 'Just what we need — experience,' said Texas sardonically.

'Be fair, you chaps,' came a new voice from behind me. 'You all had to start some time. How d'you do, Blacking. I'm "B" Flight's commander.'

The speaker was a tall Captain, quietly-spoken, aged, I thought, about twenty-four. I shook his outstretched hand and felt encouraged at having met him.

'Come and get some grub while it's going,' chipped in Harrison, 'then we can take a walk over the airfield.'

By this time I was hungry and the food, though plain, was good. As we sipped our coffee Harrison said, 'I thought it might be a good idea for you to see what lies beyond the boundary — where the River Authie is — then when we come back you can watch the bombing-up and sit in on the briefing. It's as well for you to have a clear idea of what goes on on the ground before you get in the air.'

As we crossed the road and started to walk down the northern edge of the airfield, which seemed to have a slight slope to it, Harrison said, 'That's the control tower,' pointing over towards a small sandbagged structure to the right. 'You get your take-off signal from there, in Morse Code,' he added.

Suddenly we heard an engine sound approaching. It seemed to be well up, heading for the airfield — probably a Hun, on a reconnaissance, or perhaps a quick strafing attack. We dived for the boundary and got under the nearest screen of bushes and undergrowth. At that moment the engine cut out and the aircraft, which we could now see against the bright summer sky, went into a vertical dive, the scream of wires bracing getting higher and higher as he rushed earthwards.

'He'll never pull out,' cried Harrison. 'Either he'll kill himself or some of us as well. It's a Spad,' he added, as the diving machine got nearer. But at that moment, perfectly judged, the French pilot pulled out of his dive just over our heads, went into a steep left-hand turn round the camp area, his bracing wires still screaming as the speed fell off and the machine took the strain of the turn, and landed — on the road, coming to a perfectly judged stop behind the 0/400s, so we couldn't see who got out.

'What a cheek!' said Harrison. 'I presume he knows the CO — or has some jolly good excuse.'

We continued down to the river, whose banks were broad and sloping at that point, forming a wide valley. 'Very useful,' commented Harrison. 'Probably why they chose this field for 0/400s. It enables you to get up speed a bit after take-off before climbing. Particularly helpful when there isn't much wind.'

I looked back towards the line of 0/400s, being serviced after last night's operation. The field looked quite large from the bottom end, but no doubt much smaller when one was rolling down it towards the river with a load of bombs on board. I should soon see . . . Just then there was the sound of an engine starting up, and a single-seater machine taxied out in a determined fashion for take-off. 'That's the squadron's BE12,' observed Harrison. 'We'll know by the take-off who's flying it. It if behaves erratically the CO is probably flying — he likes to test the air before an operation.'

The BE12 seemed to have some difficulty in keeping straight. Then, with a sudden burst of throttle it gathered speed across the field — towards us.

'Look out!' Harrison yelled. 'Duck!'

We flung ourselves down on the grass, just as the elderly biplane roared overhead, airborne at last.

'Silly blighter,' observed Harrison. 'He must have seen us and done that deliberately. I'll bet it was the CO. Let's go up to the other end and then we can watch the bombing-up and see him land from the only safe vantage point — behind him.'

Most of the 0/400s, when we got near them, seemed to have bomb trolleys near or underneath them. 'That's a usual bomb-load,' remarked the ever-informative Harrison. 'Those are 112-pounders — sixteen of them. The gunlayer — by the way, old boy, remember that 207 is a Naval squadron and a lot of nautical terminology survives; forget about this brand-new Royal Air Force while you're here — the gunlayer also has about a dozen twenty-pound Cooper bombs on a shelf in front of him, for dropping on searchlights. As an alternative to the sixteen bombs, I hear we may at some point carry a really big one — 1,650 lb — on special missions. The old machine'll go up like a lift when that drops.'

'I see,' I said faintly. I began to feel like what I was — a nineteen-year-old, a million miles from the exuberance of flying training back in peaceful England.

Suddenly there was a whoosh over our heads, as the returning BE12 just cleared the line of 0/400s. From our rear view we could see it diving for the ground, until at the last moment the pilot appeared to rein it in like a horse. (If this was indeed the CO, perhaps that explained the cavalry boots.) The nose reared up, the tail came down and — as the machine lost speed — hit the ground with a thump.

'I'll bet he's broken his tail-skid again,' observed Harrison, as if used to the performance. 'You'd better collect him, lads!'

While some of the AMs bumped out towards the unfortunate BE12 in a Crossley tender, Harrison and I walked back along the line of 0/400s which were being bombed-up and generally got ready for the night's operation.

'Hello, Tex,' he said suddenly.

There was the character I had met in the Mess tent.

Texas nodded to me, then shouted up at the front cockpit, 'Harold!'

A face emerged, rather red as a result of bending down, and its voice said, 'Hello, Tex. Be with you. Just checking the bombsight.'

'This is Blacking — just joined us,' said Texas as Lt Harvey climbed down the ladder.

We shook hands and Harvey said, looking at Harrison with a twinkle in his eye, 'You know, you just couldn't do without us, you pilots. All you have to do is to get the old crate off the ground and back on to it. When it comes to finding the target and getting you back here again . . .'

Just as that moment a despatch rider on his motorcycle roared along the road behind us, then turned left with a screech of tyres towards squadron HQ. 'That must be our orders for tonight,' said Harrison. 'Blacking's going to sit in on the briefing, to get an idea of what we do. Are you on tonight, Tex?'

'I think every crew is,' answered Tex. 'The pressure's beginning to mount, with the Hun going on the offensive. We've got to do all we can to slow them down and bring them to a halt. You've come at a crucial time, Blacking, so the sooner you and Harrison can get yourself operational, the better.'

'Steady on,' said Harvey, 'the poor chap's hardly unpacked his bag yet. But he's got a good mentor in Harrison.'

'You haven't flown at all out here, have you?' said Tex as we walked along towards squadron HQ. 'You really ought to get a bit of practice in getting in and out of this field, and take a look at the area in daylight. I'd suggest that to the CO — he's quite reasonable. And I think your crew would appreciate it — eh, Harrison?'

Privately, I'd been thinking that I didn't want my first take-off in France in an 0/400 to be by night, from a strange field, with a full crew and a load of bombs and ammunition on board.

'Is that the usual procedure for new pilots — to get in a bit of daylight familiarization?' I asked.

'Well, there isn't any set pattern,' said Tex. 'I forget what happened when the last new pilot arrived. But have a word with the CO after briefing.'

By now we'd got to the hut, which was already almost full, with about thirty aircrew waiting to be briefed — most of them smoking, some with RNAS uniforms, others wearing RFC insignia and a few with the new RAF badges. There was a pretty animated buzz of conversation as we squeezed ourselves on to a bench at the back, and the front of the hut was barely visible through the blue haze and crowd of heads. As I strained to get a glimpse forward, a figure stood up and the chatting suddenly died down. ' "B" Flight's commander — Captain Brinden,' I heard the ever-helpful Harrison say *sotto-voce* in my left ear. I saw a good-looking fellow, a pilot, with an air of authority.

'Gentlemen,' he said, 'the CO will introduce tonight's briefing.' Major Folliott didn't waste any words; with a precise manner, and in those rather clipped tones I had already heard, he began, in a quiet, almost confidential way.

'Gentlemen,' he said, 'the Hun is beginning a major offensive.'

There was a sudden stir and a few whistles, but I got the impression, from what Tex had just said, that most of the crews knew this already. 'GHQ told me this this afternoon,' the CO went on in his deliberate manner. 'There's a big build-up of supplies, and our Intelligence people have got good information about plans for a big push in a last effort to throw our Armies back. It's going to be hell for the boys on the ground, so it's our job to do all we can to help them, by getting into the air every night and pounding the hell out of the Huns' supply lines and communications, while the DH4 squadrons keep up the offensive by day. Tonight the target is the railway station at Valenciennes, where a lot of Hun equipment is piling up. We've got to do all we can to destroy it, because the Army has been told there's no retreat this time, so we've got to take the weight off them. It may even be, if things start getting worse, that we shall have to do two sorties in a night — so long as there is sufficient darkness. Tonight it's all ten aircraft, with the normal bomb-load of sixteen 112-pounders; a maximum effort to create as much confusion as we can behind enemy lines. Captain Brinden will now give you a detailed description of the target, before you start working out courses. Good luck.'

He uncovered a blackboard behind him; on it was a chalk sketch of the lines, sidings and warehouses, showing in which direction they ran, and with an arrow indicating a line of approach.

'We shall come in from the east,' he said, 'and if you can identify your target, drop your eggs on the run-in then turn away to the southwest and head back for our lines. If you miss it on the first run, turn away to the north and come round again for another go. The first man over the target after me should see the flares I drop. All being well we'll bomb in the order in which we take off, so don't straggle or get lost. Any questions?'

'What's the wind, sir?' said a voice on the other side of the room.

'When the balloon check was done it was about 240°/15,' Brinden answered. 'That means you'll get there pretty quickly, but it'll take a long time coming back.'

'Take-off codes?' asked Tex, sitting next to me.

'Lieutenant Harvey has them,' responded Brinden. 'Collect after this briefing. Observers, check that you have your list of lighthouse bearings.'

'What are they?' I asked Harrison in a whisper.

'Letters flashed by lighthouses across France,' explained Harrison. 'We navigate by them. I'll show you the list.'

'Any more questions, gentlemen?' Brinden's voice cut authoritatively above the rising hubbub of conversation. There was a momentary silence. 'If not, that concludes the briefing. Good luck tonight.'

There was a scraping of boots and benches on the rough floor as everyone rose, standing while the CO and his flight commanders left the hut. 'We might as well go to the Mess,' said Harrison. 'Everyone will be busy from now on working out their courses, kitting themselves up, having a meal and then out ot the aircraft for final checks.'

I followed him through the door and out into the beautiful evening, feeling rather disembodied — as if I were half there, on this airfield in France, and half not.

'It all must seem a bit strange to you,' Harrison commented, as if reading my thoughts. 'Squadron life takes a bit of getting used to, but when once you get into it, there's nothing like it.'

The Mess tent was deserted except for the barman, a fresh-faced young corporal.

'Yes sir?' he asked Harrison, responding to a familiar face.

'Make it two beers, corporal, as we're not flying tonight — unless you want something stronger, Blacking?'

'No,' I said. 'Cheerio, Harrison. Here's to our professional association.'

He raised his glass, drank, and looked hard at me.

'What made you come into this flying game? Surely you'd have been better off in your regiment — what was it, London Rifle Brigade?'

'Well,' I said, 'when I was offered a commission I was asked whether I wanted to fly. My answer was "yes" — and here I am.'

'But what happened in between?' persisted Harrison, in his quiet but determined way.

I took another pull at my beer before answering.

'The Air Ministry sent me for medical examination, which somehow I managed to pass, though it was pretty stiff, especially that thing they strap you in and then roll and spin and loop it at an alarming speed. Once I got through that, it was No 2 RFC Cadet School at Hastings where all the trained men went.'

'You mean, those who'd already got some war service in?'

'Yes,' I said. 'New recruits went to No 1 Cadet School, which was at Farnborough. It was because of Bloody April, last year — you remember? — which proved the need to gain air supremacy on the Western Front, that an expansion of the RFC was decided on — which was how I and many others got the chance to get into flying.'

'Have another beer,' said Harrison. 'Corporal! But what did you do at Hastings? Surely not drill and PT all over again?'

'Exactly that — for everybody, and we were a mixed lot — British, Canadian, South African, New Zealander — even a few Foreign Legionnaires, Britishers released by the French Army. Under Regular Army WOs and Sergeants, discipline was extremely strict, and we were at it from dawn till 9 pm. With square-bashing, route marches, PT and lectures.

'One RSM with a florid round face and waxed moustache was an absolute bastard and made our lives hell. The course lasted six weeks, during which time we were billeted in empty hotels and boarding-houses, stripped of all carpets and comforts, and the night before we left some of us collected twenty empty dustbins and blocked up the old RSM's door with them. By the time he got out we were on our way to Denham.'

'That was where your flying started?' put in Harrison.

'No, that was ground training,' I explained. 'Lectures on the theory of flight, navigation, map-reading, gunnery, techniques for attack and defence — everything you could possibly learn about flying without actually getting into the air.'

'I'll bet that was about as tough in its way as Hastings had been,' observed Harrison quietly.

'Well, Denham was a pretty deadly place,' I said. 'Uxbrige was all right, but it was swarming with Red Caps; however, we took chances at the weekends. Once away from the camp, second lieutenant pips replaced the white shoulder bands we used to wear and we made for Uxbridge, booze and beauty. On one occasion four of us became aware that we were being shadowed by an RFC captain, so we hopped on a bus, and to our dismay he got on too and produced a notebook and pencil. "Are you Denham cadets?" he asked officiously, and as our faces fell at being caught out of bounds he roared with laughter and said "So am I".'

By this time the Mess dining room — that part of the tent laid out with trestle tables and benches — was starting to fill up with pilots and navigators coming in for their pre-flight meal, which seemed to be mainly bacon and eggs, with tea and bread and butter.

'We'll go out and watch the take-offs when they're ready to go,' said Harrison. 'Tell me about your flying, after you left Denham.'

'Well, after a week's leave I went to Ternhill, where I was attached to No 132 Squadron, a training squadron, later re-numbered 13 TDS — training depot squadron. By the way, when Denham had taught us all we could learn on the ground, we were allowed to decide which kind of flying we favoured. I chose bombers.'

'Why did you?' asked Harrison. 'Surely fighters would have been much more exciting?'

'I think bombers offered a bit more of a challenge. Everybody wanted to go on fighters, and often they lasted only a few days when they got to a squadron at the Front.

'Anyway, when we got to Ternhill we were divided into two Flights. One was on pusher-type aircraft, the 'Rumpety', as we called the Maurice Farman Shorthorn, the other on tractor-type, the DH6 or 'Clutching Hand'. I was put into the Rumpety flight and my instructor was Captain Smith, MC, a Scots red-head with a temper and a vocabulary to match. He had variegated ribbons on his helmet, showing that he had been a flight commander in France, and boy, could he fly!

'We did about two-and-a-half hours dual, then one evening he took me up for landings and take-offs. After the fifth circuit he climbed out and said, "Off you go!" and walked away. I took off and landed safely, but damaged the undercarriage, which had a skid on it in a Rumpety, when taxying in. However, that didn't impede my progress, and after thirty hours and two crashes I began night flying.'

'Wait a minute,' said Harrison quietly. 'What did you do in that thirty hours' flying? It sounds a lot. And what happened in those two crashes? You don't look very much damaged.'

'I've got the details in my log book,' I said. 'The hours were mainly on cross-countries, droning along over the Shropshire countryside, and I don't think the crashes were very serious. It was when I started night-flying and had to go farther afield that things became interesting, like finding airfields in the Chester, Liverpool and Manchester areas — strange territory, even though they weren't very far from Ternhill.'

Behind us the squadron crews, in their bulky flying-kit, had had their meal and disappeared. There were only about half-a-dozen pilots and navigators left (the gunners, being NCOs, ate in their own Mess) and the subdued buzz of conversation had almost died away.

'Let's go out and see what's happening,' said Harrison, turning as he got off his stool at the bar. He'd been listening patiently, I think as much as anything to reassure himself about this brand-new, inexperienced pilot who had just arrived on the squadron and with whom he was going to fly.

Outside the dusk was just beginning. The beautiful summer day seemed to be crumbling into darkness; outlines were getting blurred, but across the road there was a quickening of activity, figures moving about with a sense of purpose. The 0/400s, looking even bigger as their shapes became more indistinct, were each a focus of attention; aircrew and groundcrew milled round them in an orderly way, checking tyres, pitot head, bomb racks, control surfaces and propellers, flashing torches here and there all over the aircraft. Each one had two wooden ladders propped at its side, one at the front and one at the rear; at some of the ten bombers the first two crew members were already climbing bulkily in — the gunlayer at the rear and the pilot at the front — and one or two had mechanics on the wings ready to wind up the engines.

I stood back with Harrison at the end of the row, getting the scene into perspective. I'd never before been on an operational station, and this was what my training had prepared me for — to disappear into the night with a load of bombs and two fellow crew members, heading for enemy territory. I glanced down the field, which didn't look very long, towards the slope down to the river valley. 'They'll be off in a few minutes,' said Harrison. 'Once the leading aircraft goes the others will follow at five-minute intervals.'

Just then there was a throaty burst of engine firing, and a cloud of blue exhaust smoke billowed back from the 0/400 at the far end of the line: the 375 hp unit whirled the four-bladed propeller and the throttle, opened wide for starting, was pulled back to a healthy idling, then the procedure was repeated on the other side, though not before a second bomber had made a successful start and the whole line gradually roared into life.

I could see the legs of darting figures, and the ends of cockpit ladders being removed, the mechanics suddenly appearing in front of their aircraft to give a thumbs-up signal. Then one of them darted under a wing to pull away the chocks from in front of the big main wheels, there was another thumbs-up sign, and after a second or two the grass behind the end 0/400 was flattened as the engines were opened-up. Slowly the big machine moved forward and gathered speed, running down the slope. I thought it was never going to get off, and Harrison must have sensed what I was thinking, because he suddenly said, 'There she goes,' as the 0/400 rose, slowly (it seemed) but confidently, clearing the river valley by what looked like about thirty feet then banking to the right.

'They're heading for the first lighthouse,' remarked Harrison as the bomber merged into the dusk, still turning to get on its north-easterly course.

'Lighthouse?' I queried. I knew that 207 had been a Naval squadron and that some nautical terminology remained, but surely to talk of lighthouses was taking tradition a bit too far.

'Well, they're really lights which flash out identity letters,' explained Harrison in his kindly way. 'You only have to read the letter to know exactly where you are at night.'

'Doesn't the Hun try to shoot them up?' I queried.

'Well, he has tried, but without much success. It would need some pretty accurate bombing or some deadeye shooting by scout pilots, who aren't very confident themselves about finding their way about at night, at least over any sort of distance. They don't mind trying to shoot us down, when they're not very far from their own bases.'

Just then the second 0/400 opened up; it was getting darker now, and pinpoints of light shone out — some white, some red or green, some moving and some still. I thought back to my night-flying days at Ternhill, but this was altogether more purposeful and dramatic. The bomber lumbered forward, again seemed to gather speed only slowly, then just to gain a bit more height and bank to the right.

'It's a full squadron tonight,' commented Harrison. 'Ten are going off.'

'Is that the usual number?' I almost shouted as the roar of engines opening up came closer to us, the line of aircraft diminishing one by one.

'That's the whole of each flight,' Harrison shouted back. I could just hear him, because the 0/400 at the end of the line nearest to us had signalled that he was ready to go: the chocks had been pulled away and as the grass flattened out in his slipstream, the gunner waved and we were enveloped in a dusty whirlwind that shut out sight and sense. As it subsided we saw the bomber, far down the field, heading for the left-hand hedge. Then, at the last moment the pilot pulled it off and banked sharply to the right, then levelled his wings as he lumbered away over the valley.

'Sh--,' exclaimed Harrison through his teeth, 'that was a near thing. One of our new pilots — Torres, I think. Well, they're all on their way. Let's go back and have another drink; they'll be gone for about three hours. Would you like to watch them come in?'

'I would,' I said somewhat pensively as we walked back to the Mess tent.

Seeing the big bombers go off into the gathering darkness had given me a lot of food for thought, especially that last shaky take-off.

'Harrison,' I said as we crossed the road, 'you've been so kind and helpful to me today, that in return I must be perfectly frank with you. Tell me, is your regular pilot on leave? Obviously you don't want to fly with a beginner if an experienced chap is available.'

'No, he's not on leave,' Harrison replied. 'He got a Blighty one — on our last raid he was hit in the leg by ack-ack, but although in pain and with a boot full of blood managed to bring the aircraft back and land it.'

'With a little help, I suppose?' I ventured.

'Well, the worst thing was that he was weak through loss of blood, and it was all he could do to land the thing. After the effort he more or less passed out. They took him off to hospital at Abbeville and he's still there — so I'm spare.'

'And landed with me,' I said. 'I've had far too little experience on Handleys to fly them on operations. I'm going to ask the CO to transfer me to a Fee* squadron. If he won't do that, you must get yourself another pilot — an experienced one. I don't want to be the cause of your losing your life on operations.'

Harrison stopped and looked me in the eye.

'Obviously those take-offs have shaken you a bit,' he said, 'especially that last one. You'll get things into perspective tomorrow, after a night's sleep, and when you fly around the area in daylight. After all, I often helped my pilot to land and can do the same for you — it's a team effort. Come on, let's have that drink.'

The Mess tent had a quiet, subdued feel about it; there was a whiff of tobacco-smoke in the atmosphere, but more of departed spirits — a hint of laughter hanging in the air, echoes of conversation broken off suddenly, of voices whose owners were now somewhere high up in the cold, hostile darkness. There was one figure at the bar and Harrison introduced me.

'Blacking, this is Captain Bishop, our engineer officer. He's responsible for keeping our aircraft serviceable.

'Captain Bishop, Second Lieutenant Blacking is a new pilot who's just joined us after training at Ternhill.'

As we shook hands I noticed that Bishop looked older than other members of the squadron he wore glasses and his hair was greying round the sides, thinning on top, while his eyes had the keen look of those used to peering into engines and fuselages.

'Have a drink, Blacking,' he said crisply. 'Welcome to the squadron.'

I took the beer he proffered, as he said to Harrison, 'How long did you say you think they'll be tonight?'

'About three hours, I think,' Harrison answered. 'But there's always the possibility of stragglers.'

Bishop took out his pipe and started filling it in a ruminative way. 'We shall see,' he commented, half to himself.

'Captain Bishop and the CO always see the last aircraft back,' Harrison said, 'or wait for a message that one of them is down somewhere. That can take a long time if it's difficult to get through to the squadron.'

'I remember that occasion when one of our kites came down near that scout squadron,' said Bishop. 'Were you here then, Harrison?

* FE2b

They had a devil of a job convincing them they were RAF, because there'd been a lot of Huns around there in British uniforms and the airfield was on the look-out for imposters.'

'Did the crew eventually get back here?' I asked.

'Oh, yes,' said the captain. 'We sent out a tender when we heard where they were, with a sergeant and a couple of air mechs. They supervised the towing-in of the 400, then checked the rigging and ran the engines. Everything was in working order, even the undercarriage, because they'd landed in a rough ploughed field, but when the mud had been cleaned off the oleos and skid they were found to be undamaged — which says a lot for the Handley's construction.'

'Is the serviceability good?' I ventured, feeling I ought to keep the conversation going with this man — much older than ourselves, I thought — in whose experienced hands and eyes our safety might depend on one of these nights.

'It's very good,' Bishop replied, looking at me in a very direct way, his left hand round his tankard and his right forefinger over the stem of his pipe. 'Both the Rolls-Royce and the Sunbeam are reliable,* and as for rigging, we know how to handle that, provided the pilots tell us exactly what they want.'

I stored that one up in my mind for future use, then I said, 'What about the bombs. Do you get any hang-ups?'

'That's not really a matter for me,' said Bishop. 'We have an armament officer, Lieutenant Westoby. I expect you'll meet him . . .'

Before he could finish the sentence, there was a shrieking whine and the 'wumph' of an explosion outside, the staccato ting-a-ling of an alarm bell, voices shouting, a car engine starting. The lights in the Mess tent were doused and we all rushed for the door, knocking over stools and chairs *en route*. Just as we got there, another 'wumph' and a flash flung us to the ground, and we heard the sound of an aircraft engine dying away into the distance.

'That was a near one,' said Harrison as we picked ourselves up.

'I'd better go and look at the damage,' Captain Bishop announced as he set off towards the road, Harrison and I following. 'If there are any craters on the airfield we've got to fill 'em in damned quick.'

The scene had changed from when we were out before dusk watching the take-off; everything was dark and lights were flashing here and there, with voices and shouts of command trying to bring order out of confusion.

* The 0/400s had either Rolls-Royce Eagle (375 hp) or Sunbeam Maori (275 hp) engines.

'Sergeant Burley!' called Bishop as soon as he got to the tent which was his office. The sergeant seemed to materialize out of the blackness; most probably he had got there a second or so before Captain Bishop.

'Sarnt Burley, take three AMs in a tender and work your way down the left-hand side of the airfield then in towards the centre, to see if there are any holes. If there are, mark them with red lights and set about filling them up with ashes or rubbish. I'll go down the right-hand side. Get me two or three AMs.'

'We'll come,' said Harrison.

'No, thank you,' Bishop replied. 'This is a task for the engineers. Drivers!' He was beginning to give commands for the airfield repair operation, and Harrison took me by the elbow.

'We're not wanted here, so we might as well go back to the Mess, or do you want to get on your bed for a while, until the first aircraft comes back?'

'Do you think they'll get any craters filled up in time?' I asked.

'Yes,' he said, 'it's a regular drill. The most difficult part is finding them. The field is a very big one, when it comes to driving around it in the darkness looking for holes in the ground. We may as well go to the Mess. If the CO or adjutant want us to do something they'll jolly soon find us.'

In the Mess tent, some sort of order had been restored and the bar had an occupant, a jolly-looking fellow sitting on one of the stools.

'Hello, Porter,' Harrison greeted him. 'Meet our newest member — Second Lieutenant Blacking.'

'Hello, Blacking,' said Porter, who was wearing an observer's brevet. 'Welcome to the squadron. Hello, George. What a way to return from leave — in the middle of a raid. Must be the first one we've had. I didn't think the Hun knew where we were. Or maybe he just dropped his eggs on spec.'

'How was London?' asked Harrison. 'Did you see any of the new shows or were you out in the country, getting away from it all?'

'Well, I did both,' Porter replied. 'By the way, what are you drinking, Blacking? Drinking — Blacking. I like the sound of that; sounds ominous for the future. Anyway, two halves, eh? Charlie! Yes, I saw one new show — what was it called? — *The Geisha Girl*, I think — something like that; and I went down into the country — you mightn't have known there was a war on there, as far as the food was concerned. But there were fewer chaps about, more women doing men's jobs; lots of available girls.' He took a pensive swig of his beer, half sighed, then said, 'When are they due back, George?'

Harrison looked at his watch.

'All being well, the first should be in in about half an hour,' he said. 'So there's time to get you a welcome-back drink, Peter, before we hear the first engines.'

'Where've you come from, Blacking?' Porter asked.

'From Ternhill,' I said, 'where I flew Rumpeties — but I did my 0/400 flying at Stonehenge.'

'Ah!' Porter interjected. 'An experienced man, I see; just what we need to give us observers a chance to concentrate on navigation and not worry so much about the flying — or the landing,' (with a wink in Harrison's direction).

'I'm sure Blacking's an ace on landings,' said Harrison in his usual tolerant manner. 'He'll give us a demonstration tomorrow morning.'

I was just about to think up some remark which would indicate my brave self-confidence in advance of the morrow when there was a roar of engines overhead.

'They're back now,' yelled Porter, heading a rush for the entrance to the Mess tent. As we got outside, there was a disappearing whirr of propellers and a swish of black wings and struts overhead. The moon had risen, lighting up the night, and down the centre of the field was a line of lights, one after the other, disappearing into the distance, with one short line at right angles marking the beginning of the landing path.

The 0/400 had swung into a left-hand turn and began his run downwind. Everything else was in darkness except for the lights of the landing tee. 'If the Hun is about they're extinguished and you have to wait,' said Harrison, reading my thoughts again. 'It's just the sort of night when they might come over again. Let's hope we get everybody back first.'

Behind us the first of the squadron aircraft to return had straightened up on his approach and came in over the tents. I could just see the observer hanging out over the side, looking for the landing lights. The 0/400 looked huge in the darkness and seemed to be much too high; I thought he would never get into the field. But he settled down smoothly and soon stopped, the tail bumping up and down as the skid ran over the rough ground, and with a burst of engine the big aircraft did a 180° turn and taxyed up towards us, making for the end of the line where the aircraft had been parked before the operation.

There he swung round again, smothering us with a little gale of grass and dust, and throttled back to idling, then the four-bladed propellers flicked round for the last time and stopped, and there was that crackling sound of hot metal cooling, a smell of oil and of cordite. As we reached the aircraft the pilot pushed up his goggles and leaned over the side.

'Have a look at the gunner,' he said. 'I think he got one over the target, but we don't know how bad he is. Be careful with him.'

The AMs had already propped a ladder up to the rear cockpit and Harrison climbed up it. The gunlayer was slumped down in the left-hand corner, his face was white and as he managed to look up he said, 'They got me, sir — underneath.' Harrison called down, 'Give me a hand. I'll have to get in to help him out.' As he climbed over and got in his foot slipped; there was blood on the cockpit floor. Steadying himself against the side, he got his arms under the gunner's shoulders, but it took all his strength to lift him, such was the dead weight of the half-conscious, severely injured airman who had lost so much blood on the flight back from the target area.

I got up to the top of the steps but Porter said, 'No, let me, I'm used to this — and I'm bigger than you.'

I came down and stood at the bottom of the ladder while Porter went up. While he and Harrison struggled to get the gunner over the edge of the cockpit the pilot, Captain Halfer, 'A' Flight commander, and his observer Lieutenant Ronald had organized a stretcher which was laid out on the grass.

Gradually Harrison manoeuvred the gunner into Porter's arms and I gave some support from below. Porter laid him on the stretcher and Captain Halfer knelt by him, but the gunner was too weak from his long ordeal and the excruciating effort of being lifted out of the cockpit. His face was deathly pale and his left leg up to his thigh soaked in blood. Somebody brought a blanket to cover him and the stretcher was carried away.

'What happened, sir?' asked Porter.

'Shrapnel as we were coming away from the target, I think,' said Halfer. 'A burst right underneath us. Some fragments must have come up through the aircraft and caught poor Ellis. I felt the tail lift, so it was pretty close. A good thing we'd dropped our bombs.'

'You've got a jagged hole right through the rear cockpit floor, sir,' said Sergeant Burley, appearing out of the darkness. 'We'll have to check in the daylight for holes in the rear fuselage and tailplanes.' Just as he finished speaking there was another sudden roar of engines and a black shape overhead.

'Here comes No 2,' said Harrison. 'There should be eight more to follow, all being well.'

Again the 0/400 disappeared into the darkness; then as it came round its sound increased again and the next minute its shape appeared above the tents. It crossed the road with a burst of throttle and floated down the lights of the landing tee, towards the far end of the field. Then there was a single burst of power as it turned, taxying up towards the line. We watched as it reached the roadway and ran parallel with it before aligning itself with Halfer's aircraft, manoeuvring itself into place with a final engine roar that had us turning away as the slipstream hit our faces.

'Any casualties?' called Halfer up to the cockpit; he had got there before any of us, and the propellers had scarcely stopped turning.

'Sir?' said a voice from above. The pilot had pushed up his goggles and lifted up the flap of his flying helmet. But after three hours of deafening engine noise, the slipstream and seeing the glowing coals of bursting shells, he just wasn't attuned to ordinary human conversation. An AM had put up a ladder and after a few moments the pilot climbed out of the cockpit and down it. At the bottom he pulled off his helmet; he had a shock of fair hair, a fresh complexion — heightened where his face had not been protected by helmet and goggles — and very bright blue eyes.

'Sorry, sir,' he said, 'just couldn't hear a thing.'

'I asked if you had any casualties, Billing.' The flight commander repeated his question.

Lieutenant Billing shouted up in the direction of the rear cockpit. 'Are you all right, Corbett?'

The gunner's head appeared. 'Yes, sir, thank you. No trouble.'

'No, sir, we had no bother at all,' Billing said to the flight commander. 'How about you?'

'A hit up the rear,' Captain Halfer replied. 'I'm afraid poor Ellis copped it. We were very lucky it missed the petrol tank. Shrapnel, I think. We can assess the damage better in the daylight.'

By now Halfer's own aircraft had had its wings folded back and covers put on the engines. Billing's crew had gathered together their maps, pads and rations and were trudging over towards the flight offices when the third 0/400 to return appeared with a roar of engines out of the blackness of the night. As it came overhead a red Very light soared upwards from the front cockpit.

'Burley!' shouted the flight commander. 'Stand by for this one. Either they've got a bad casualty or a hang-up. Be prepared for one or the other.'

It seemed an age, I thought, before the aircraft re-appeared; it had been engulfed in the darkness again, its engine noise dying away, then growing louder as it came up the downwind side of the field and banked towards us. The approach seemed careful, and the pilot judged his touch-down so that he held the machine off the ground as long as possible, letting it sink gently on to the grass. Then, instead of turning to the right to taxy back up the field, the aircraft turned to the left, taxyed a little distance to be clear of the landing path, and stopped.

'He needs help', said Captain Halfer. 'Get a tender and some AMs out to him, Sergeant Burley. We must clear the field as quickly as possible.'

I watched the lights of the Crossley tender racing towards the 0/400. 'The fact that he didn't want to taxy probably means that one of his bombs is hanging up,' Harrison explained. 'This sometimes happens and you can't do anything about it in the air. The great danger is that it will fall off when you land, but they seem to have avoided that.' I noticed the swift, experienced movements on the flight line and the darting lights of torches round and underneath the aircraft down the field. 'Come across to hear about the raid,' said Harrison. 'They should all be back within the next thirty minutes.'

As we walked to the road and along it from the flight line we could hear the engines of the fourth aircraft to return. It did what seemed to be a rapid cricuit. 'That must be Tex,' commented Harrison, 'he's a dashing pilot, never averse to cutting a corner, but really very safe.' By the time we reached the Mess tent it was on its approach, with a confident final burst of power before gliding in over the landing tee. Again I got the impression that such a big aircraft would never get in to the field. But the next thing we heard was an engine roar as it turned and started to taxy up to the flight line. Inside the Mess was the blue haze of tobacco smoke in the bright light as we opened the door and the quiet but determined hum of conversation.

'How strongly defended was the target?' a voice asked. It was the CO, Major Folliott, standing by the bar and questioning Captain Halfer. 'Well, sir,' said the flight commander, 'there were the usual flaming onions and shrapnel, as we found out to our cost. I told you about poor Ellis. I think they had our altitude. Certainly they held us in the searchlights for a bit, but I managed to evade them and Ellis gave as good as he got.'

'Good show,' said the major. 'I hope there are no more casualties.'

'We're waiting for the tender to come back,' Halfer replied. 'Ah, here's Bishop.'

'One of the 112-pounders got hung up under Lieutenant Kerr's machine, sir,' announced the engineering officer without being questioned. 'He taxied clear of the tee and we went down and disengaged it safely.'

'Thank goodness for that,' said Major Folliott, brushing the back of his finger across his moustache — a gesture which somehow sorted with his trim military appearance. 'Is the bomb safe?'

'Yes, sir. The armourers are bringing it up now.'

'How many aircraft are still to come in?'

'Four now, sir. The rest are all back in the flight line.'

'Would you like to go out and watch the last aircraft come in, Blacking?' Harrison asked. I nodded and with an 'Excuse me, sir' he led me out of the Mess tent into the darkness, under a great whirr overhead as another 0/400 made its approach across the road.

'Do you make a squadron report to Wing Headquarters after every raid?' I said as we walked towards the flight line.

'Yes we do,' Harrison replied. 'If everything was pretty straight-forward it goes by despatch rider, but if there's something special that HQ should know, for example, if one of the crews should spot a Hun airfield with aircraft rising up from it, which we hadn't known about before, then it's plotted and one of the pilots or observers goes to HQ in a motorcycle sidecar, with the despatch rider, to make a verbal report on it. That's done as soon as possible after the last 0/400 has come in, because if it means a new target this will affect the planning for our next raid. The day boys — the DH4s — will go over and photograph it the next morning.'

'They have a pretty hazardous job,' I said as we reached the flight line where the aircraft which had just landed was taxying into place.

'Yes, they do,' Harrison replied in his fair-minded manner, seeing any question from both sides. 'They have to watch out for Fokkers and Albatrosses and Pfalzes, though they get protection from the SE5s and Camels, and they have only one engine — so if that's hit, down they go. But the whole idea of reconnaissance is to try to get back safely, so they don't take any unnecessary risks. The DH4 bomber boys have a harder time, because they've got to concentrate on hitting a target despite the ack-ack and looking out for Hun fighters. On the other hand, we have the hazards of darkness, navigating from lighthouse to lighthouse, without seeing the ground after we leave it, and having to come down in the dark if we get hit so badly — or if the pilot is so injured — that we can't make it back here.'

'He always has his observer to help him,' I said, looking at Harrison and recalling how splendidly he had aided his previous pilot in such a predicament.

'It's a team effort, as I said before,' said Harrison shortly.

Counting the one which had just taxyed up, there were nine 0/400s now on the flight line, half of them with their wings folded preparatory to being pushed back into the hangars, whence they would be towed out again in the morning for inspection and servicing by the fitters, riggers and armourers.

'Here's the last man!' Harrison's quick ears picked up the engine note just before I did, just before a great black shape materialized over the tents, giving a fierce burst of throttle. 'He's low,' as the 0/400 skimmed the road, touched just beyond the angle of the Tee, bounced, seemed to hover, steadied with another sudden application of power then settled down. There was a silence. 'Phew!' commented Harrison, 'that must have been Torres, back from his first operation — you remember his rather wayward take-off.'

'Well, he's down in one piece,' I said, feeling none too sure of myself. At least Torres had piloted an 0/400 on a raid, while I had yet to have my first experience.

'We'll see him safely up here, then it'll be time to turn in,' Harrison answered, without any comment, looking at his watch. 'It's getting on for midnight. You've had a long day, Blacking.'

As the bomber piloted by Second Lieutenant Torres, the 'new boy' ('new boy' until I arrived, that is), felt its way in the darkness up to the flight line, I wondered what my emotions would be in the same situation. It arrived, swung into place with a burst of throttle, the engines steadied to a tick-over, the propellers flicked for the last time and stopped; the AMs put up the ladders and Captain Brinden, 'B' Flight's commander, who had appeared out of the darkness, looked up and waited for the pilot to pull off his helmet.

'How was it, Torres?' The face that appeared looked young, pale and strained, but somehow elated. 'All right, sir; we delivered our eggs, I think, with the squadron's compliments. But I didn't care for those flaming onions you warned me about.'

'Come up to the Mess and see the CO,' said Captain Brinden. 'He'll want to know how you got on.'

'Best have a chat with him tomorrow, when he's digested the experience,' Harrison advised. 'Let's go back to the tent. Nothing more will happen tonight, once the aircraft have been put away.'

As we walked along the road I looked up into the night sky: everything appeared so peaceful — we could have been in an English country lane; yet a few miles to the east lay the battle area, where two great armies had been locked in dreadful warfare for nearly four years, and we had only to fly for an hour or so, threading our way across France, then into Hunland, to be in the midst of vicious destruction hurled up at us from the ground, while we unleashed our own form of destruction on some target far below.

Harrison, tactfully, didn't speak. Not until we were getting ourselves into bed did he say quietly, 'I expect the CO will get you into the air tomorrow, so you can see the lie of the land around here and familiarize yourself with the airfield. So a little cross-country and circuits and bumps will probably be the order of the day. Goodnight, Blacking; sleep well.'

'Goodnight, Harrison,' I replied, 'and thank you for taking me around today.'

I lay back but couldn't sleep for a long time. I recalled Ternhill and Stonehenge, and the journey to France — not as a soldier in the London Rifle Brigade but as a pilot in the Royal Air Force, a member of a night bomber squadron. Training had been one thing, but this was real, part of the great offensive which might win the war. At least, I thought, I was in a comfortable bed, unlike those poor fellows in the front lines. I would do my best to be a good pilot for Harrison, as the 'new boy' on the squadron.

2

A Funeral and First Flight

'Tea, sir — seven-fifteen.'

I'd been dreaming, I think, of schooldays back in Bromley, of the stern schoolmistress who used to rap us over the knuckles or press up under our chins if we couldn't pronounce our words properly. In mid-afternoon she used to have a cup of tea without milk, and an arrowroot biscuit, brought to her; and in my dream this was just being put down on her desk when the batman touched my shoulder and put down the tea.

'Morning, Blacking,' said Harrison. 'It looks a good day again.'

I took in his face, the tent-pole with jackets hanging on it and a flash of sunlight through the entrance and remembered where I was — No 207 Squadron, Ligescourt, with its 0/400s taking-off into the darkness, returning over the tents some three or four hours later. Suddenly all I had heard and seen yesterday came back to me. Did all that happen only yesterday?

'He's a good lad, Peters,' Harrison remarked, propping himself up on an elbow and sipping his tea.

'Peters?' I queried.

'Tom Peters, our batman, regular and reliable as an old clock. His parents are Wiltshire people, good yeoman folk. He's worth his weight in gold.'

Just then Peters came in with some shaving water.

'I'll use this first,' said Harrison, springing out of bed, 'and give you a few more minutes to finish your tea. Peters, you'll bring some more hot water for Mr Blacking.'

'Yes, sir,' said the disappearing figure.

'Breakfast is fairly flexible, as those who were on last night don't get up early,' Harrison remarked from behind his lather. 'But we'd better report to HQ to see if there are any duties for us to do. I expect we shall be flying this afternoon.'

When we stepped out to go across to the Mess tent the morning air was fresh and sweet; the grass sparkled; there had either been an early shower or a heavy dew.

Few members of the squadron were in evidence at breakfast; they had either been in or were not 'surfacing' until lunchtime. I found the tea, bacon, eggs and bread and butter with plum jam in tins, satisfied my appetite; it was plain and wholesome. When we'd finished an almost silent meal (apart from Harrison's 'Morning, Coop' to the Mess waiter — the English tradition of early morning reticence was well preserved, with one or two officers turning over the pages of old copies of the *Illustrated London News* with their pictures of the Western Front and Allenby's advance through Palestine), Harrison said, 'Unless you want another cup of tea we'll go across now; there may be a flying programme up and the Adj will let us know about any special duties.'

'Hello, Harrison,' said the Adjutant, Captain Pennington, when we entered his office and saluted. 'I see you've been taking good care of Blacking.'

'I hope, Adj, he'll take good care of me in due course,' Harrison replied quickly, 'so it's a bit of self-insurance to tell him all I can about the squadron — before he starts finding things out for himself. We wondered if there were any duties, and no doubt the flying programme will be up soon.'

Captain Pennington, who had a neat, likeable face with keen but friendly eyes, took a paper out of the 'in' tray on his desk and looked directly at me.

'You'll be sorry to know, Blacking,' he said, 'that we had a casualty last night — Sergeant Ellis.'

'We were on the flight line when his aircraft came in,' I replied. 'He seemed pretty badly hurt. How is the poor fellow?'

'I much regret to inform you, gentlemen,' Pennington said in measured tones, 'that Sergeant Ellis did not survive the night. He'd lost so much blood on the way back from the target that he passed out after the effort involved in getting him down from the aircraft, and never regained consciousness.

'The practice is, Blacking, for a funeral to take place as soon as possible after death — for obvious reasons, which I won't enter into now — and Sergeant Ellis is to be buried at Hesdin at eleven ack emma. As you know, we are fairly short of officers not engaged on operational duties, and as you are free this morning the CO has detailed you to represent the squadron officers. Harrison will tell you what has to be done.'

With a nod Captain Pennington dismissed us, taking a sheaf of papers out of his in-tray; he obviously had many other things on his mind that morning. As we walked out of his office, into the sunlight Harrison said:

'This means you'll have to go to Hesdin. It's a little place about seven miles north of here. I'll check with the MT, but I think a car will pick you up at the Mess at ten o'clock. You have to wear a black arm-band — the Orderly Room will provide you with that — and when you get to the cemetery, contact the Padre who's taking the service and say you're representing 207 Squadron. There'll be a firing party with a sergeant in charge. All you have to do is to accept his salute and give him permission to carry on; then afterwards, the same thing in reverse — permission to dismiss.'

I went back to the tent after Harrison's briefing to tidy myself up, and the next hour-and-a-half seemed to drag by horribly slowly. I felt as though I had the responsibility for the whole squadron on my shoulders, although I'd done nothing yet to justify it, which made me think myself something of a sham.

However, I realized that if I were going to be worthy of the squadron, whatever might happen once I started on operational flying, I ought to make as good a show as possible on its behalf. So I made sure I was looking smart, for there is nothing like putting on an appearance, whatever one's feelings might be, and was at the Mess tent well before ten. I sat down in one of the wicker chairs and picked up a copy of *The Times*. But I had barely had time to read the main story — it said something about 'Major German Offensive Ludendorff aims for a break-through' — before a voice said:

'You're Blacking, aren't you — the new pilot?'

The speaker was a tall, thin captain, with slightly protruding teeth and a smiling expression, he had quick, alert eyes which looked as though they wouldn't be likely to miss anything, whether human or mechanical. Fortunately I remembered my meeting with him yesterday.

'Yes,' I said, 'and you're Captain Bishop, the Engineering Officer.'

'True,' he responded, extending a hand. 'My job is to ensure that the 0/400s stay in the air, as far as is mechanically possible. They're not bad old crates, but the problem is supply — getting the right spares. Most of them seem to go straight down to the Independent Force. Those people at the Base Depots seem to forget we exist.'

'We're not part of the Independent Force, then?' I queried.

'No,' said Bishop, '207 is on its own, in co-operation with the day-bomber boys, the DH4s. Although we do the same kind of job as the IF — strategic bombing, getting behind the Hun lines to destroy his supplies and disrupt his communications.'

'I thought you were only interested in keeping us in the air,' I challenged him. 'You seem to know all about the squadron's role.'

'I can hardly help knowng,' replied the engineering officer, with a laugh that brought out a lot of cheerful creases in his face, 'since I've been here longer than anyone else; in fact I came in with the 0/400s when this squadron got them, when it was No 7, a Naval squadron, before this Air Force business started. So I'm as old as the Ark!'

'Were you originally with the Navy?' I asked.

'Not as a seaman,' said Bishop, 'but as an aircraft engineer. I . . .'

Just then the sound of a car horn interrupted our conversation; it came from the entrance to the Mess and I said, 'I'm sorry, Captain Bishop, that must be my transport — perhaps we can talk some other time. I'd like to hear more about the origins of this squadron.'

'Cheerio, Blacking,' the engineering officer replied with a half wave. 'Good luck on 207.'

I was glad to have met him on an off-duty basis, it gave one confidence to realize that the maintenance of our 0/400s was in such good hands — at least the aircraft shouldn't let us down, whatever else happened on operations.

'Second Lieutenant Blacking?'

The driver was at the Mess entrance with a highly polished staff car, he held open the rear door and I got in, feeling like a general.

'It's about half an hour's ride, sir,' he said as we rolled through the camp entrance and turned right on to the road. On our left were the aircraft, already being serviced for the night's operations.

As the sights and sounds of the squadron fell away and we moved northwards through the French countryside, I reflected on how much had happened to me during the last twenty-four hours. I had already forgotten England and become involved in the war again. Yet, once away from the Royal Air Force (I still couldn't get used to that title), even the fighting seemed unreal. The farms, the fields, the trees, the cattle, the ever-changing shapes of summer clouds in the sky, were the reality; they would still be here, still going on, when every man and machine of war had disappeared from this landscape.

'You're a new officer, aren't you, sir?' asked the driver, breaking into my reverie.

'Yes,' I said. 'In fact I only arrived yesterday, posted here after training.' I suddenly realized, when I had begun to gain a little confidence, just how new and raw I was.

'What's it like in Blighty now, sir? Is the food shortage as bad as we hear?'

'How long is it since you were there?' I countered, looking at him. A corporal, he had a wizened, outdoor kind of face, full of wrinkles; his cap band was under his chin, he wore puttees and his boots were highly polished. He looked to me like a regular soldier.

'About nine months, sir, for a week's leave; but I came out here in 1915. Things were different then, before the Somme.'

'I know,' I said. 'I was in the infantry, before transferring to the Flying Corps, in the London Rifle Brigade. People cheered then when they saw us; we were heroes, and things were easier on the home front. But the U-boats have made things difficult now. There are lots of shortages, there's hoarding, nearly every family has someone serving and they're sick of the long casualty lists. Now, after all the battles, the Jerries are on the move again. We've got to stop them for good this time. I think the Air Force will help to do it, now we've got air superiority at last.'

For a while we drove in silence, passing the odd military vehicle, though strangely there wasn't much sign of the war in that area. Suddenly the driver said, 'We're nearly there, sir,' and I saw a sign which said 'Hesdin'. He seemed to know where the cemetery was, having probably done this journey many times before; and as we turned in at the gate I got the impression of what seemed to be a field of white crosses. The padre was already there; I saluted and told him I had come to represent the squadron. He had one of those likeable faces, not sad, nor jovial, but amenable to every occasion; the sort of parson, I thought, that men at war would respect. We had just exchanged greetings when a gun carriage wih a coffin on it, and an escort party, appeared; and in a few moments the padre began, with his rich intonation: 'I am the resurrection and the life, saith the Lord:

he that believeth in me. though he were dead, yet shall he live: and whosoever liveth and believeth in me shall never die.'

I looked from the open grave to the Flanders sky as the burial proceeded. Yesterday Sergeant Ellis had been alert, fit, intelligent, part of the front line of a new Service; now he was — I heard the padre say it — 'our dear brother here departed', and some wife or family back in Blighty would be receiving the dreaded message about their husband or son being killed in action. So thin was the thread, out here, between life and death that at any moment it could be snipped.

'The grace of our Lord Jesus Christ . . .' As the padre spoke the words of the blessing a breeze ruffled his surplice and a skylark started up in a neighbouring field: I thought it was Ellis's soul ascending heavenwards. Apart from this rising song there was a silence, broken by the escort party dismissing themselves with a salute and marching off.

'You're going straight back to Ligescourt, Blacking?' asked the padre as he took off his clerical attire and became a khaki soldier again. 'Or will you come into the estaminet for a drink? Your people generally do.'

'All right,' I said. I was eager for any new experience, especially one favoured by my new squadron. 'You'd better come in the staff car; you can tell the driver the way.'

'Did you know Ellis?' The padre's curiosity was inevitable, even if it was only a conversational opening gambit. Either way, I had to disappoint him. 'No, I only got to the squadron yesterday, and they sent me along here this morning because I'm not yet committed to any duties.'

'You haven't flown yet, then?'

'No, but I probably shall tonight, it depends what operations are planned and how they make up the crews.'

'Were you out here before?' His curiosity seemed insatiable; I got the impression that asking questions was probably part of his professional technique.

'No. I was in the London Rifle Brigade but too young for service overseas, then when offered a commission I was asked if I was prepared to fly and said 'yes' without hesitation. So I was sent off to London for approval as potential flying material.'

'Was it hard to get accepted?' the padre asked. He wanted to know everything; what flashed into my mind momentarily was that tomorrow he might be burying me — so I might as well let him have the story while it was still available.

'Well, the medical was pretty thorough,' I said. 'It was done at the Air Ministry and apart from the usual checks for sight and hearing and nervous reactions and so on — I didn't like the pointer being run up the soles of my feet — it included being strapped into a sort of earthbound aeroplane, which performed at an alarming speed. I felt that if I passed that test I could get through anything.'

'Presumably you did,' commented my ecclesiastical inquisitor, half to himself, as the driver negotiated a rough bit of road. We were just reaching the turning which led to the cemetery, and there was another car ahead of us and one behind, whose occupants seemed to have been engaged in similar sad duties to ours. 'Take the next left,' the padre said briskly; then, to me, 'Sorry to have interrupted your story.'

'There isn't much to add,' I put in quickly, feeling that as I hadn't done anything in the air it was tempting Providence to say too much. 'I was posted to the No 2 RFC Cadet School at Hastings, from there to Denham for ground training — all the theoretical stuff— and then to Ternhill for flying. That's all, really, apart from the final thing at Stonehenge; navigation and bomb dropping.'

'I wanted to fly,' said the padre, half to himself, 'but once you get into this sky pilot job you've as much chance as a snowball in hell in getting out of it. It seems they're short of us. Here we are, driver; this red-brick place on the left.'

Inside, after the brisk, fresh air, it was suddenly hot and smoky; a sea of khaki figures, an almost deafening noise after the silence of the cemetery, voices raised to make themselves heard one above the other.

'How's business, padre?' said a cheerful red-faced sergeant with a large wink.

'Too brisk, I'd say,' responded my companion. 'So I don't want to see you in an official capacity, my friend,' a rejoinder which got him a laugh as we pressed our way towards the bar. Clearly the padre was used to talking to, and being talked at by, all sorts and conditions of men.

'What'll you have, Blacking?' he asked as he made it to the counter.

'Well, as I shall probably be on the list for tonight when I get back I'll make it a grenadine,' I said.

'Nothing like the brandy here,' said the padre, ordering himself one. 'But perhaps some other time.'

'You must come to the squadron,' I said. 'See us while we're alive, not when we're dead.'

Almost immediately I bit my tongue. That remark wasn't in the best of taste. But the padre took it in his stride. 'We're rather like doctors,' he replied. 'We see men at their best and at their worst in these conditons; and we learn to keep our personal feelings to ourselves. I'd like to come; I've had very good reports of 207.'

'I must get back,' I said. 'If I'm on tonight I want to get acquainted with the crew I've got to fly with.'

There were signs and sounds of a celebration developing. One of the other funeral parties had quickly turned itself into a party of revellers; this was a customary reaction. But I felt that as I was so new on the squadron I'd better not get involved. The padre seemed a part of it all; the hotter and noisier it got, the more he beamed. I excused myself. Pushing and easing my way through the motley crowd of Army and RAF chaps, wreathed in the blue haze of tobacco smoke, I'd just about reached the door and caught a glimpse of the driver outside with the Staff car when a strong hand grasped my elbow and a voice said, 'Well, well, Blacking, what are you doing here?'

I looked round in the direction of the voice and recognized one of my Stonehenge fellow-trainees, Oscar Darke, with whom I'd finished up in a bed of cabbages on the outskirts of Bath at the end of a night flight in an FE2b.

'Hello, Oscar,' I replied. 'Still navigating hapless pilots around?' That was unkind of me, I realized, but I couldn't resist it on the spur of the moment. Our last association was too freshly ingrained on my mind. Getting lost on a simple cross-country so near to the end of one's course had hurt my pride.

'Well, you might say that,' said Oscar quite cheerfully, 'only there isn't any room for mistakes here, is there? I think I learned my lesson.'

I began to feel a bit more tolerant. On the flight that ended in disaster for us, Second Lieutenant Darke had made every mistake in the book, including knocking the battery over when he turned to resume his seat after handing me a slip of paper with a compass course for Stonehenge written on it, and so putting out the cockpit lights, which didn't help at all. No man could go on making so many mistakes, and no doubt Oscar had realized that if he didn't mend his ways he'd get chucked out of the newly formed RAF.

'What are you doing now?' I asked. It seemed to say much for his persistence and determination that he had survived so far.

'DH9s,' he replied simply. 'No 99 Squadron. It's a day bomber and reconnaissance unit.'

I knew what that meant. The DH9s, single-engined, with a two-man crew, did the same job as we were doing, bombing targets well into Hunland, but did it by day, without the protective cover that darkness gave to us. I'd heard that they were having a rough ride.

'What brings you here, then, Oscar?' — as if I didn't really know the answer.

'The same sad duty as yours, I expect,' he answered, 'giving some of our chaps a decent farewell. We lost two-and-a-half crews the other day. It was a really bad show and squadron morale is at rock bottom. This can't go on.'

I suddenly felt quite desperately sorry for Oscar Darke. He seemed to be about ten years older than when I'd last seen him, although that was only a few months ago, and his features had crumpled into a kind of premature maturity forced on him by events. He'd lost that careless, boyish look he had at the training school. When he asked, 'Look here, Blacking, you will have a drink with me, won't you?' I thought of all the reasons why I shouldn't: I'd already said goodbye to the padre, I'd been in the estaminet too long already, the driver was waiting and I had to get back to the squadron in case I was on flying duty. Instead, I said, 'All right, but only a grenadine,' and with a kind of desperate relief he turned to fight his way through the bodies and the smoke to the bar. I hoped the padre couldn't see me. He seemed to be doing a good line in ecclesiastical public relations with the red-faced sergeant and a couple of Tommies, and when young Darke reappeared with a couple of glasses I took one and wished him well.

'All the best, Oscar. Don't forget you might be in the PBI. I had a dose of that.'

'I remember you telling me,' he replied. 'But you haven't yet told me what you're doing now.'

I recalled I'd countered his first question with a similar one to him, which he'd answered. So I told him about the 0/400s and how I'd been put on them although what training experience I'd had had been on FE2bs.

'Come and see us at Ligescourt some time,' I said. 'It's always good to know how the other half lives.'

'I will, I will, thank you.' He seemed grateful for the idea, but had a faraway look, as if he realized it might never come to fruition.

'Oscar, can I get you another drink before I go?'

'No,' he said, 'I'll take one off you when I come to your Mess. We'll have a party. I'll bring some of the boys over — if there are any left.'

I slapped him on the shoulder. 'Cheerio, Oscar. Keep your pecker up.' But when I got out into the sunshine again, and on the drive back to the squadron, his last remark stuck in my mind.

3
Over the Lines

When we drove into Ligescourt airfield the 0/400s were already lined up along the right of the road, being got ready for the night's operations, some with their wings spread and others with them still folded back. Here and there little groups of air mechanics were working on the aircraft, and the engine of one of them was being run up; we caught the blast of the slipstream as we drove behind it.

I thanked the driver when he dropped me at my tent (just managing to remember which it was, not yet being quite familiar with these new surroundings), and with a cheerful 'Good luck, sir,' he slid off in the staff car. I had a feeling I was going to need that luck.

The tent was tidy, rather stuffy in the heat of the afternoon, and deserted. Then, as my eyes became accustomed to the canvas gloom of its interior I noticed a piece of paper on my bed. The pencil-written message was brief:

'You're flying tonight with Captain Musgrove — as his gunner. Call in the squadron office. H.'

I sat down on the bed. What I'd half expected was now to become a reality. I was going to have my first experience of operational flying. This was the initial stage, a back-seat taste of what it was like over the lines at night. Then I'd do some flying with my crew, and next would come our first operation together.

Harrison's advice about calling in at the squadron office was sound, like all the advice he gave. Then I would know our take-off time, and when the briefing was, which would give me an opportunity of looking over the guns in the rear cockpit of the 0/400, and of learning from the armourers about the kinds of ammunition they loaded into them. I picked up my cap from the bed and made my way over to squadron HQ, in the wooden huts where I'd 'booked in' with Harrison yesterday. I was just looking at the list of crews detailed for operations, on a sheet of paper pinned to the notice-board, when Captain Bishop the engineering officer came out from the squadron offices.

'Wotcher, Blacking,' he greeted me cheerfully, with the accent on the '-er'. 'Got you down already, have they?'

'Well, I'm flying as Captain Musgrove's gunner tonight to get some over-the-lines experience.'

He peered at the board.

'Yes, I see. Musgrove, Tring, Blacking. That's a good team.'

'I wonder if you can introduce me to the armament officer,' I said, on a sudden inspiration. 'I'd like to get a good look at the guns and see the types of ammunition they fire.'

'Of course, Blacking. I'm on my way to the flights now. Done any gunnery before?' he asked as we strode over to the flight offices.

'In the London Rifle Brigade, as a Lewis gunner, but not in the air.'

'Then you'll add a new dimension to your experience tonight,' said Bishop. 'Here we are. Hayes!'

His call was addressed to the inside of an office marked 'Armourers'; though his voice wasn't stentorian it was authoritative, used to being obeyed, and after a few seconds' interval a stocky lieutenant appeared, wiping his fingers on an oily rag.

'Harry, this is Second Lieutenant Blacking who's just joined the squadron. He's flying with Captain Musgrove tonight as his gunner. Could you show him the guns and ammunition we use?' With that parting shot, Bishop disappeared towards the line of 0/400s being readied for operations.

'I can't myself,' said Hayes apologetically. 'As you see', looking at his hands, 'I've got problems. Corporal Connor!!'

A tousled red head and a fresh complexion, followed by some oily overalls, appeared behind him. 'Sir?'

'Connor, Second Lieutenant Blacking is to fly tonight with Captain Musgrove, as his gunner. Take him along and demonstrate the gun positions in the rear cockpit, explain how the ammunition feeds and the different types we use. And show him where the Cooper bombs are stowed.'

'You've just come on the squadron then, sir?' asked the corporal as we walked over towards the Handleys, three or four of which still had their wings folded back.

'Only just,' I said, still feeling very much the new boy. 'In fact I arrived late last night and attended a funeral this morning.'

'Sergeant Ellis?' put in Connor.

'Yes. I was asked to go as one of the few officers available. I didn't know him, of course.'

'I knew him well,' the corporal said. 'He could have stayed on the ground, but all he wanted to do was to get into the air. He thought that by making a fighting contribution he could help to bring the war to an end. You couldn't have met a nicer, gentler chap. Let's try this one, sir.'

We'd reached the line of aircraft and were looking at A2. It was only when we got close that I realized once again what a big machine the 0/400 was, its black paint giving it a sinister, purposeful appearance. Connor got a ladder and set it against the side.

'Up you go, sir, then I'll show you the gun and its ammo and the bomb stowages.'

I climbed up and got over the side into the rearward-facing seat. The 0.303 inch Lewis gun was mounted directly in front of me on a cross-member, which I could hold on to and which would also help to keep me in my seat, I thought, mentally taking advance stock of emergency situations.

'You're familiar with the Lewis, sir, I take it?' Connor's head had appeared over the side and he began his explanations forthwith.

'Three drums of ammunition are carried — tracer, incendiary and ordinary. The first is the best against fighters because you can see where your shots are going. You also have eight twenty-pound Cooper bombs, here' — he pointed to a bomb-rack in front of the gunner's cockpit — 'for dropping on searchlights.'

I took hold of the handles of the gun and moved it around. Some twenty feet from me, at the end of the fuselage, was the Handley's assembly of tailplanes, fins and rudders, like some gigantic box-kite. With the tailskid on the ground all this assemblage was mainly below me; in the air it would be up at my level and I must be careful to keep it out of the line of fire.

'You'd better have a look at the front gun position too, sir,' said Connor.

I climbed out and he took the ladder round to the nose, where twin Lewis guns on a Scarff ring, allowing them to rotate through 360 degrees, pointed menacingly towards the sky.

'You get up to this one through that hole, sir,' Connor explained, pointing to a hole in the underside of the fuselage, just aft of the pitot tube which supplied the flow of air to the airspeed indicator in the pilot's cockpit. 'Up you go.'

This was much harder to get into than the rear gunner's cockpit: first, you had to squeeze up through the hole (which seemed to me difficult enough in uniform, never mind when wearing flying clothing), then immediately bend yourself into a right angle to get through the entry hatch into the cockpit. Once there, sitting in the seat with the Scarff ring round me, I looked down over the side at the ground about fifteen feet away.

'All right, sir?' asked the ever-helpful Connor from far down below. Then, mirroring my thoughts, he added, 'Normally we fly a three-man crew, and as it's the tail that needs protection, I expect you'll be in the rear cockpit tonight. In an emergency, the observer could crawl through from his seat beside the pilot and operate the front-cockpit Lewis guns.'

'Thank you, corporal,' I said and ducked down, facing rearwards, to get through the hatch, mentally noting that I wouldn't like to do that in flying kit, on a dark night, with the aircraft bucking about. Then I got through the hole and down by the ladder.

'Hello, Blacking,' said a familiar voice behind me, 'I was told you were here.'

'Hello, Harrison,' I greeted him. Thanks for your note. I went over to the squadron offices, looked at the board and then thought I'd better familiarize myself with the guns and ammo before the briefing. What time will it be?'

'I think it's at six,' Harrison replied. 'That gives time for the observers to work out their courses before the take-off, which will be at about seven-fifteen. You'd better come over to the mess and get a meal while you can, then meet up with Captain Musgrove and Lieutenant Tring just before the briefing. Then I think we'll be doing some local-area work tomorrow afternoon, to familiarize you with the airfield. That's if everything goes right tonight.' Then he looked at me quizzically, realizing he might have said something tactless, and quickly added:

'Feeling nervous?'

'Well, I can't say I'm feeling all that brave. It'll be a strange experience — the first time over the lines, and at night. How did you feel?'

'Pretty worried, I admit,' Harrison replied. 'But you're lucky because Musgrove is probably the most experienced pilot on the squadron. He wouldn't be a flight commander if he weren't.'

We'd reached the Mess during this conversation. It was nearly deserted, but there was a chink of plates and a bustle in the background, and a steward appeared.

'Just dinner for Mr Blacking, Edwards,' said Harrison. 'He's flying this evening. I'll have mine later.' Then, to me: 'You must be hungry — all that way to Hesdin and back, and nothing since breakfast, though no doubt you had a drink after the funeral.'

'I did,' — recounting the story of the chaplain who'd taken me into the estaminet — 'and met up with a friend who's on DH9s, on 99 Squadron. Those boys have a tough job, doing what we do but in daylight, and with only one engine.'

'They do indeed,' said Harrison, 'and I think their morale gets pretty low at times, with the losses they have.'

The steward put a plate down in front of me; its contents looked like hash, accompanied by carrots and fried potatoes. As I looked at it, I realized how hungry I really was and tucked in, Harrison tactfully remaining silent until the sweet came. It was plums and custard, and I did that justice too.

'Coffee, sir?' asked the steward at my elbow.

'Yes, please. How are we about time for the briefing?'

'You needn't gulp it,' Harrison said. 'We're all right. I'm glad you enjoyed your dinner, after a while there's not much novelty about the menu, but the food's good and we're much better off than those poor chaps in the lines — as you know.'

'I do indeed. As if the mud and the lice and rats weren't horrors enough, every other minute death might come whistling over the top. I'm lucky to have got out of the PBI.'

I drank the last of my coffee and picked up my cap, feeling I ought to show a determination I didn't really possess.

'Come on,' I said. 'I'm ready.'

As we walked along to the offices I saw that the number of 0/400s on the line had increased: There were seven there now, and another was being slowly drawn across from one of the flights.

Inside the offices the benches and chairs in the small briefing-room were already full, and we had only just found seats when the major appeared and went up to a table at the far end. Behind it was a blackboard with a large-scale map pinned to it, showing the present positions of the Allied and enemy armies, and — I presumed — the target we had to attack. For, well into Hunland, there was a large red circle.

'Gentleman,' said the major as the buzz of conversation died down. 'Tonight's operation is against a main ammunition dump which GHQ want destroyed. It's about sixty miles beyond the lines and you'll know when you hit it. Your bomb load will be sixteen 112-pounders. Here's the target' — he used a pointer to tap the circle on the blackboard — 'and the weather will be overcast, with cloud at about 8,000 feet and no moon, so there shouldn't be any fighters, but the searchlights will be looking for you, and the target is likely to be strongly defended. Captain Musgrove will be leading — altitude, 5,500 feet to 7,500 feet, aircraft stepped-up by 200 feet according to order of take-off. Time of take-off, first aircraft, 6.45, the rest at five minute intervals. On return, check with Doullens lighthouse for an all-clear to land. The Tee will be switched on for each aircraft, then off as soon as he's down — we don't want to give our position away to the Huns. The colour of the night is red; fire it if any of our own searchlights pick you up. Any questions, gentlement? . . . If not, carry on with your flight planning, and the Crossley tender will pick up the first crews at 6.15. Good luck tonight.'

As the major finished his briefing and the buzz of conversation resumed, Harrison said, 'You'd better make your number with Captain Musgrove and Lieutenant Tring is probably with him. Yes, there they are.'

I recognized the quietly-spoken captain I'd met the night before and went across to him. 'Captain Musgrove, I'm to fly with you tonight as gunner.'

'Yes, Blacking,' he said. 'Meet our observer, Lieutenant Tring.'

I shook hands with a dark, lively-looking fellow with a twinkle in his eye, who said with a Scottish accent, 'I'd heard you were bringin' up the rear. Mak' sure you keep your eyes well peeled and if any searchlights come up, shoot straight doon them — or drop your Cooper bombs on them.'

Musgrove himself was equally forthright, though in a less colourful way, just commenting, 'That's the best advice you could have been given, Blacking. We'll have our work cut out at the front, so we depend on you to guard our rear. Have you got your flying kit?'

'I'll see to that,' cut in Harrison.

'Good, then be ready for the tender at 6.15. We'll look out for you then.'

Somehow I felt confident in these two, Musgrove with his quiet-spoken manner, Tring with his determined sense of humour.

'Let's get you kitted-up,' Harrison said, as he led the way out of the briefing room and took me along to one of the wooden huts which was the clothing store. Here I was fitted with fleece-lined trousers and jacket, a pair of flying-boots, a helmet and gauntlets, with silk gloves to be worn inside them, and issued with a revolver and compass. I felt like one of H G Wells' Martians* in this get-up, and about twice my normal size.

'We'd better go back to the tent so I can leave my shoes and cap there,' I said, but Harrison dissuaded me. 'You don't want to walk around too much in that gear; I'll take them back while you go to the briefing-room. The tender will be up soon.'

At the sight of other flying-clothed characters in there I didn't feel so strange, and although everyone looked different from his normal self, managed to identify my pilot and observer, Tring with his maps on which our tracks had been drawn.

'All set?' said Musgrove briefly.

'Yes,' I replied, feeling excessively warm, but realizing I should shortly welcome every ounce of this protective clothing.

'Flying rations,' Tring observed as he handed me a cardboard box. 'Not to be consumed before take-off. I won't tell y ou what they are — leave you to be surprised by the discovery.'

'Tender!' yelled a voice from the door and the crowd of bulky figures swayed towards it. 'First two crews.'

'That means us,' said Musgrove. 'Come on, Blacking, let's get aboard.'

Outside, the sky was just beginning to darken and the air getting colder as the Crossley bumped towards the first 0/400 in the line, which grew bigger and bigger the nearer we got to it, towering over us when we stopped. Torchlights were flashing as AMs moved around it and I could see a ladder set up against the rear cockpit. Feeling ungainly and self-conscious, I climbed up and eased myself over the side. It seemed strange to sit there looking backwards over the tail and across it towards the squadron offices and tents. Not being morbid about it, if I survived this trip I would be sitting in the front cockpit for the next one.

* *The War of the World* had been published in 1898.

I glanced round. Tring was just climbing in to his left-hand seat, and gave me a thumbs-up as he did so; I could just see Musgrove's helmet — he was having a last word with the mechanics before climbing up the ladder. To me he seemed a complete professional, old and self-assured; in fact he was about twenty-three and operationally very experienced. I was nineteen and completely inexperienced.

Between my cockpit and theirs were the bombs — sixteen of them. I flashed my torch over the racks and counted them and, on either side, the engine nacelles which the pilot and observer had to the left and right of them. As Musgrove settled himself in his cockpit, one of the AMs climbed up on the lower starboard wing to start the Rolls-Royce Eagle with a winding-handle. Musgrove gave him a thumbs-up and after a few hesitant coughs it fired and I felt a slipstream of cold air rushing past my right ear. After a couple of minutes this procedure was repeated on our port side and I felt myself shut in by parallel rackety blasts of what seemed like a hurricane — and so far, the engines were only being warmed up! I would have to endure this for about the next three hours, and the only possible means of communication between me and those in front would be by hand signals, by torchlight or by scribbled notes wound along a pulley.

We sat in this noisy static situation for some time, while Musgrove and Tring checked their instruments (I could see torches flashing about inside their cockpits), and looking round and ahead beyond the nose of the aircraft I noticed a steady red light — an Aldis lamp. Suddenly it changed to green and Musgrove started to open-up the throttles (the engines had previously been warmed-up by the AMs, before we came out). The 0/400 rolled forward, slowly at first, then increasing in speed. The tail began to come up. I glanced at my watch. It was 6.45 on that late summer evening. We were on our way. With its Eagles roaring at full take-off power the 0/400 cleared the river on the northern boundary. I looked back through the box-kite-like structure of the tailplane at the airfield with its line of bombers, the next shortly to begin its take-off run, and the huts and bell-tents beyond, a view I might never see again.

As we turned to starboard, climbing and turning to gain an easterly heading, the last remnants of daylight were being withdrawn to the west through broken cloud; the weather was unsettled and the night sky dark and threatening.

I checked my three Lewis guns visually, cocking them and getting the feel of the trigger pressure through my gloved fingers. I decided to wait until we were over the German front line before firing warming-up bursts, otherwise they might be misunderstood by our defences.

Still climbing and turning, we reached about 5,000 feet (I estimated, for I didn't have any instruments in the rear cockpit), and looking out over the starboard side I saw the lines far down below; not the ghastly tracery of earthworks and trenches, since it was now too dark for that, but the flashes of opposing gunfire as far as the eye could see which betokened 'the hour of hate'. I thought of the infantrymen in their muddy, lice-ridden, explosive, rat-infested, barbed-wired, machine-gunned, horrendous, hopeless existence, waiting for the next order to advance into the death-trap of no-man's land, in another abortive push to gain a few yards at the cost of a thousand lives. I was lucky to be out of that, and in the hope of saving just a few Allied soldiers I aimed my guns towards the German front line and fired a triple burst down on some invisible enemy positions.

Then we were in complete darkness. Behind the lines no lights were showing. I peered forward and could just see the outline of helmeted heads in the front cockpit; I couldn't miss, on either side of the fuselage, the red-hot glow from the exhaust pipes. Reckoning that we were probably not very far from our target I scanned the dark sky for night-fighters, both above us and through the V-aperture in the floor. Then suddenly, ahead of us, a pencil-thin searchlight beam shot out of the darkness and began to probe the sky. We must have been picked up by the German warning system and its anti-aircraft defences were looking for us, heading that night's procession of bombers. The white beam of light, swinging slowly around and etching the cloud contours, came towards us in a menacing, robot-like way. I knew it would catch us and wondered what Captain Musgrove, with all his experience would do.

Suddenly we were lit up by what seemed to be a million candle-power illuminations. We had been caught not only by the original searchlight but a dozen more which joined in as soon as we were pinpointed. In seconds bursts of archie were coming up towards us, and shells bursting around us. But just as quickly Musgrove reacted, putting the big aircraft into a steep, sickening, corkscrewing dive to escape both searchlights and flak. Fortunately I'd anticipated what he might do, and held on tight, but I was terrified by the experience and the steepness of our dive left my stomach far behind; it was like being on a nightmare big dipper, whizzing down into the blackness in a vehicle over which one had no control. But we escaped the searchlights, Musgrove levelled-off the aircraft and after a minute or so climbed back to 5,000 feet, and my nerves steadied. I kept my hands on the guns in case of night-fighters, and peered continually around into the enveloping darkness. The excitement had caused my adrenalin to rise, and I didn't feel cold or hungry; I was even ready for what came next.

More searchlights suddenly pricked the blackness — about four of them, on either side of us, moving. Presumably they were on vehicles, racing along roads which seemed to be converging, as if we were flying into a funnel. As we entered it and they held us there for a second or so, following Lieutenant Tring's advice I dropped half my Cooper bombs into the intersection of the searchlights, and as we passed over it sprayed the area with my guns, which proved an effective deterrent, for the lights wobbled and went out.

But ahead of us now — it couldn't be much farther — lay the target. Musgrove swung the aircraft to port; he was bringing it into wind, on the compass heading given him by Tring, who was now in his front cockpit ready for the bombing run. The German defences, however, were ready too, as the CO had warned us they would be. Up through the darkness, on either side of us, came flaming onions — chains of green phosphorous balls fired from synchronized guns, so that they arrived simultaneously, doubling the enemy's chances of setting the aircraft on fire. They lit up the night sky hideously; one hit from them would mean the end of us.

Musgrove kept the aircraft on a rock-steady course and we emerged from this dreadful accompaniment into another horror, an intense ack-ack barrage, sending up balls which burst just below and around us, rocking and buffeting the 0/400. We were over the target all right, so intense was the defence, and at the end of our run-in Tring dropped a stick of eight bombs. Seconds later there was a huge explosion down below; it looked as though we had hit the ammunition dump. Musgrove heaved the aircraft into a port turn and I peered down into the darkness. Following the explosion, a great cloud of smoke was billowing upwards.

The ack-ack seemed to have ceased momentarily as we completed our circuit and lined up again for another run-in, but as soon as Musgrove steadied on his course the bursting shells again invested the aircraft — but once more we were lucky, and Tring's second stick whistled down into the smoke and flames, Musgrove pulling the 0/400 round while his observer and I peered downwards to observe results.

This time, he steadied the 0/400 on a reciprocal heading, and I saw Tring come back from the front into the pilot's cockpit with a torch which he shone down into the bomb rack to check that none of our load had got hung up. I looked too, and there was nothing left. If there had been, we would have had to lash them up before landing. At least dropping the 112 lb bombs made us less explosive. Our job was finished and all we had to do now was to get back to Ligescourt, through the shellfire, the searchlights, the flaming onions, the archie on the wrong side of the lines, and possible night fighters.

As the burning target receded I scanned the dark skies. Suddenly, over to the port side, the clutch of searchlights which had tracked us on our way in pierced the darkness. I hadn't switched them off then, though I might have scared the crews. I caught sight of Musgrove looking round towards me, and pointing downwards with his left arm. Almost at the same time he heaved the aircraft over into a diving left-hand turn, heading for the searchlights. I knew what he meant; they were trying to illuminate one of our following 0/400s and Musgrove wanted me to put them out with the remaining Cooper bombs and my Lewis guns. He was going to fly into and across the searchlight beams to try to protect our squadron colleagues.

In our dive, the blazing white candlepower rushed up to meet us. As we hit the beam I released the remaining eight Cooper bombs then grabbed the three Lewis gun handles. Musgrove whipped the aircraft into a climbing turn to port, ramming open the throttles and taking advantage of the airspeed gained in the dive. The gravitational force pulled me down into a corner of the cockpit, but I fought to keep myself upright and to aim my guns down into the searchlight beams, giving them a long burst of fire before the physical effort required finally beat me. However, by then we were climbing up into the darkness again, with the searchlights extinguished, perhaps only temporarily, but we may have saved one crew. Now we had no more bombs, but still possessed some ammunition.

Musgrove continued to climb as we regained our heading. I was sure we were going higher than before, and suddenly felt chilled and shaken — a reaction to the frightening new experiences of the last few minutes. I slumped down in a corner of the cockpit and felt for my flying rations, which I examined with my torch. Tring had said he wouldn't tell me what they were, so I should be surprised by the discovery; they consisted of biscuits, chocolate and dried fruit, which I munched greedily. The excitement and the cold had made me hungry.

I'd barely finished eating when more searchlights suddenly pierced the black sky directly ahead of us, and Musgrove looked round again, gesturing; he was going to go to the left of them. As we got abreast of them there was a c-r-rump, c-r-rump on our starboard side and the aircraft was tossed about by the force of the explosions. Then a sickening green chain of flaming onions lit up the nearby sky. Musgrove put the nose down to escape the barrage and headed for the lines in a south-westerly direction.

As we left the searchlights and the barrage behind us he steadied the 0/400 on course again. We must have been at about 3,000 feet, by then, and deserved some luck, which we seemed to get — at least, no bad luck, because no archie came up at us. All we had to do now was to find a lighthouse which would lead us to Ligescourt. We banked to the right, heading northwards, keeping our altitude at about 3,000 feet.

For a time nothing happened; we stooged on expectantly. Then, a sight for tired eyes, a dash-dash-dot-dash suddenly became visible in the darkness over to our right. It was 'Q' — Doullens — and Musgrove banked towards this oasis in the night, the flashing lights becoming brighter as we neared them. He crossed over the top of the lighthouse and banked left into our last course, for Ligescourt.

I strained my eyes into the darkness, looking for a sight of the landing tee which would be put on for us. Just then I remembered something I ought to have done, and which would help to ensure our safety — I should fire the colours of the night. I picked the Very pistol out of its clips, held it as high as I could and pulled the trigger. Two stars, one red and one white, shot up into the dark sky like a rocket fired at a Guy Fawkes bonfire party in the garden at home before the war. I put back the pistol and peered forward towards where I imagined the airfield to be.

As if in answer to our self-identification — for we should be the first aircraft back — the illuminated tee appeared out of the darkness, ahead and slightly to our left. Musgrove aimed for it, reducing height, and aligned himself with the tee; then, keeping it on his left, flew upwind of it and turned to come downwind, still losing altitude.

I watched his technique with fascination, for I would have to do this myself soon, admiring the way in which he judged his last turn so as to align us with the tee, and watching how Tring hung over the side to advise him of our height in the final stages. I saw the huts and tents with their lights pass below us, felt the throttles pulled back so that the propellers were just turning, and held my breath when we seemed to hang just above the ground. Then there was a rumbling and a scraping as the wheels and tail-skid seemed to touch down together. It was a good three-point landing, perfectly judged and well done, considering all that Musgrove had been through.

He opened-up the throttles, swung round to the left and taxyed quickly up the field to keep clear of the next aircraft coming in. As we got up close to the flight line, air mechanics ran out to take hold of our wing tips to guide us in and turn us round, marshalled by torches. As soon as we had turned, Musgrove switched off the engines, the tail was raised and we felt ourselves being pushed backwards. There was silence except for the busy shouts of the groundcrew, glad to have their aircraft back in one piece (torches were being flashed over the wings and fuselage, looking for damage), and the crackling sound of hot metal cooling. Someone put a ladder up to my cockpit, then a face appeared and said something. I was deafened after the sudden cessation of engine noise, but remembered to lift up one flap of my helmet. 'Guns all right, sir?' shouted the face into my ear. 'Yes,' I said, 'and all the bombs gone.'

The AM retreated, to leave me space to get down the ladder. When my feet touched the grass, my whole being seemed to be quivering as it came into contact with the solid ground and mentally I gradually adjusted to the sights and sounds of military normality around me, getting out of the way just in time as the AMs folded back the wings. Musgrove met me as I came out in front of the tailplane. 'Sorry you had such a rough ride for your first one, Blacking,' he said. 'That last diversion, before we crossed the lines, was because F-8s were attacking the airfield from which a Hun circus was operating, and some of their scouts would undoubtedly have been airborne. So it was no place for a peace-loving 0/400, especially after what seemed to have been a good attack. We shall know from the DH9s' photographs tomorrow.

'We'll go and report and then have a drink in the Mess before turning in.'

I walked with Musgrove and Tring across the road towards the HQ, feeling bulky and clumsy in my flying kit. Though I was with them I hardly felt aware of anything they were saying; I could still hear the roar of our engines, and see the blackness of the night lit by those terrifying flashes. As Musgrove pushed open the door of the hut and led the way in I felt suddenly blinded by the light inside. Then we were engulfed in a hubbub of voices, and shrouded in a congenial, smoke-laden atmosphere. I realized that what had been unique to me (and indeed was, for everyone's experience was different in its particulars) was a routine of life for these bomber crews; that they simply described their trip to the Intelligence Officer, as Musgrove was already doing, and went off to bed. We joined him by the table as he talked and the IO wrote. Another 207 operation was being recorded for posterity in his report.

'How were the defences?' the IO asked.

'Pretty lively,' said Musgrove. 'Ask Blacking. He was seeing them for the first time.'

'I can't offer any comparisons,' I put in, 'not having had any previous experience; but I thought they were very alert, both the 'lights, which caught us first, and the HE which followed them, and especially the flaming onions, which were not only terrifying but came up close on both sides of us.'

'Was there anything new, Musgrove?' the IO asked.

'No I don't think so. Only perhaps the speed with which they moved their searchlights. They seemed to be tracking us.'

The IO made a quick note. 'All right gentlemen, thank you. If there's anything further you think of, let me know.'

'That's it,' said Musgrove, 'we can get to bed. Thank you, Blacking, you did well. Goodnight.'

As I went through the HQ door into the night and the sudden cool silence I looked up towards the dark sky, where less than an hour before we'd been engaged in a deadly combat. It was hard to imagine that what we were looking at now was the same arena, that for years it had been the scene of fights to the death, by day and night, and yet could look so peaceful.

'You'll be glad to get some rest.' Tring's voice came from behind me, breaking into my reverie. 'You've had an exciting day. Your baptism of fire.'

'Well, I don't regret it. It had to come some time — this is what we were trained for.'

'You couldn't have had a better captain than Musgrove. Even so, one needs a bit of luck. Goodnight.'

'Goodnight, Tring.'

His figure swung away into the darkness as I found my tent. Its flap was open and Harrison was presumably fast asleep. I didn't want to disturb him. It didn't take me long to get out of my flying kit and into bed, and I was so relieved to find myself in comfort and safety once again that as soon as my head touched the pillow — or so it seemed — I was fast asleep.

4

Familiarization

A fly woke me, landing on my forehead. When I brushed it away it did a quick take-off, a zooming circuit, then alighted on the blanket about three inches from my nose. In concentrating on his manoeuvres I collected my thoughts, starting with a quick glance at my watch, which said 8.50. I looked across the tent. Harrison's bed was empty; it was also made. He must have been gone some time. Suddenly I heard a voice. 'Mr Blacking!' it said, and a shadow darkened the entrance to the tent, embodying itself as Tom Peters, our batman. 'Mr Blacking! Ah, you're awake, sir. Beg pardon for troubling you after your night flying, but there's a Mr Darke here to see you — Second Lieutenant Darke, from 99 Squadron.'

'Oscar!' I said, half expecting him to appear. 'Where is he, Peters?'

'In the Mess, sir. Shall I tell him you'll come over?'

'Yes,' I said. 'Bring me some shaving water; I'll be there as quickly as I can.'

What's Oscar doing here? I wondered, peering into the mirror attached to the tent pole while I had a rapid shave and wash. Has he been transferred to 0/400s or is this only a social call? I tied my tie, pulled on my uniform and gave my hair a quick brush then hurried over to the Mess. Oscar Darke was sitting in one of the wicker chairs looking at a copy of *The Sphere;* he was in uniform, not flying kit.

'Hello, Oscar,' I greeted him. 'I thought you'd had a forced landing.'

'No,' he said. 'You remember when we met at Hesdin — yesterday — after the funerals, you said, "Come and see us at Ligescourt some time." Well, we had no operation today, or rather I hadn't, so I thought I'd seize the opportunity.'

'You did right,' I answered. 'Welcome to 207 Squadron. I'm sorry I wasn't around when you arrived, but as you guessed or were told, I was flying last night.'

'I'm sorry I woke you,' said Oscar.

'That's all right. I'd have woken soon, anyway. Have you had breakfast? Or could we offer you a cup of tea or coffee?'

'Could I have some coffee? — but don't let me spoil your breakfast.'

While I ate bacon and egg, still with the sights and sounds of last night's operation horribly vivid in my mind, Oscar sipped his coffee. He looked pale and drawn, rekindling the impression I'd formed of him at Hesdin.

'How are you getting on?' I said.

I think I knew; he was hating the daylight bombing raids on DH9s. I think I also knew why, after having met me, he'd seized the opportunity of coming over to Ligescourt. He wanted to change to 0/400s and hoped to be able to join 207 Squadron, through an introduction from me. But he gave nothing away in his reply, merely saying:

'All right, 99's a good squadron. I couldn't wish for a better bunch of fellows. But we've had some back luck recently, as I told you. I — I . . .'

'Hallo, Blacking. Had a good sleep?'

The voice that interrupted him was Harrison's, cheerful as usual.

'Sorry, I didn't mean to butt in,' he said. 'I went to the tent expecting to have to wake you. When I found you'd gone I thought you might be here.'

'Oscar, this is Lieutenant Harrison,' I put in, adding in explanation: 'Second Lieutenant Darke from 99 Squadron. We trained together — I think I told you.'

Harrison nodded. 'Glad to see you. We wouldn't normally meet, the day boys and the night boys. Two different worlds. Blacking, the CO would like to see you. He wants to get you off on some familiarization — this morning, if possible.'

'I'll go right over,' I said. 'Oscar, can you hang around for a bit? I shan't be long.'

He nodded and Harrison sat down at the table. 'Leave him to me. We can talk about the pros and cons of day or night navigation.'

As I made my way over to HQ I wondered what plans the CO had in store for me. Clearly the squadron weren't wasting much time in getting a new pilot operational. They needed every possible crew, with the Germans on the offensive again, to help to turn the tide. I knocked on the Adjutant's door, then I heard the sound of his voice. He seemed to be finishing off a conversation in angry terms and banged the 'phone down.

'Come in!' he almost shouted, still upset by something he had heard. 'Ah, Blacking. The CO wants to see you.'

His urbane manner re-asserting itself, with the flexibility of a bank manager's temperament, he got up and tapped on the adjoining office door. Half opening and peering round it, he said, 'Second Lieutenant Blacking, sir,' and motioned me to enter, shutting the door behind me.

'Morning, Blacking,' the Major greeted me as I saluted. 'How did you get on last night?'

'All right, sir. It was a bit frightening. But Captain Musgrove's a very experienced pilot.'

'You know the kind of thing you're in for, then?'

I nodded. 'Yes, sir.'

'All right. Then as you probably know, we've got a big task on. The Huns have started a major offensive. They're aiming to drive a wedge between the British and French armies, and we in the air have got to do all we can to try to stop them. The scout squadrons are out every day possible, low-level strafing; the DH4s and 9s are also out daily, bombing; and we put in our punch at night. To make it effective we must get every serviceable aircraft in the air whenever we're given a target: railway sidings, ammunition dumps, stores parks, factories — and this means always having enough crews available at all times. That's where you come in. This means getting into the air today, with your observer, familiarizing yourself with the field and the area, then doing the whole thing again at night, using one or two lighthouses, so you can find you way back here.

'The aircraft you use will be one prepared for the night's raid, so don't bend it. When you come down the AMs will check any snags you might have found, then refuel and arm it, with bombs and bullets. Any questions?'

'No sir,' I said. I didn't feel there could be any, after such a comprehensive briefing.

'All right, then. See your flight commander and he'll arrange a machine for you. Take your observer with you — never fly solo — and don't go anywhere near the lines.'

I saluted and stepped out of the CO's office.

I thought I'd better collect Harrison, as he would be coming with me, so I first went back to the Mess, where he and Oscar would still be arguing about navigation.

'The CO's asked me to see the flight commander about an aircraft,' I said, 'and you're to come with me.'

'All right,' responded Harrison in his straightforward way, getting up from his chair and saying to Oscar, 'We'll continue the argument. Excuse me.'

'Any chance of coming with you?' asked Oscar.

I looked at Harrison. I didn't know the rules on the squadron about taking passengers on training or test flights.

'We'd have to ask the flight commander's permission, then it's up to the aircraft captain to say if he wishes to take an extra body,' Harrison averred, looking at me.

'You'd better come over to the flight offices with me, Oscar,' I said, 'then if the flight commander agrees you'll be ready to get aboard.'

As we walked across the grass I looked up at the sky. The weather was unsettled, the sky a summer embodiment of Shakespeare's 'uncertain glory of an April day' — a line I'd remembered from my schooldays — with lots of white, moving clouds which threatened showers.

We found Captain Musgrove talking with the cheerful engineering officer, Captain Bishop.

'Aircraft?' said the latter. 'At this time of day? I've got a lot of old crocks which we'll just about manage to get into the air tonight.'

'How about Blacking doing an air test?' the flight commander queried.

'Well, there's B2.' Bishop consulted the blackboard which showed the squadron's serviceability state which was reported to Wing HQ every morning. 'She had a mag drop on the starboard engine last night but I think it's been cleared. Chief!'

Flight Sergeant Arnett materialized out of the workshops.

'B2. Is she serviceable now?'

'Yes, sir. We're towing her across shortly.'

'All right,' said Captain Musgrove. 'Blacking can give her an hour's flight. What time do you want to take off?'

Harrison looked at his watch and I consulted mine. It was 9.45. How about 10.30?' I suggested.

Captain Musgrove agreed. 'Have a couple of AMs out there for starting, Chief, and make sure you check on the weather,' he added looking at me, 'and Harrison will see you don't get lost. And don't break the aeroplane. They're in short supply, and every one is needed just now.'

'Could we take a visitor from 99 Squadron as a passenger?' I asked. 'He's asked for a flight and could ride in the gunner's position.'

'If he's happy to fly with you,' said the flight commander, looking me squarely in the eye, 'then it's all right with me.'

'We'd better get our kit,' put in Harrison, a cue to leave the flight commander and Captain Bishop to their interrupted conversation.

As we walked back towards the flight offices, Oscar said, 'Thank you, Leslie. I've always wanted to fly in one of your night monsters. Could I borrow some kit?'

'If we can find someone small enough,' Harrison commented, looking at Oscar, who was about five feet four.

By the time we managed to suit him, and get into our own flying kit and check on the weather — a front was expected to pass through, but not until later in the day, hardly affecting an hour's local flying — thirty minutes had passed and by the time we'd trudged across to the aircraft it was 10.20. Two ack emmas were waiting to start us up.

'Would you help Mr Darke into the gunner's cockpit?' I said to them. 'He's coming as a passenger. By the time you've got him settled we'll be ready to start.'

Then I climbed up the front ladder, crouched my way through into the cockpit and settled myself in the right-hand seat. Harrison followed.

'I think you'd better do a few turns around the local area first,' he said, 'then I'll give you a course to take you to the lighthouse we'll be using at night.'

One of the AMs, on the port wing, handed across the strap he'd removed from the wheel-grip on the control column. As an instinctive reaction to this tangible proof that the controls were free I heaved on full right and then full left aileron, peering along to the outer ends of the top mainplane as I did so, to see the ailerons go up and down. Then I tried the elevators and rudders, pulling the control column hard back into our laps (Harrison was too experienced a hand to be taken by surprise at this) and jabbing the rudder pedals to left and right. As I looked back towards the tail empennage, Oscar Darke gave me a cheerful thumbs-up from the gunner's cockpit.

Another thumbs-up came from the port wing, where the two AMs

— one on either side of the Rolls-Royce Eagle VIII, holding the starting-handle — were ready to turn the engines. I pushed up the port magneto switches and opened the throttle about an inch, then put my thumbs up. Slowly the big four-bladed propeller began to turn, then the engine gave a deep cough and fired. I caught it with a slight jab of throttle, which I then eased back, to make the slipstream less uncomfortable for the men on the wings, while they pulled out the handle, and slithered off to the rear, reappearing on my right to start the starboard Eagle, which was a bit reluctant, but went at the second go. When both were running and the AMs were clear, I closed the radiator shutters and checked the starboard oil pressure indicator on the engine nacelle, while Harrison checked the port indicator; then I used the metal knob on the throttles to open up each engine slightly, till both were ticking over quite fast. After a few moments I ran each of them up in turn, checking them on separate magnetos, finally pulling back the throttles to ensure that there was no cutting-out at low rpm. All seemed well and we were ready for the off. I gave a final thumbs-up to the AMs, waving to them the 'chocks away' sign, then pushed the metal knob steadily forward to open up both throttles, and we began to move.

There was a little way to go before we reached our take-off point, the beginning of the landing tee, so I swung the 0/400 first to the left and then to the right, scanning the sky for any other aircraft. There was no one on the 'bandstand' (as we called the sandbagged control-tower) at this time of day, so we relied on a visual check. All was clear and I lined up for take-off, pushing the metal knob forward to open up the engines. The long grass field was slightly inclined downwards, helping us to gain speed. I kept my eyes on the slope at the end of it and on the airspeed indicator in the cockpit.

As our speed increased — 20, 30, 40 mph — I pushed hard forward on the control column to bring the tail up. Then, when I felt it clear of the ground, eased back to lift the nose. The wheels stopped rumbling on their oleos, I felt the elevators bite on the slipstream, and we were off, clearing the airfield boundary at about a hundred feet.

I could feel Harrison watching me, he was naturally anxious to see how his new pilot performed. So I decided to do everything as correctly as possible, and climbed the 0/400 straight ahead at a steady 55-60 mph until we reached 1,200 feet, then I levelled-off and let the airspeed settle at about 70 mph. At the same time I synchronized the engines, using the metal knob on the throttle. As we were by then a good way upwind from the airfield (steering about 280 degrees, I noticed from the compass, which was my only other cockpit instrument, apart from the AS1 and altimeter) I decided to turn back, so as to get a good look at the local area before going in for a landing. I indicated with my left thumb to Harrison what I intended to do, and we both instinctively looked round to see that the sky was clear; then I pulled the control wheel hard over to port.

For a moment or two, it seemed, nothing happened. With the Handley's hundred-foot wing span, you had to allow time for the message to get along the control cables to the ailerons; what you had to avoid doing was to go on putting on bank, thinking that nothing had happened. I remembered, just in time, to ease off the bank a bit as we swung over into a forty degree turn, which I continuted, undershooting a bit to enable the compass to settle down, until we were on a due easterly heading which should take us back to Ligescourt. In that direction, we seemed to be going a good deal faster, and I remembered that the front which would be passing through would be preceded by a freshening westerly wind. We'd better watch the weather — there seemed to be a good deal more cloud coming up.

Harrison touched my shoulder and pointed downwards. There was the river, the valley, the airfield, the huts, hangars and aircraft. I let them all slide by under the nose, held a steady heading for a few moments (as if on a bombing run, I thought), then put us into a 180 degree port turn, glancing backwards and seeing Oscar hanging over the side, making the most of his Cook's tour of Ligescourt. The airfield looked extremely small, with the camp on its approach and the river valley at its end. I decided to make my first landing descent a long steady one, so as to judge it correctly. The best thing to do was to keep the circuit fairly wide, to let the HQ and the tents pass under the port wing, and then to start a descending turn to port, lining up with the tee.

But the wind had freshened since we took off, and I was further out than I'd anticipated, so I kept the power on as we descended so that the speed wouldn't drop if I tried to stretch the glide: 1,000 feet — 800 feet — 600 feet — 400 feet — down we came, the AS1 registering 90 mph — 85 mph — 80 mph. This was too fast, so I eased both throttles back with the metal knob: 75 mph — 70 mph: that was better: 65 mph — 200 feet as the camp started to pass beneath us and I could see faces looking upwards. I concentrated now on the field and our airspeed — 60 mph as we crossed the road — and on the flare-out, sitting high up there in the cockpit, nearly twelve feet above the ground. At the right moment (as I judged it) I pulled back the control wheel. The Handley's undercarriage touched and she bounced; I gave a quick bleep of throttle and she steadied, then sank down on three points. We didn't run far.

'Now we'll go off to the lighthouse,' I shouted to Harrison, at the same time looking round to see that the field was clear, and turning the aircraft to port with the throttles then taxying back to the take-off point. We stopped across wind and I glanced back through the wing at Oscar in the gunner's seat: he stuck his thumb up cheerfully, so I was relieved to see he'd survived my first landing at Ligescourt.

'Steer 080 to the lighthouse,' Harrison yelled above the roar of the Eagles. I gave him a nod then twisted the metal knob on the throttles to bring us into wind. I paused a second to glance at the sky behind us. All was clear so I opened up and we gathered speed down the field; a steady pull back on the control column and we were airborne.

The wind was fresher now and there was more cloud. As we climbed up white puffs of it flew by the Handley's nose. To the west the sky looked dark and threatening, but as we turned on to an easterly course it was bright and clear ahead. As I kept the aircraft in its turn Harrison nudged me and pointed over his left shoulder.

'Better watch the weather,' he shouted.

'How long to the lighthouse?' I countered.

'About seven minutes,' he mouthed into my left ear.

'All right, we'll go there then straight back to the airfield.'

Harrison had his map on his knee and looked over the side. 'Make it 070 degrees,' he yelled. 'This is a strongish wind.'

I put on a bank to port but nothing seemed to happen so I put on a little more. Then the ailerons responded to the message and I realized I'd over-corrected, not allowing for the time-lag. We'd turned on to 060 degrees, so I made a gentle starboard correction and managed to settle down on a steady heading, though with a cross-wind component it was starting to be gusty. But this was good practice for the sort of weather we might meet at night on operations.

At 2,000 feet we could see for miles across the Flanders countryside. I looked over to the right where the lines were, but apart from the occasional burst of archie you couldn't tell there was a war on down there, and that thousands of soldiers were embroiled in a life-and-death struggle. We were fortunate to be able to fly clear of it from time to time, and to fight our war in another element. Probably hundreds of aircraft were up over the lines dogfighting, or on reconnaissance or bombing missions, but in the vast acreage of the sky we couldn't see one of them.

'There it is,' shouted Harrison, pointing forwards and downwards.

I peered ahead, but could see nothing particular in the French countryside, dotted with farms and long poplar-lined roads.

'You'd better turn on to a reciprocal, allowing for the wind,' he yelled: 'try 280 degrees.'

This time I swung the Handley into a port turn, easing it off so as not to overshoot the heading, and trying to imagine returning from a raid, using the lighthouse as a homer. We were buffeted by the wind, and suddenly a rain squall hit us, drenching the cockpit and obliterating our view. I held the aircraft as steadily as I could, concentrating on the AS1 (90 mph) and the altimeter (1,800 feet); then, as quickly as it had enveloped us, we were out of that sharp shower. But there were more of them on the way.

'Better get down,' shouted Harrison in my left ear. 'It doesn't look too good.'

I nodded assent and pushed the control wheel forward — 1,700 feet, 1,600 feet — down to 1,200 feet, our speed increasing to 110-115 mph. Then another shower hit us, the rain stinging our faces and the horizon completely disappearing. Harrison thumped my left shoulder and pointed over the side. I knew what his gesticulations meant: we were back within sight of the airfield, though I could see nothing of it.

'We'd better keep flying around until this one passes through,' he yelled, his face and goggles streaming with the wet.

I gave him a thumbs-up and thought that, if we flew on to the west of Ligescourt we might find a clear patch, and follow that in for a landing before the next shower came. So we droned steadily on and after a few moments the sky cleared.

'I'm going in now, before the next shower,' I shouted. 'Keep a good lookout.'

I pulled the Handley into a turn to port, holding it in until the compass came round to ninety degrees, then straightening up. Harrison kept peering over the side, until he biffed me on the shoulder and yelled, 'We're on top of it now. Go a bit more to the right!'

I put on starboard bank and we veered away for a few seconds. Then he signed to me to come left again and I went into a port turn, just catching sight as I did so of the tents, the airfield and its river boundary. We were now at about 1,000 feet and I continued a descending turn until we were downwind, when another shower hit us. This was a time for concentration and coolness; we had to get down, and we had to get down safely. Fortunately, that seemed to be the shower that just gone through, for as we continued our turn into wind for the approach the weather cleared; there was even a watery burst of sunshine.

I pulled the throttles back with the metal knob and we settled into a glide at about 65 mph, which should take us right down to the grass, if I'd judged it right.

I noticed the rain-saturated tents as we sailed over them, then we were across the road and the ground was coming up fast. I closed the throttles and eased back the control wheel, and this time I got it right, for the wheels and the skid seemed to sink down together in a perfect three-pointer. One was lucky some times!

As we taxyed up the field the propellers whirled up spray from the grass, which had had a good soaking. The AMs were there to marshal us in and I swung the aircraft round in response to their signals and switched off.

I followed Harrison out down the ladder. Oscar was already at the front to greet us.

'Thank you very much, Leslie,' he said. 'I think I'll put in for a transfer to 207. I like these big aeroplanes.'

'Any complaints, sir?' one of the mechanics asked me.

'No, I don't think so: everything seemed to be working well.'

'We'd better report to HQ,' put in Harrison. 'They'll put us on the rota now you've had a shake-down flight.'

'Are you going to stay for lunch, Oscar?' I asked him.

'No, I don't thnk so, Leslie; I'd better get back. Can I mention your name when I put my application in?'

'Of course,' I said. We were just crossing the road and there was another shower on its way. 'Have you got transport back to your squadron?'

'Yes, thank you. Cheerio, Leslie; cheerio, Harrison — I enjoyed that flight.'

'Goodbye, Oscar. Don't forget to drop your flying kit in.'

He looked refreshed and happy, but I wondered what lay in store for him — and for me.

'There's one problem,' observed Harrison as we walked across the wet grass towards squadron HQ.

'What's that?' I asked, thinking that he was about to make some shrewd comment on my flying.

'We need a gunner,' he said. 'We'd better tell the flight commander you're back safe and sound, then see what he has to suggest.'

Captain Musgrove wasn't visible in the HQ; he was talking with the CO. So we doffed our flying kit and waited till he re-appeared.

'Hello, Blacking,' he greeted us. 'Glad to see you brought him back safely, Harrison.'

'Rather the other way round. We had a bit of a buffeting,' Harrison commented. Then he added, 'We need a gunner to make up the crew. Who do you suggest?'

'What about the corporal you had up to the time King got wounded?' countered Captain Musgrove. 'You seemed to make a good team.'

'So we were,' said Harrison, 'and the trouble is, Corporal Pilcher's so damned good, all the other pilots want him. But if you could say the word, and if he likes the idea, he could team up with Blacking and myself — I'm sure he'd prefer to be with a regular crew again.'

'I'm agreeable, Harrison,' the captain put in. 'Find Pilcher and see what his feelings are about a new crew. Then let me know if you're going to operate together.'

Another shower hit us as we stepped outside and set off to see the armourers; we'd been lucky to get that flight in before this front started to come through.

We found Corporal Pilcher up to the armpits in oil. He was cleaning a twin Lewis gun, taken from the front cockpit of one of the Handleys.

'Glad to see you're sprucing up my guns, Charlie,' said Harrison.

'Yes sir,' the corporal responded. 'There's nothing like keeping things in good working order — especially if you're going to have to use 'em in an emergency.'

He was a small man, with ginger hair and freckles, of a reddish complexion and with a cheerful, pugnacious expression.

'How would you like to fly with Mr Blacking?' Harrison came straight to the point, introducing me with a nod in my direction. 'He's just joined the squadron after training in England, and I can vouch for his capability.'

Corporal Pilcher gave me a very direct look; not unkindly or inquisitively but as if he were summing me up in a glance. Then he turned to Harrison.

'Well, if you say so, sir, it's all right by me. I'd rather be in a regular crew again, where you can work up an understanding. Otherwise there could be misunderstandings at the wrong time.'

'I agree,' said Harrison. 'I'll tell the flight commander. He'll probably want us to make a night familiarization flight before our first operation. We've just done a day one. But it will depend on the weather and on aircraft availability. You'd better keep an eye on the notice-board, Pilcher.'

'Yes, sir,' the corporal replied. 'We'll meet again soon then, Mr Blacking.'

I gave him a wink and a smile. I liked his character, and could feel confident with him in the rear cockpit. A gust of rain lashed one of the windows in the armoury.

'What shall we do?' Harrison asked. 'Wait for this shower to go through or run for it?'

But the question was answered for us. At that moment the door burst open and two wet-looking figures appeared, taking-off their caps and shaking them — Captains Brinden and Bishop, our flight commander and the squadron's engineering officer.

'Hello Harrison, Blacking,' Brinden nodded to us. 'Well, have you fixed it — have I a new crew?'

'You have,' said Harrison. 'Corporal Pilcher has agreed, and we told him there might possibly be a night familiarization flight before we go on operations.'

'Correct,' Brinden confirmed briefly. 'But everything depends on availability of aircraft. If tonight's show should be cancelled by GHQ because of the weather, and if the weather should then improve locally, then you could do it after dark this evening. You'll just have to stand by and see what happens.'

'In the mean time,' I put in, 'we'll go over the night-flying procedures. The more I can get clear on the ground, the less confusion when we're in the air.'

'You couldn't have a better mentor,' said Brinden, nodding towards Harrison. 'Work things out between you, and attend tonight's briefing anyway.'

As I opened the door a fresh gust of rain-laden wind hit the side of the hut. We pulled our caps down and made a dash across the wet grass to SHQ.

'Let me explain,' Harrison began, still breathless. 'This is the procedure we follow: every aircraft is allocated a recognition letter or number at briefing, and this is flashed from the control tower, giving you permission to take off. Once in the air we head for Doullens, our 'home' lighthouse. Are you quite clear as to how this system of lighthouses works?'

'Yes,' I said. 'I think so. But I'd be glad if you'd explain it.'

'Well,' Harrison went on patiently, 'scattered over Northern France is a chain of about twenty-three lighthouses, most of them with recognition letters and a few of them with numbers, which they flash in Morse code at frequent intervals. Doullens, our home lighthouse, is 'Q', and we know the magnetic tracks to and from all the others; so we head for 'Q' when we set out, and back to it when we return. When we get there after returning from a raid we have to ask for permission to land, in case Ligescourt is being bombed.'

'Doullens is south-east of here, isn't it?' I asked.

'Yes,' said Harrison, 'I see you're getting to know the local area. In fact the River Authie, which forms the north-eastern boundary of this airfield, flows through Doullens. We could have followed it this afternoon if the weather had been better.'

'There's one other thing I'd like to ask you,' I added, 'and that's for your help in night touch-downs. I find it a bit difficult to judge my height . . .'

'You seemed to manage all right this morning,' Harrison interjected.

'I mean at night; and it would be a great help if you could hang over the side and call out our approximate height above the ground.'

'We'll see how it goes,' he said cheerfully, though I got the feeling that he might have been a little dismayed at the idea of his new pilot not being able to get an 0/400 down at night. 'Are you clear now about the procedures? They're really quite simple.'

'Yes, thank you, George. When we do our night familiarization we could fly to 'Q', then away from it, then turn back and simulate the procedure of returning from a raid. I wonder what the weather's going to do?'

'Looks just about the same — or worse.' Harrison had stood up and was peering through the window. 'All we can do is wait for the briefing. In the meantime' — he glanced at his watch —'lunch. We've done a good day's work this morning. Come on, beat you to the Mess.'

Although we didn't have time to look around as we sprinted across to the big marquee, the general impression one got was that it had set in for the day. A wind-blown shower swirled against the canvas as we reached the entrance. There was a general impression of midday gloom with ragged dark clouds down to the horizon.

'I'm afraid we've got to assume we'll be flying,' said Harrison as we made for the bar, 'so it's grenadine or lemonade.'

'I'll have a lemonade, thanks,' I heard myself saying. Grenadine now reminded me of Hesdin and the funeral I attended.

'There you are Leslie. Cheers,' Harrison intoned as he took the glasses from the barman. 'Here's to our new crew.'

'Corporal Pilcher in particular.' I enunciated the syllables and raised my lemonade with appropriate dignity. 'May he never have a stoppage.'

'Indeed,' said Harrison. 'And that reminds me. After lunch, we've got an important job to do.'

'What's that?'

'We've got to get you kitted-out with your own flying clothing. I'd nearly forgotten that.'

'Well, we can do it this afternoon. If we do fly today it won't be until the evening.'

'Let's eat,' said Harrison. 'I'm famished after this morning's unusual activity.'

After lunch, which was hash, with locally bought vegetables (cabbage and potatoes), followed by stewed apples and custard, we made a quick dash across to the flying clothing store. It was still raining, though not heavily, but there was plenty more around and the wind blew in gusts.

'Are you there, McTavish?' Harrison shouted, banging on the wooden counter.

Beyond it, out of reach in the recesses of the hut, were wooden shelves. On them were piles of clothing, arranged according to type. Everything was very neat and seemed to reflect the custodian's view of life — that it should be carefully arranged and labelled.

'Mac —'

'Sirr?' said a voice, closely followed by its owner who materialized from among the shelves, as if he had become part of them. His expression was quizzical, his eyebrows bushy, his complexion weather-beaten, his hair dark; a brown overall signified complete professionalism.

'Sergeant McTavish. Mr Blacking's a new pilot on the squadron. Will you please fit him up with flying gear?'

Harrison's request met with a dour but instinctive response. The dark eyes across the counter looked me up and down, making mental measurements. Then their owner disappeared among his shelves, returning from time to time to place another heap upon the counter. All this without a word. Finally, when the piles placed there had almost obscured him from view, Sergeant McTavish made room at one side of them to place an inventory form on the counter, entering every item with its reference number, memorized from long experience of the numerology and terminology of Service stores.

'Sign here, sirr,' he said, reversing his pad with its carbons and pushing it towards me. 'If any of yon don't fit, we can change 'em. It's Simpson's on the Somme, ye ken sirr.'

I signed. 'Thank you, sergeant. I'll try them on and hope not to trouble you again.'

'Just a moment,' Harrison put in with his characteristic quiet determination. If I was Hamlet he was certainly Horatio. 'Let's see what we've bought before we leave the shop; then we shan't come back with any complaints, eh, Mac?'

Sergeant McTavish maintained a dour silence while Harrison turned the items over, enumerating them as if talking to himself: Sidcot suit*, fur boots, helmet and goggles, woollen socks, silk gloves and leather gauntlets. That seems to be the lot. But we'll be back with anything which isn't the right size to change it, Mac.'

'Verra well, sir,' said the sergeant. 'I'll expect not to see ye again, but if I do, I'll noo what ye want.'

With the flying clothing under our arms we made a quick dash back to the tent through the wet afternoon, with grey, lowering clouds all around. I made a rapid check of all the items, taking off my uniform and pulling on the Sidcot suit, which fitted me confortably; then the woollen socks and fur boots, the helmet — which seemed a bit tight at first, but moulded to the shape of my head as I pulled it down — and the gloves, one layer on another.

'Sergeant McTavish has a good eye for sizes,' I said.

'Long experience, I think', Harrison suggested. 'At least you don't have to bother to take anything back. You can keep it all here until we go over for briefing this evening. Then I'll find you a locker. Till then, you might as well relax.'

I took off my new flying kit and folded it up. Then I lay down on the bed; there seemed to be nothing more to do for the time being, and it was a wet afternoon. Harrison stretched out on his bed. 'Might as well make the most of it,' he said. 'There's tea at five. I won't disturb you

* Named after Sidney Cotton, its designer, an Australian who served in the RNAS.

before then.'

I lay looking up at the at the canvas and hearing the pattering of the rain. I could just see, through the tent flap, drifts of grey cloud scudding past. What was it like in the lines right now, I wondered, as they faced another night of rain, cold and discomfort? Anything we could do to shorten the war would help to bring an end to the awful sufferings of the men on the ground. Eventually I drifted off and found myself walking through some quiet, leafy countryside in early spring. Birds were singing and every now and then one of them flickered through the trees, so swiftly one could scarcely follow his flight. Above the wood was a fresh April cloudscape, against a background of brilliantly blue sky. Shafts of sunshine which filtered through the branches shimmered and were broken from time to time as a breeze ruffled the woodland. I felt free and happy despite the rifle slung over my left shoulder, a belt of ammunition across my chest and a haversack over my right shoulder.

Then the woods fell silent; no birds sang or flickered through the branches. The trees thinned out and I noticed that they were bare of leaves; the sky darkened and it began to rain; I could hear thunder — or was it gunfire?

Suddenly I found myself on a downward slope, but kept on walking. The skies were darker still now and the rain came on harder than ever. Steep, straight banks rose up on either side of me, until I realized I was walking below ground level. It had become muddy under foot and a grey rat slithered across the bottom of the trench. I'd automatically put my bayonet on my rifle and brought it to the ready, as the sound of gunfire increased. Somehow I wanted to get up the side of the trench, to see what was going on, and when some steps appeared I climbed up them and got over, sinking to my knees in mud at first but pulling myself up again. Then there was a blinding flash, a fountain of mud and earth spattered over me and I fell forward on my face. As I looked up I saw other figures rising and falling and half-running on either side of me, until a burst of machine-gun fire mowed them down and I pressed my face into the mud.

I felt someone touching my shoulder. The terrible sounds of battle seemed to die away and I heard a voice calling my name. I looked up, expecting to see mud. My face was deep in the pillow of my camp bed and the voice was Harrison's.

'Come on, Leslie,' he was saying. 'It's time we went over to the Mess. You went right off.'

I looked towards the triangle of the open tent flap, and the sodden skies outside it. 'Is it still raining?' I didn't expect any answer to this banal remark, made as I swung my legs over the side of the bed to put my shoes on. Somehow each little mundane action was a wonderful relief after that frightful dream. I didn't care whether it was raining or not. I just wanted to be with ordinary people again, to take away the nasty taste of my traumatic experience.

'All right,' I said, 'let's go.'

Harrison looked at me but said nothing. The air outside was refreshingly sweet and clean. In the Mess tent the hot cup of tea I drank tasted like nectar, the bread-and-butter and jam like ambrosia. I couldn't explain how relieved and exhilarated I felt. A line from one of the Psalms came into my mind: 'Even like as a dream when one awaketh . . .'

Harrison must have wondered what was going on, but he was too polite and tactful to make any comment; until he said in his quiet, matter-of-fact way, 'We'll go across to Headquarters when you're ready, to hear the briefing for tonight, then we'll know what we're going to do. If operations are off, there's bound to be a party; but if we're flying we can join it when we get back. Ready?'

I nodded. I was now prepared for anything, so long as it meant being with the squadron, and flying.

'Wing has decided to cancel tonight's operation,' said the Major.

An ironic cheer went up from the lines of benches. It had hardly died down when the CO continued, 'But this raid will be put on tomorrow night, if the weather improves. There's to be no let-up in the pressure on the Hun. We've got to take the weight off the boys in the line.'

For a second my awful dream came back to me. Then I heard the major say, 'Provided the weather improves locally, there'll be some training flying tonight, for new crew familiarization. Any questions?'

There was a moment's barren silence.

'Thank you, gentlemen,' said the CO, to the accompaniment of benches scraping the ground as his audience stood. 'Dismiss.'

'That means we're on,' said Harrison in the sudden burst of conversation, 'and you'll have to bring your flying kit across — we forgot it.'

'I'll check with old Bishop first on what aircraft we're to have. When do we take off?'

'As soon as it's near dark,' Harrison replied. 'The time should be on the board.'

I found Captain Bishop in the aircraft parking area, which was crowded with 0/400s because none had been towed out to the take-off point that afternoon. He was with his senior NCO, Flight Sergeant Arnett (whose name I happened to remember from our morning visit to the Servicing Flight), a cheerful Northumbrian — to judge from his Geordie accent.

'Hello, Captain Bishop,' I said. 'I'm to fly on local familiarization tonight, as there aren't any operations. Can I have an aircraft?'

'You are, are you?' the engineering officer retorted, clearly implying that all his 0/400s had been serviced and stabled for the night. There were to be no ops and there would be a party in the Mess, so he didn't want this desirable state of affairs to be upset by a new pilot demanding an aircraft to fly around in after dark. But Bishop's essential good nature re-asserted itself after this momentary irritation (expressed facially rather than verbally).

'Well, we'd better find you something to fly. Which is the nearest aircraft to the field, Arnett?'

' "B2", sir, I think,' said the flight sergeant.

'All right, have her towed out, with a couple of AMs for starting. What time do you want to take off, Blacking?'

'About eight o'clock.'

'And how long will you be up?'

'Say an hour and a half.'

'Have the AMs go out there with the aircraft for line-up at 7.45 and tell them they must be ready for the last landing from 9.15 onwards to see Mr Blacking in.'

'All right, sir. "B2" is fully fuelled. There'll be no bombs but the gunner will be responsible for his ammo and his Very cartridges.'

'Right,' said Captain Bishop. These engineers didn't waste any time or words. I got the impression I could trust their aircraft. 'Who is your gunner, Blacking?'

'Corporal Pilcher,' I answered.

'And a very good man too — you were lucky to get him. Well, "B2" will be ready for you. Have a good trip and bring her back safely.'

'Thank you, Captain Bishop,' I said, nodding to Flt Sgt Arnett, who had one of those open, confident faces with a wide grin and obviously enjoyed looking after aircraft. 'Eight o'clock then — provided the weather doesn't worsen in the next two hours.'

It was still blowing, and raining, as I walked back to the tent to get my flying kit. There was a ragged dark sky all around, but it was less gusty and over towards the west there was just a hint of brightness, as if the front had nearly passed through. I picked up the kit, clutched it in my arms and made my way back to the Headquarters.

Harrison was there and greeted me: 'Hello, Leslie. I've got a locker for you. Now you're really a member of the squadron.'

'How about Corporal Pilcher?' I asked as I was pushing my stuff into the locker. 'How do we let him know?'

'He happened to come in here while you were over there checking on the aircraft — so I told him. We meet here at 7.30, so in the meantime we can get something to eat. I've worked out magnetic courses from and back to the Doullens lighthouse, so you can get a trial run. And I've checked the weather — still showery.'

'You're a good chap,' I said. 'Remind me to buy you a drink when we get back.'

I felt rather clumsy and cumbersome, wearing my flying boots and Sidcot for the first time, as we walked out to the aircraft in the dusk. Corporal Pilcher was carrying his Lewis gun and several belts of ammunition; Harrison had his maps and torch; I felt quite empty-handed. '2' looked lonely, standing there by herself. When we got up to her — looking bigger and bigger the nearer we got — the two AMs were sitting on the wings ready to start. I went up the ladder first, crawled through the tunnel and got across into the right-hand seat, easing my way into it to find the most comfortable position. Harrison followed closely, and as soon as he was in and seated I checked the controls for freedom of movement by pulling the wheel hard back, then fully over from left to right, and exercising the rudder pedals.

'Are the wings locked?' I asked the AMs.

'Yes, sir,' said one of them, indicating the locking pins.

'Then we're ready to start.'

As they turned the handles in slow but quickening rhythm, I eased the port throttle forward; then the engine fired, the four blades of the propeller turned, and I felt the power communicate itself to me. The AMs scrambled down, got up on the starboard wing and the procedure was repeated. No trouble at all.

'Don't forget to give me that visual check when we get close to the ground on landing,' I shouted across to Harrison.

'I won't,' he yelled. 'Your first course is a hundred degrees — one hundred. Turn left after take-off.'

I set 100 degrees on the large compass on the floor, and opened the throttles gradually to warm the engines up. I could see the two AMs standing out in front of the aircraft, over to the left, waiting for a thumbs-up. Then I opened up the port engine and tested the magneto switches, throttling-back quickly to make sure it still ran smoothly, and followed the same procedure with the starboard engine. All was well, so I gave the thumbs-up sign to the AMs, waiting for them to pull away the chocks then opened up enough for the aircraft to move forward a few feet. It was now quite dark. A green light shone out from the control tower. I looked round at Pilcher to see that he was all right and got a wave from him, looked across at Harrison who gave me a thumbs-up, then I opened the throttles by using the metal knob in between them and pressed the control column forward to get the kite-like tail up.

She came off the ground almost without my noticing, and we headed into the night on a steady climb, the River Authie passing as a dull gleam below us. I put '2' into a turn to port when we'd reached 700 feet, being careful not to overbank, but waiting until the ailerons reacted at the end of those long wings. Gradually we came round and I checked the bank so that the compass would settle down, until we were about on course. Harrison was peering forward into the night, I was concentrating on my height and airspeed.

After a few minutes he thumped me on the shoulder and shouted, 'There it is!'

A white beam pointing straight upwards and stabbing the darkness was flashing dash-dash-dot-dash. It was 'Q', the Doullens lighthouse, so I headed over towards it at about 1,000 feet. There was broken cloud some 500 feet above us.

'Turn on to 050 — oh-five-oh,' Harrison yelled when we were over

Doullens, vigorously pointing over to his left. I realized that this course would take us away from the battle front — a safe precaution on a training flight. Heaving the control column over, I put us into a turn; the 0/400 was a heavy aircraft and the reaction from the control surfaces, which were a long way from the cockpit, was slow. The important thing was not to put on too much bank and then overshoot the turn.

We steadied on the north-easterly heading and I noticed that the sky was becoming a good deal cloudier. Even at 1,500 feet (I'd let the aircraft ease itself up a bit) we were brushing through the bases of what seemed to be a considerable cloud mass. Evidently we were catching up the weather which had passed through Ligescourt that afternoon. I became convinced of this when a shower started to spatter the windscreen, then increased in intensity, drenching the occupants of the cockpits. The red and green wingtip identification lights glowed brightly in the rainy darkness. To give an indication of my feelings about this murky weather I pointed to the left. Fortunately, Harrison quickly got the message — we had already developed a good understanding as a crew. 'Two-three-oh degrees,' he shouted; the reciprocal course would take us back into clearer conditions.

Once again I heaved on the control column, this time for a big turn — 'doing a one-eighty,' as they used to say. Gradually we went round. I concentrated hard on keeping the airspeed constant, not losing or gaining any height. As we steadied on the new course the rain eased off, and after a few minutes the sky cleared. We both realized that we should soon see the Doullens lighthouse flashing its letter, but nothing pierced the darkness. I saw Harrison looking at his watch. He must have timed our last leg to the turn, and now our time was up, even allowing for a head wind; so we should see something. We did, both of us at once. Over to our left was a steady red light, which glowed like an ember in the surrounding blackness.

'That means we're not to land,' shouted Harrison. 'There must be a raid on. We'll have to orbit.'

I realized what this meant: round and round Doullens until the 'Q' came up again, keeping the 0/400 on a steady turn at a constant height. It was good night-flying practice. After about ten minutes we got our first glimpse of the stars as the cloud broke up and the rain area moved away. I was contemplating their beauty, while trying to concentrate on piloting the aircraft, when Harrison hit me on the shoulder and yelled, 'There it is!'

Over to the left, a dash-dash-dot-dash punctuated the dark sky.

'Steer two-eight-zero,' he shouted and put the new course on the compass grid ring.

I eased the aircraft into a turn and we headed for Ligescourt, only about ten minutes' flying from Doullens. Harrison was the first to spot the lights of the landing tee, enthusiastically pointing just over to our right, and I hoped he hadn't forgotten to lean out and monitor our height on the approach. I turned towards the airfield (we were upwind of the tee) and as we got nearer to it saw the River Authie shining in the darkness. Gliding down to get to circuit height, we crossed the river and I pulled the 0/400 round to enter the downwind leg, held it long enough for the lights to disappear under the port wing, then went into a descending turn, pulling back the throttles and straightening up when the tee appeared ahead. All I had to do was to judge the approach correctly — not too high, not too low, and level out at the right time, helped by Harrison's guidance.

I kept my eye on the lights, aiming for the first of them. Harrison hung over the side, waiting for the moment when I should pull back on the control column, to ensure that I didn't do so too soon or too late. We were over the camp, swishing down towards the road. Harrison gave me a thumbs-up and I heaved back on the elevator control. The wheels rumbled satisfyingly on the grass. We were back.

When we got to the end of our landing run I swung the 0/400 round and we taxyed up the field with the lights of the tee to guide us. At the top of the field two torches were being waved in a circular motion, and when we got near them this changed to a side-to-side one.

'That means switch off,' said Harrison. He didn't need to shout any more. When the propeller blades had whirred round for the last time, all we would hear was the crackling of the exhaust pipes as they started to cool down.

Then one of the AMs shouted up from the ground below, 'We thought we'd seen the last of you, sir, when the raid started.'

'Was it bad?' asked Harrison.

'A few bombs and all the lights went out,' said the voice. 'But it lasted about half an hour.'

Harrison led the way down the ladder and I followed. The AMs had already started folding back the wings and the tractor was ready to tow the aircraft away. Corporal Pilcher had extracted himself from the rear cockpit and we made our way over to the squadron offices.

'Thank you, corporal,' I said en route. 'I expect you knew what was going on.'

'No thanks, sir,' responded the gunner in his honest and cheerful way. 'I didn't have anything to do except to keep a sharp look-out. I realized what had happened when we couldn't see the lighthouse.'

'There you are,' put in Harrison — for my benefit, but I'd already realised it — 'the best rear-crew man in the squadron. Always calm, always efficient. Will you put up with us, Pilcher, if we get you there and back in one piece?'

'If you don't get us lost, Mr Harrison, and if Mr Blacking gets us up and down safely, then I'm happy,' said the corporal phlegmatically. 'So I'll see you tomorrow, sir' — addressing me, before he disappeared into the darkness. We'd reached the HQ hut, but it was deserted.

'I reckon there's a party on,' Harrison said. 'Let's get rid of this kit and go over to the Mess.'

We set course for our tent and hung up our flying gear then made for the Mess. It was clear from the noise that 207 had been stood down for the night. Instead of the sombre scene I'd got used to there, with quiet conversation, grenadine being drunk, meals eaten quickly and people coming and going purposefully, everybody was there, someone was banging away on the piano the tunes from the latest London shows, the air was thick with smoke and everyone was talking or singing at the top of his voice.

Harrison and I pushed our way to the bar. In no time at all we were equipped with pints of beer and talking or singing as loudly as everyone else. I found Captain Pennington, the adjutant, standing next to me swaying slightly.

' 'lo, Blacking,' he said. 'How's the jolly old squadron, then? Not so bad, eh?'

The last few days, and all that had happened, flashed through my mind in a second. I thought how, from my own brief experience, a squadron had two levels of operating: the air, where what happens is a private matter for the crew involved, and on the ground. Crews didn't say what had happened to them, except in writing an official report. Otherwise they laughed it off, as now. Everybody was interested in doing the job, and surviving.

'Not so bad,' I said.

5

The Vegetable Seller

When I woke up I could hear the sound of rain steadily drumming on the canvas of the tent. I looked across towards Harrison. He was still asleep, almost invisible under his blanket. I had a hazy recollection of a party, which I thought about for some time, but finally couldn't remember anything about. Then I thought of getting up, but this seemed to be a matter for serious consideration — in giving it which, I fell asleep again. I was awakened for the second time by a voice calling 'Mr Harrison!'

At the second time (or was it the third?) time of asking my observer stirred and responded unenthusiastically: 'Yes?'

'Mr Harrison, it's the vegetable sellers' day. Can you come sir?'

I recalled, from the depths of my second slumber, that Harrison, among his many quiet attributes, was PMC (President of the Messing Committee) and therefore responsible for the quality of food in the officers' mess — and so for making local purchases.

'I'll be over in about ten minutes,' said Harrison, who had emerged slightly from his cocoon, dismissing the messenger.

'Leslie, would you like to see how the local economy operates?'

I fancied that Harrison, courteous though he was, had a slightly vindictive motive in suggesting this. He was perhaps less concerned, at that moment, about increasing my experience of life on a squadron and rather more about seeing to it that, if he had to get up, I should get up too. This mean reflection, however, lasted only a microsecond, and the pause before answering could have been put down to somnolence.

'Yes, I don't mind,' I heard myself saying. 'It would be interesting.'

'Come on then. Let's get over there before they get into an Anglo-French argument about prices.'

We washed quickly, left shaving till later and pulled on our uniforms. On the way over to the mess Harrison explained. 'We buy our vegetables from a local farmer, who brings them up on his cart, then we haggle about the prices. He always wants to charge far too much. Sometimes he brings his daughter with him, and she's just as sharp as he is. What's more, some of our lads have taught her the worst of the English language, so she can bargain in pure Billingsgate, without really understanding what it means.'

At the back of the big brown marquee which formed the mess a horse was grazing, still between the shafts of a two-wheeled wooden farm cart which was loaded with vegetables — potatoes, cabbages, carrots, turnips, swedes. Nearby, with his thumbs stuck in the arm-holes of his black waistcoat, was a florid man with a wide moustache, pointed at the ends, wearing a shirt without a collar, grey trousers and large black boots, arguing volubly in French with one of the mess cooks, who was answering taciturnly in English, though neither party seemed to understand the other.

However, it wasn't the farmer (as I took him to be) who caught my eye, but a girl who was leaning back on the vegetables sucking a stem of grass, whom I assumed to be his daughter — and if so, one of his most successful and beautiful crops.

She had a mass of chestnut-brown hair, dark eyes that seemed to smoulder as they looked at you, a tan to her skin that spoke of sun and wind and rain, and a figure that her plain white dress showed off in its mature naturalness — the figure of incarnate womanhood, with a full bosom that couldn't be concealed, and hips that had an unaffected swagger, showing off their unique femininity. Her legs were long and brown and bare.

'Monsieur Briand, comment ç'a va avec vous?' said Harrison, approaching with his hand outstretched. 'Tout va bien, eh?'

This diplomatic enquiry seemed to pacify the farmer — who beamed and put out a great brown fist.

'Et combien pour les legumes aujourdhui, monsieur?' went on Harrison, seizing the opportunity of getting down to business as soon as possible.

'Le temps fait mal,' countered the farmer defensively, using the traditional ploy of blaming the weather. 'Et la guerre' — shrugging his shoulders and holding out his hands — 'tout les choses sont très difficiles.'

I caught the girl's eye. She had a half-mocking, half-admiring look which was irresistible.

'Jeanne,' said her father, 'que pense tu?'

'Que les Anglais demandent le bloody lot,' came the reply, without hesitation.

Now, I'd seen Shaw's *Pygmalion* and remembered Eliza Doolittle's famous epithet — uttered after she been schooled to appear in public. But Jeanne had learned her English from the mess cooks and was using it in its proper environment.

'Monsieur Briand, peut-être un pour boire . . . ?' put in Harrison, indicating the rear entrance to the mess — words and gesture which were not lost on the Frenchman as a means of concluding amicably the argument about prices.

I found myself left alone with Jeanne, and very diffidently tried out my schoolboy French. 'Est votre ferme loin d'ici?' I began.

'Non!' exclaimed Jeanne, her eyes widening with surprise that one of les Anglais didn't know exactly where it was. 'C'est près d'ici', she added scornfully.

'Avez-vous beaucoup de vaches?' My question was asked more because 'vaches' was one animal name I could remember, rather than because I really wanted to know, although I could have gone on for ever asking questions of this beautiful creature. No wonder the cooks had tried to teach her English — even of the worst kind.

'Non! Pas de vaches — même une seulement pour du lait. Nous avons des cochons et des poules et des chiens et des chats. C'est tout.'

'Et beaucoup de legumes,' I added, pointing to the cart.

'Et beaucoup de legumes,' she echoed, and we laughed. Her voice had a two-tone quality, rather husky in an intriguing way when speaking, but musical when she laughed.

There was an embarrassing silence, while Jeanne chewed on her stem of grass again in a relaxed way, half smiling at me. I couldn't think of anything else to say, and was searching my mind for some French agricultural phrases I might have learnt as a schoolboy, when the situation was saved by the re-appearance of Harrison and the farmer, obviously in cordial agreement.

Jeanne hardly needed telling that the price had been settled. At a nod from her father she started unloading the vegetables into the buckets and wooden boxes and sacks the mess staff supplied. She was strong and energetic, a marvellous embodiment, I thought, of beauty and vigour, but quite natural and unsophisticated.

With Harrison, as PMC, and the cookhouse corporal keeping an eye on the produce as it was unloaded to make sure it was all of good quality, I could afford to be an onlooker, and I was day-dreaming when I heard a voice say, 'How about a trip to Berck Plage?'

Realizing that it was Harrison's, I pulled myself together. I was being offered another new experience. 'Yes,' I said. 'Is this a duty?'

'Well,' Harrison replied in his polite and careful way, 'it's another of my duties as PMC. We go there for groceries, especially butter. I have a pass, as the town is out of bounds to troops because of you-know-what, and I generally take somebody with me as a safeguard. If we're not flying tonight it would be a good chance to stock up the mess.

'They'll be checking the weather soon, and if HQ doesn't order any operations it would be a good chance to go. We could get ourselves ready in the meantime.'

We were sitting in reverse positions — Harrison in the right-hand (driving) seat, myself in the left-hand seat of the Crossley tender, bound for Berck Plage and its groceries. There were to be no operations that evening, unless some should be ordered at very short notice and in defiance of the weather, which was still south-westerly and stormy. In any case, we should be back by the early afternoon.

I pulled up my great-coat collar against the wind and the rain blowing in through the side of the vehicle and gazed out at the French countryside as we drove north-westwards. Most of the traffic was going the opposite way to us, towards Abbeville and Amiens, probably with supplies for the big push that was soon to end the war. In many respects everything looked just as it must have done in peacetime — as I'd thought when I went to Headin for the funeral; the poplars lining the long straight road, the villages and the farms like the Briands', where Jeanne had grown up, where the seasonal round hadn't changed for centuries, but the customers for produce were now the English, who'd played a large part in whatever education she's had.

We'd left Ligescourt about noon and it was going to take us about three-quarters of an hour to the coast. When we turned off the main road there were twenty bumpy minutes to go to Berck Plage.

'Getting bored?' Harrison shouted. It was nearly as noisy in the Crossley as in the Handley Page, so we made little attempt at conversation. 'Won't be long now; you'll smell the salt sea breezes soon.'

Gradually the countryside changed from the pastoral kind — meadows and woods and streams — to that more spiky, tufted, windswept type which occurs the nearer you get to the sea, where the trees are sparse and stunted and seem to lean away from the prevailing wind. The buildings, too, seem to be whiter, counteracting the glare of sunlight which has that special quality of brightness by the seaside.

However, this wasn't a holiday jaunt. The landscape got more windswept, the buildings whiter, and we were rattling through the streets of a small seaside town where one could smell the ozone and catch glimpses of a grey and stormy English Channel. But the market, when we got to it, was agricultural — well stocked with butter, cheese and eggs which Harrison bargained for and bought with experienced charm and which I helped to load into the back of the tender.

'Like to look at the sea?' he then asked. We drove towards the front and Harrison parked with a great pull on the ratchet of the brake lever.

The sea was grey, its wave tops whipped into a white foam from which smokey plumes blew. The horizon, beyond which lay England, was misty and faded into obscurity. I felt decidedly homesick, thinking that over there lay peace and security, desite wartime privations.

Along the deserted shoreline of Berck Plage wandered the ghosts of peacetime summers past — ladies with white parasols, children with hoops, young men wearing boaters and ogling the girls, older men sipping their aperitifs and swapping saucy postcards. Behind us lay north-east France, a great arms-dump, full of shells and bombs and guns and aircraft, thousands of acres of churned-up earth and men in their millions living in mud and filth and dying obscene deaths.

Harrison must have read my melancholy thoughts.

'Let's get back to the squadron,' he said.

6
Bomber Pilot — The Long Night

The frontal weather system that had swept through with low cloud and gusts of rain and had held up our operations cleared overnight and around midday the dispatch rider from GHQ arrived with our orders, which weren't supposed to be known until briefing at five o'clock. However, a strong rumour (which Harrison heard and told me) started going around that the Valenciennes marshalling yards were our target — a short-range target but a 'hot' one.

Following our first flight together as a crew, the squadron party, my encounter with Jeanne the farmer's daughter and our trip to Berck Plage, I'd felt part of the squadron — which was a happy one, made up of a friendly bunch of youngsters (average age twenty-two); but I hadn't yet proved myself on an operation.

Lying on my bed in the tent that afternoon, trying to intercept a solitary zooming fly, I suddenly recalled some lines by that splendid Roman poet, Horace, which I'd learned at school:

> Aequam memento rebus in arduis,
> servare mentem, non secus in bonis,

which I always translated as

> Remember to keep a steady mind
> in difficult circumstances, not only in good ones,

and which seemed to be a suitable motto to apply in my present situation, as captain of a big bomber aircraft with two fellow crew members. I was musing on this when Harrison's form darkened the tent flap.

'Leslie,' he said, 'I've got news for you.'

What could this be, I wondered; a reprimand from the CO, a posting, or a change of crew? By this time Harrison had come right in, taken off his cap and Sam Browne belt and thrown himself on his bed, so it couldn't be all that important.

'You're Orderly Officer tomorrow,' he said.

'That means,' I replied, half to myself, 'that we must be flying tonight.'

'A correct assumption, I think,' Harrison added quietly. 'So any rest we can get between now and briefing will be beneficial. That's if these flies will let us.'

I'd almost stopped worrying about flies, tiresome and persistent though some of them were, and must have dozed off, because somehow I found myself back at school, on a hot summer afternoon, and teacher was giving us a geography lesson — which happened to be all about France, its people and its countryside. He'd just mentioned Valenciennes, and used his wooden pointer with such force that it made a hole in the map, when I heard him call my name out. I must have dozed off at my desk, for I heard him call me again, 'Leslie! Leslie!' Then he was shaking me by the shoulder and I sat up suddenly.

'Leslie,' Harrison was saying, 'briefing's in ten minutes. You'd gone right off.'

'I thought I was back at school, and I'd dropped off in class.' I held my face in my hands, making that awful transition from sleep to sudden wakefulness.

'Well, don't fall asleep in the next class or teacher won't be very pleased. We'd better get across there.'

The fresh air revived me, and by the time we got to SHQ I was feeling quite chipper. The briefing-room was already nearly full, and in about two minutes the CO came in, our benches scraping on the floor as we stood to attention.

'Be seated, gentlemen,' said Major Folliott. 'Well, after the hold-up in operations because of the weather, we've been given a special task tonight — to make a mess of the marshalling yards at Valenciennes, where the Hun is assembling most of his supplies for the big offensive. We've got good reconnaissance photos, which show heavy loads — ammunition mainly. So if your bombing is accurate you should be rewarded with a big bang.'

There was an ironic cheer at this remark, and the CO continued: 'Yes, gentlemen, the target area is a fairly small one. Within it are the main lines themselves, sidings filled with rolling-stock, and warehouses alongside them. What Wing requires is saturation bombing, to hit everything and so weaken the Huns' offensive. We are to put up every possible aircraft. Any questions?'

'What information have we on the defences, sir?' asked Captain Brinden.

'We're told they'll be pretty hot,' said the CO, 'both from the ground and in the air — night fighters, I mean. The Hun is just as anxious to stop us interfering with his supplies as we are keen to stop them getting through. So watch out for fighters, particularly if you're late in the bombing order, when they'll have had time to get up.'

'What about the weather?' Harrison put the other question that had been in my mind.

'It should be clear now this front has passed through,' the CO answered, 'but in the calm conditions behind it there may be mist forming, so watch out on your return — we're going in after midnight, when the Hun will least expect us, so you'll be getting back in the early hours. First take-off will be at 11 p.m., the last at 11.50.'

There was a sudden buzz of conversation at this. Usually the squadron took off after dark and was back well before midnight, but there was clearly a special reason for the timing of tonight's attack. Wing were building-in a psychological factor, hitting the Hun just when he probably thought we weren't coming.

'Any more questions, gentlemen?' The CO's voice, thin and precise but authoritative, rose above the hubbub, which died down. 'Then I suggest you get your order of take-off from the flight commanders, work out your courses and get some rest before the operation.'

'What about the ack-ack defences?' said one voice, almost as an afterthought.

'We hope the late start will catch them napping,' replied the major curtly.

There was another buzz of conversation, while the implications of this were digested. Then the CO said 'Any more?' and when there was silence added: 'Well, good luck, gentlemen.'

'You'd better check our take-off number,' Harrison suggested as the briefing broke up, 'while I work out the courses. Ask Brinden.'

I looked around for the flight commander and spotted him in one of the little groups. What he had to tell me wasn't very encouraging. '"A" Flight are leading so we shall be going off second,' he said, 'and as you're the newest crew, Blacking, I'm afraid you'll be taking off last.'

I wished I hadn't asked, but I'd have shortly got to know anyway. When I found Harrison, poring over his map, and told him he replied in that quiet philosophical way, 'Well, someone's got to be last, but we'll have problems — not only the fighters but the weather.'

'The weather?' I echoed.

'If mist is going to form, as we were told, it's going to form later rather than sooner, and we shall be the last to get back.'

'I see,' I answered reflectively. 'That means that if we evade the fighters, which by that time will be like a hornets' nest disturbed, we'll still have to feel our way back through the fog.'

'Exactly,' said Harrison. Then he added brightly, as another thought struck him, 'Have you got your mascot yet?'

'No — what is it?'

'A black cat. All 207's aircrew wear them. We'd better get you fixed up — let's go over to the clothing store. They should have one there. Get your helmet.'

As I went across to our tent I mentally summed-up the situation created for me by the briefing: a difficult target, being the last aircraft to bomb, and making sure of the protection of the squadron mascot. That would mean meeting the lugubrious Mac again, king of the stores.

When I rejoined Harrison he remarked, almost casually, 'We're jolly lucky to be here, you know, rather than in the lines. I know it's a matter of chance, from the moment we start to take-off, whether we'll come back or come down. But when we do get back we're assured of a comfortable dry tent. How superstitious are you?'

'Not very,' I said.

'Not at the moment; but I think you might become so. Most of the chaps on the squadron swear by its black cat as a symbol of good luck.'

We'd by now got to the clothing store, which, when we opened the door, bore its usual deserted look: an empty counter and silent shelves, behind which the custodian could be completely concealed.

'Sergeant McTavish!' called Harrison, in a voice of stentorian command I'd been unaware that he possessed. There was silence for a while and he was just about to call again when the sergeant appeared from behind the right-hand shelving.

'Can I help ye, sirr?' he enquired in the sort of tone in which he might have bid us 'guid aerternoon' in Rothiemurchus, or wherever his home was.

'Sergeant, have you got a squadron badge for Mr Blacking?'

McTavish looked at me for a moment, as if he were summing-up my size for a shirt or cap, then disappeared without a word. He reappeared, after a few minutes' search, and banged something down on the counter in front of me.

'There you are, sirr,' he said. 'It's the last one left.'

'It' was a piece of black felt, about one and a quarter inches wide and two and a half inches deep, depicting a black cat with its tail up ('rampant' I suppose was the heraldic term), with red glass beads for eyes and wearing a red collar. So this was 207's mascot.

'Thank you, Sergeant McTavish,' I said.

He nodded. 'I hope it'll always bring ye safely back, Mr Blacking. Hae ye got a needle and thread to sew it on with?'

I nodded in turn. 'Yes, thank you. Come on, Harrison.'

'Where's the correct place to wear it?' I asked as we walked back.

'In the centre of the front of the helmet,' Harrison explained, 'although as the cat is looking to his left, by rights he ought to be on the left-hand side. But everyone wears them on the front. So get busy with your needle, Leslie.'

It took me about twenty-five minutes, because leather isn't the easiest of materials to get a needle through: but at last my black cat was proudly positioned, and I felt a member of the squadron.

Harrison looked at his watch. 'Time to get some supper, I think. Then we'll go to HQ and find Corporal Pilcher, to check that he's organized.'

The Mess was pretty quiet, with one or two chaps at the table, nobody at the bar and a few figures lounging in the wicker chairs reading magazines. We ate our bully beef and potatoes, graced by some chutney, and sipped our tea, in silence. There was an air of tenseness which I suppose preceded every operation. I took my tea over to a chair and picked up an *Illustrated London News*. It seemed to consist entirely of stories about the war, both in Europe and the Near East, illustrated with photographs or artists' impressions.

I heard the chair next to mine creak and turned to find Captain Bishop, the engineering officer, sitting there. 'See any of the latest shows, Blacking, before you came out? I'm going on leave next week and hope to visit one or two. Anything worth seeing?'

I racked my brains. I sometimes found my mind went blank at the simplest question, especially when I was trying to concentrate on the night's operations. 'What about *The Passing Show*?' I said with a sudden flash of inspiration.

'Capital,' said Bishop. 'I'll try that.' Then, seeing Harrison coming over, he added, 'Good luck tonight.'

Harrison nodded to the genial EO. 'I think we ought to be going,' he said. 'We'd better get back to HQ to look at the met,' he reiterated impatiently, glancing at his watch. 'It generally comes in about 8 o'clock.'

I noticed that his manner, and that of other members of the squadron, was changing with the advent of an operation. Characters like Harrison's, normally relaxed and gentlemanly, became tense and time-conscious, always looking at their wrist-watches and assessing where they were or ought to be next. I judged it to be a preliminary mental muscle-flexing for their forthcoming aerial combat, and decided that I would act in the same way after I'd been on the squadron for a bit longer.

Those thoughts, of course, took only about a millisecond to come and go, such is the marvellous mechanism of our brains and minds, and as what must have appeared to Harrison an instinctive reaction, I said, 'All right. What's the next thing? You know the routine.'

'Well, we work out our compass courses when we know the winds,' Harrison answered as we set off across the grass to HQ. 'You work them out and I work them out, and they have to agree; then we can be sure they're correct.'

There was a sudden burst of noise and light as we got inside the HQ, and it looked as thought the met had just been put on the board. Some pilots and observers were crowding around and jotting it down. As they moved away to work out coursers we got a look at the forecast winds and clouds; the former were going to be light, the latter broken remnants of the front which had passed through. Harrison pointed out the landing forecast for our return: fog forming in the early morning.

'That'll affect us,' he commented. 'It could be a bit tricky.'

I'd never thought myself much of a navigator in the mathematical sense, though I could do it in the calm of a ground environment, and this time (luckily) it came off. Harrison's courses and mine matched to a degree.

I'd spotted Corporal Pilcher's cheerful face almost as soon as we got into the HQ. 'Everything all right?' I asked.

'As far as humanly possible, sir. I understand we're taking off last.'

'That's right — at 11.50. So we'll have to look out for night fighters; they'll be thoroughly aroused by then.'

'Never mind, sir. I'll take good care of 'em, and Mr Harrison's a good shot with the front gun.'

Privately I realized that the weak link in the chain was myself, in the middle with no experience. So I said, 'Well I'm lucky to be with such a good team.'

'I'm going to the map room,' Harrison put in. 'You could come with me, Leslie, to get the list of lighthouses. They've probably changed since the last op. Then we can re-check our compass courses, before going out to look over the aircraft.'

'That'll be in about half an hour, I should think,' I suggested, mainly for Corporal Pilcher's benefit.

'All right, sir,' said Pilcher. 'I'll see you here in twenty-five minutes.'

Harrison and I set off for the map room, a hut abut fifty yards from squadron HQ, and while he checked the magnetic courses I copied out the list of lighthouses and their magnetic bearings from 'Q' (Doullens), our point of departure and — we hoped — return.

'How's it going?' a voice said over my shoulder.

I looked round. The voice belonged to Captain Bill Brinden, commander of 'B' Flight, a big, good-looking fellow who radiated a considerable air of confidence.

'Hello, Bill,' said Harrison. 'I think you met Leslie Blacking, my new pilot — at least briefly.'

'I did,' Brinden acknowledged with a nod towards me. 'I just wanted to wish you luck on your first operation, Blacking. You'll be the last to bomb, but I'll be hanging around until you've cleared the target. You've got a very experienced crew in Harrison and Pilcher; couldn't be better. Don't forget though — keep to your height, then we'll all get back safely. All the best.'

'Thank you, sir,' I said, responding more from instinctive politeness than because I really knew what to say. Despite the flight commander's reassuring cheerfulness I felt a good deal of trepidation.

'We'd better go over to the aircraft and set the bombsight,' Harrison put in when Brinden left us. As we walked over the grass towards the gate with its sentry and across the road, he added, 'He's a first-class flight commander. In fact they both are — good leaders, and very experienced in this kind of operation.'

When we got to the 0/400 (ours was '5') Harrison climbed up the ladder then crawled through into the front cockpit. I followed him but got into the right-hand seat, so I was behind him, as we would be on the bombing run.

'5,000 feet isn't it, our altitude?' he asked, half turning round.

'That's right,' I answered. Instinctively we were almost shouting at each other, as we would be doing in a few hours' time, in the darkness with the engines running. But it was still a beautiful summer evening, the only sound an occasional lark or a motor-vehicle, the only movements those of figures clambering in and out of aircraft parked in line down the side of the field.

This reverie lasted, I suppose, barely five seconds before being broken by a voice from down below: 'Everything all right, sir?' The flight sergeant's open, weather-beaten face looked up at me. 'We've finished our checks, sir, but let me know if you find anything.'

'Hello, Arnett,' sid Harrison from the front cockpit. 'You've met Mr Blacking.' The flight sergeant nodded to me. 'I'm sure we'll find everything in order if you've been over it.'

'The bombsight's set,' he added, turning round to me. 'I'll check the front gun — they should all be loaded — then we'll look over the bombs.'

After a few moments he crawled through the tunnel back into the cockpit and then we looked down at the bombs, sixteen 112-pounders, fused at the nose and tail, held in position by their two little 'propeller blades'. In their racks they were a neat and menacing load.

'Let's hope none of them hang up,' commented Harrison, 'otherwise I shall have the tricky business of trying to release them.'

'What about the rear guns?' I asked.

'Corporal Pilcher will see to them,' said Harrison. 'they're the tools of his trade.'

'Already checked, sir,' said a voice from down below. Corporal Pilcher had been chatting with the flight sergeant. 'Guns clean and in good order, ammunition on the belt — 2,000 rounds in all, tracer and explosive. I checked Mr Harrison's guns too, before you came up.'

'Thank you, Pilcher,' I said. 'It's good to have two professionals in the crew. Then we've nothing more to do except to get into our flying kit?'

'No. Let's get out of here. We'll be seeing enough of it later on.' Harrison was already halfway through the tunnel and I followed him down the ladder.

'Thank you, flight,' I said. 'We'll see you later, Pilcher — about 11 o'clock at HQ. Take-off is 11.50.'

It wasn't far from our aircraft, at the end of the line, to the road and into the camp. 'We might as well go to the Mess for a meal,' Harrison suggested.

First we went back to the tent to get into our flying gear: a Sidcot suit of waterproof grey cloth, fur lined and with a fur collar, and sheepskin lined boots with thick rubber soles. I left my three pairs of gloves, and my helmet with the 207 cat badge, on the bed ready to put on. Both of us gave our Sidcots a good shake before we put them on. Harrison had advised me that during the day earwigs tended to get into the fur, then come out at night when we were airborne.

'Let's go to the Mess,' he said. 'The high tea isn't very exciting, but it's nourishing, and we need nourishment for the next few hours.'

As we walked across, the contrast between our lives and the existence of the men on the ground came suddenly into my mind once again. Here we were, able to sit at table to eat our meals, almost as if we were at home, in preparation for what might be two or three hours' discomfort, fear, danger — a concentrated period of apprehension, alertness, cold and perhaps terror. But when we got back we could take off our clothes and get into bed, and sleep in safety. There was no mud, lice, bayonets, rats, cold and wetness or trench fever in our lives, which were civilized by comparison with theirs.

Harrison might have wondered what I was thinking about. He probably just surmised that I was preoccupied with thoughts of the night's operation, my first on the squadron. But in the short time I'd known him I'd realized he had a gift for reducing tension by making some commonplace remark, relating to practical things.

As we ducked under the entrance to the Mess tent he said, 'We mustn't forget to pick up our packed rations here. They're often very welcome on the return trip, when you've time to feel the cold.'

There weren't many people about, and nobody at the bar. Those who might have been drinking, because they weren't flying, were busy elsewhere, and the flyers just didn't drink before an operation. But there were one or two figures at the tables. Harrison and I steered towards a couple of chairs and sat down. One of the other observers nodded to him. There seemed to be nothing to say.

I didn't know whether I was hungry or not, but reason told me it might be a long time before we ate again, and I was a normal, healthy nineteen-year-old living an outdoor life, so I tucked into my bacon and eggs when it came. Harrison, a bit older and experienced in these occasions, looked at me a bit quizzically while he sipped his tea and said, 'A penny for your thoughts, Leslie.'

I realized I'd said nothing for a long time and that he was psychologist enough to know I was probably preoccupied and worried, but I was determined not to let him see it.

'They wouldn't be worth it. I was just thinking about breakfast at home, and how long ago that seems. The world's changed since 1914.'

'It certainly has,' Harrison put in. 'Nobody would have thought, when I was in my teens, that hundreds of people would one day be flying around. Even the motor-car was a rarity then, you could hear one coming, then it rattled past and left a great cloud of dust behind it. Have you read Kenneth Grahame's *The Wind in the Willows*?'

I nodded. 'It came out when I was at school.'

'Then you'll remember Mr Toad and his enthusiasm for motor-cars. After he and his friends had been scattered by one he was left sitting in the middle of the dusty road murmuring to himself, "Poop-poop! Poop-poop!" Then he couldn't rest until he had one of his own.'

'I remember,' I said. 'He got himself a motoring outfit — cap, goggles, gaiters, overcoat and gauntlets.'

'Dressed for the weather, like us,' Harrison commented quietly. At this sober reminder of the present my fleeting reminiscence of childhood evaporated; I was reminded of the business in hand and took a final sip of my tea.

'How's the time?' I asked.

'Nine o'clock.' Harrison looked at his watch and I checked mine. 'We might as well go back to the tent for a couple of hours. We'll hear the first take-off then we can collect Pilcher at HQ and take the tender to the aircraft.'

As we walked across the grass I reflected on the variability of time, which though constant in pace yet seems to go quicker or slower according to what we're doing. Thus here were Harrison and I on a summer evening, with darkness just falling, time on our hands but nothing to do with it. On another occasion the same time would have rushed past; there was something both physical and psychological about it.

Harrison flung himself on his bed. I thought of doing likewise; neither of us felt inclined to say anything and he was an old hand at this game. But then I had a sudden thought: I'd write a letter to my parents, one which would only be sent to them if I didn't come back from this operation. I could then update it from time to time, referring to the summer, autumn or winter, as appropriate, saying how beautiful — or how bleak — the French countryside was looking. (I suppose it looked just as beautiful, in the summer when the French Revolution began, as it had looked each summer for centuries before

— as beautiful as it now looked, in the perennial summertime during this great war.)

Although the letter was a very simple one — basically a farewell note — it took a long time to compose, or seemed to. I suppose it took about half an hour.

Harrison had tactfully kept quiet all this time, nor did he make any comment when I put down my pencil and stretched out on the bed. I must have dozed off, and had a little dream about a train going into a tunnel. It burst out at the other end with a great noise, through which I gradually became conscious of Harrison's voice.

'Wake up, Leslie, they've started; we'd better get across to HQ.'

When we got there, I blinked a little in the light and the sudden activity; but I was brought back to reality by the sight of Corporal Pilcher, with his cheerful grin.

'Hello, sir,' he said. 'Ready for the fray?'

'As ready as I shall ever be,' I replied. 'How soon before the tender comes back?'

'About ten minutes, I should think,' Pilcher suggested, adding, 'It's just gone off with one lot of crews, so they'll be going down the line now, dropping them off.' He seemed remarkably cheerful. Then he suddenly stepped back as a precise voice cut into our conversation.

'Good luck, Blacking.' The CO's handshake was firm and genuine, his smart uniform one that inspired confidence, giving the appearance of a well-run squadron.

'Thank you, sir,' I said. 'I've got a good crew.'

'Indeed you have — one of the best — and we've got good machines and good mechanics. So give the Hun what for. If we do our job properly we'll help to shorten the war for those poor blighters in the lines.'

I nodded. There seemed to be nothing to say about that: we all agreed. But there seemed to be also a world of difference, at that moment, between us in our bulging flying gear and the dapper major.

Harrison as usual saved the situation by a down-to-earth question. 'Any late report on the weather, sir?'

'No, George, much the same. You'll have to look out for mist when you get back.'

Just then a motor horn sounded outside — three insistent hoots.

'Tender!' someone shouted.

Half-a-dozen bulbous figures began to move towards the door. 'Here we go,' said Harrison. 'Allons, enfants de la patrie.'

'Good luck,' echoed round the HQ as we climbed aboard.

It was a bumpy ride across the grass to the road, and all one could see were shapes in the darkness, receding behind us — the huts, the Mess, the bell tents where we lived. I got the impression that we were leaving a life we knew — albeit a strange, unreal one — for something even more strange and decidedly uncertain.

Just across the road we stopped before going down the diminishing line of 0/400s. One of them was about to taxy out for take-off. There was a great swirl of slipstream over us as it turned to the right to go down to the take-off point. In the darkness it looked huge and black, I could hardly visualize that we ourselves would look like that in a few minutes.

Once it was clear we went on down the line to the last aircraft — No 5, the big figure on its side standing out as we pulled up in front of it. The two AMs there greeted us as we heaved ourselves out of the tender (flying kit wasn't recommended wear for riding about in motor-cars; it was much too bulky).

'Good evening, sir.' I nodded. It all sounded rather civilized, as if we were going on a pleasure flight.

'Everything all right?' I asked — more for something to say, or in response to their greeting, than because I thought anything wouldn't be all right — the squadron's mechanics were very thorough in their work.

While Corporal Pilcher got up into his rear cockpit to check his guns I walked round the aircraft with one of the AMs. There was just light enough to see most things in outline but we checked them also by the light of his torch; the tyres, to look for any cuts or creep; the bottom ailerons; the rigging; the tailplanes and rudders; the tailskid, which appeared to be sunk deep into the grass but would soon be dis-embedded when the engines opened up.

'Have the engines been run?' I said.

'Yes,' the AM answered, 'and they sounded fine. Good luck, sir.'

'Thank you,' I replied. Then I climbed up the ladder and crawled through into the cockpit. The night air felt fresh and sweet. While Harrison settled himself in on my left I looked round, first downwards at the bombs in their racks behind me, then along the fuselage at Corporal Pilcher. He was exercising his gun, making sure he had free movement with it in all directions, and checking the ammunition belt. When he saw me looking he gave a cheerful 'thumbs up' with his gloved right hand.

'How long to go to start-up time?' I asked Harrison.

'About five minutes,' he said after a quick glance at his watch, and as nonchalantly as if I'd asked him on London Bridge station what time the next train was to Clapham Junction.

The AMs were already on the starboard wing, ready to wind up the engine once I gave them a signal. We could do it verbally for the first start, but the second — with one powerplant already roaring away on our right — would have to be by thumbs-up sign.

I heaved on the wheel to check for free movement before any slipstream got on the control surfaces — backwards, forwards, over to the left and over to the right — and activated the rudder pedal, fully left then fully right. Everything was free but my was it heavy! The 0/ 400 was no scout, no Camel or SE5A, though I was sure she could be pulled around if need be, if one had the strength for it.

'Time to start up,' yelled Harrison in my right ear, in competition with the aircraft on our left which had just started.

I gave the AMs a thumbs-up sign and they began to turn the engine. It fired rapidly and when they'd slid off the wing with their handle to go round to the other side I opened it up gradually, using the twist-grip knob on top of the throttles, to 1,500 rpm.

On the port side the performance was repeated, and the engine fired after a slight hesitation. We now had two powerplants purring away and I checked their performance by the instruments on the sides of the nacelles — rev counter, oil pressure and water temperature gauges.

'As soon as he's moved out,' Harrison shouted in my left ear, indicating the 0/400 on our port side, 'we can flash our number to control — then they can give us a green to taxy forward and take off.'

I gave him a thumbs-up, which seemed to be the universal sign language, and looked down at my cockpit instruments — airspeed indicator and altimeter, neither of which were yet operative.

'One-seven-oh for Doullens after our climb-out?' It was my turn to yell at Harrison and his to give a thumbs-up response.

Our neighbouring aircraft had turned to starboard, crossed in front of our nose then turned port to line up for take-off.

'Flash our number!' I shouted, and Harrison pressed out five dots. There was a pause, as the 0/400 before us opened up and began to roll towards the far end of the field, disappearing into the darkness. After a few minutes, five steady green dots flashed from the control tower: we were on our way and I opened up the engines, using the knob on top of the throttles to ease them open. Our AMs, who had pulled the chocks from under the wheels, watched from the wing tips. I felt the wheels and tailskid ease themselves from the clutch of the grass and the aircraft move slowly forward. I also felt very high up and isolated.

With the AMs giving the thumbs-up to show that we were clear of any obstructions I opened up the port throttle and closed the starboard one to bring us round to the right, then reversed the procedure as soon as we got to the take-off tee, to swing us to port into wind. There was a steady red from the control tower — clearly they wanted to be sure that our predecessor was clear of the circuit before committing us to it — then, after some seconds, five red flashes. We were clear to go.

With a last thumbs-up (mainly for Corporal Pilcher's benefit, so that he would know what was going on — though, with all his experience, he probably knew well enough), I pushed open the throttles fully and we started to move forward, albeit slowly at first but gathering speed: 30,40, 50, 60, 70, 80 mph, when I eased back on the control column. She didn't sink back on to the ground and I kept the IAS at 80 mph, the 0/400 settling into a slow climb.

I could see dark foliage passing below us, then the sinuous outline of the River Authie. I banked right for Doullens; for a few moments I was disorientated, as we went up into the darkness. I was flying by reflex action, by instinct, by training, just following what my instruments told me.

'Turn on to 170 degrees,' Harrison shouted. Clearly we had gone further to the north-east than we should have done, while I was trying to orient myself. Slowly, heavily, I heaved the aircraft round, careful not to overshoot.

'There it is!' Harrison shouted again at me after a few minutes.

Keeping the 0/400 in a steady 80 mph climb, I stared into the darkness, then suddenly saw the steady flashing of the code: dash-dash-dot-dash — 'Q' for Doullens. It was slightly over towards our left, so I headed towards it, our height creeping up to 500 feet, our altitude for passing over the lighthouse.

Just before it disappeared under our nose Harrison called out the course from there: 'Steer 056 degrees,' he said, setting it on the grid ring of the big compass on the floor between us. He had read the figure off a sheet on his notepad, listing all the courses we were to fly that night. Our altitude slowly increased, and as it did so the air got colder. Looking out to the right, down past the Rolls-Royce Eagle whose exhaust was glowing in the dark, I saw flashes on the ground —

exchanges of gunfire between the lines, which we were just starting to cross.

Suddenly there was a sharp burst of firing behind me. I looked round, startled, ready to swing the aircraft into an evasive manoeuvre. But what I saw was Corporal Pilcher, standing up, giving his guns a warming-up. At the same moment he looked round, spotted me and gave me a grin and a thumbs-up.

'We need 5,000 feet. We shall clear the lines in about thirty-five minutes, then we shall see the searchlights,' Harrison shouted at me, mouthing the words so that I could see as well as hear them.

I looked at my height indicator. We were just coming up to 3,000 feet, and even though it had been a summer night down below, it was cold up here. I wondered about plugging in my electrically heated flying suit, but thought I'd better 'grin and bear it'. There'd be plenty to keep me warm a bit later on.

Down below were the lines, which curved in a kind of arc from north to south. The men there were no doubt getting what sleep they could, perhaps preparing for a dawn offensive.

'5,000 feet!' I yelled to Harrison. The air was calm and I pushed the wheel forward a bit to keep at our correct altitude, after climbing for so long, and to increase airspeed — which, as long as I could keep the aircraft steady, crept up towards 90 mph.

'There's the first searchlight,' said Harrison, as a thin pencil-like beam shot up into the western sky. 'We've got forty-five minutes to go to the target. Don't get caught, otherwise they'll box you in and it's a hell of a job getting clear.'

This was a long sentence, considering it had to be shouted into my left ear. I realized that Harrison was well used to communicating with his pilot in the air, and I was getting accustomed to his in-flight briefings, against the roar of the engines. I glanced round quickly to see how Pilcher was getting on: he was standing up, and seemed to be both keeping himself warm and keeping an alert eye on all quarters of the sky. He didn't miss my enquiring glance, and responded to it with his usual telepathic thumbs-up, our only means of communication at that distance, across the bomb-bay. Another forty minutes, on Harrison's reckoning, and we should be over our target. What couldn't one do with forty minutes on the ground — time for a meal, for a snooze after lunch; time enough to make a journey, even to write a will and sum up one's account. Up here, one could only concentrate on the business in hand, and wonder what lay ahead.

I felt cold, and wondered if I should have plugged in the heating to my suit. Even in this summer weather, the air temperature dropped towards freezing point at over 5,000 feet. But I forgot this when Harrison suddenly biffed me on the left shoulder and pointed, though I think I saw it almost as soon as he did — a mobile searchlight, probing the sky to the west. That meant we were getting away from the lines and nearer to our target. Its defences were hot because it was often attacked, and with tonight's good visibility there was no escaping them.

'In five minutes, steer 075 degrees,' Harrison shouted. I knew what that meant — we were to come in at an angle to our target, the marshalling yards.

I realized also that the defences would have been alerted by the preceding aircraft; they'd be waiting for 'just one more'. I held our course and checked the clock. It was four minutes to one. On the hour I would change course for the target, which we should be able to see clearly, either through smoke and flames rising, or through archie coming up.

Keeping our altitude, and an eye on the clock, at 1 a.m. I did a gradual starboard turn, steadying the big aircraft on 075 degrees. Harrison biffed me on the left shoulder. 'Now we're on course for our target, in five minutes I'm going through to the nose,' he yelled. 'Keep on course, I'll release the bombs, remember to make two runs then turn on to a reciprocal — 255 degrees.'

I gave him a thumbs-up and glanced round, giving the same sign to Corporal Pilcher, who responded. We were a team now, going into the jaws of hell, like Tennyson's *Charge of the Light Brigade*:

> Cannon to right of them,
> Cannon to left of them,
> Cannon in front of them
>
> Into the jaws of Death
> Into the mouth of Hell
> Rode the six hundred . . .

— except that we were one vulnerable, explosive, inflammable aeroplane, if we should get hit by tracer, flaming onions, or a shell.

Suddenly, over on our port side, a searchlight pierced the darkness. It probed about, this way and that, but fortunately was too far away to find us. Then I thought I saw, ahead and just to the left, smoke rising; I felt I could smell it. It could be our target.

Harrison disappeared through the tunnel into the nose, then I saw his head appear in the front cockpit. He stood up momentarily while he pushed the folding seat down, and bent forward, presumably checking his drift sight. I held our course as steadily as I could: I knew that as we got within a mile or two of the target area he would signal to me by three lights in front of him — duplicated in front of me — whether we were drifting to the left or right, so that I could cancel it out with rudder. All I had to do, apart from that, was to keep the 0/400 steady — whatever they threw up at us from the ground. Harrison would release the bombs as soon as he judged we were in range of our target. Then we'd have to do it all over again, on a second run, to drop a second stick of eight. Another searchlight lanced its way upwards, this time over to our right and a little way ahead; it was a mobile one, travelling towards us, its beam arcing through the sky. They knew we were coming and were trying to find us.

Peering over the side, I could just make out a railway line; it probably led to a junction and to the marshalling yards we were attacking. Then everything happened at once: the mobile searchlight slowly swung round and momentarily caught us in its glare; up out of the darkness came what looked like a glowing coal — then another and another, mercifully passing upwards just out of range of us, but near enough to be very frightening, and Harrison stood up in the front cockpit, ready to release the bombs, so I had to keep the aircraft straight and level.

After what must have been only a few seconds, but to me seemed like an eternity of time, I saw him pull the release handle; then he flopped down in his seat, half turned round and gave me a thumbs-up signal. We'd bombed and had to make a second run. I swung the heavy 0/400 into a port turn, holding the wheel over and waiting for the sluggish reaction from the ailerons. Fortunately the weather was still calm, so I didn't have to fight against a wind. All I had to do was to fly the aircraft in the darkness. But the Hun now knew we were there and the searchlights would soon try to find us again. There would be more ack-ack and possibly night fighters.

I didn't want to make the bank too steep, for fear of getting into a spiral. What I wanted was a steady rate of turn, without letting the nose drop. I found I needed to pull back so hard on the wheel that I had to stand up in my seat, keeping an eye on the compass at the same time, to bring us on to a reciprocal course.

What was it Harrison had said — 255 degrees? I'd set it on the grid ring, of course, and tried to visualize our path in the sky, parallel to the one we'd been flying; but the effort was rather too much, at that hour of the night, when the mind is at a low ebb anyway, and in hostile skies. I decided to bring the 0/400 on to a straight-and-level course again, then to turn gradually on to our second run-in to the target. Harrison might think what he liked, out there in front, but I was in command — searchlights, flak or fighters, come what might.

I remembered the searchlight that had been on our port side on our original run-in: it would still be there. We were in effect going round it, and mustn't be caught by it — any moment now it would probe the sky again.

Harrison would have to leave it to me how long we flew on this reciprocal leg. I was just about to turn back when he stood up and signalled with his left arm; I was ready for the message and swung the wheel over. As usual, nothing seemed to happen but gradually round we went. I then had to watch that we didn't overshoot our course. As I steadied the aircraft on its path back to the target I glanced down at the compass. It had just enough of a luminescent glow, in the darkness of the cockpit, to show me that we were on the right heading — to within a few degrees; and to confirm this, Harrison gave me a thumbs-up with his left hand.

Then it happened: a blinding flash of light on our port side — that searchlight probing again. Once it caught us the ack-ack would follow. I wanted more than anything to get away from there, but had to keep steady for our last run-in. The searchlight swept downwards, then up towards us, missed us and moved away. I kept my eye on Harrison, standing up in the front cockpit, peering over his bomb-sight. He was pointing towards the left. We must have veered off a bit, subconsciously I'd been trying to keep out of the way of that bright, searching beam. I heaved round on to our correct heading — there wasn't time to be subtle about it.

Harrison's left arm came up and steadied. I froze on the wheel, and as we ran in to the target the searchlight came round again, closer this time, caught our port wing, passed it and then came back, pinning us like a helpless butterfly. Suddenly, crump, crump — the sky was lit by phosphorescent green explosions. All around us an acrid smell pervaded the air; just before us and just behind us was the noise and flash and stench of ack-ack.

With only a few seconds to go to our target we'd become a target ourselves — for eternity, or so it seemed. I saw our aircraft's great wings lit up, all the details of the struts and bracing-wires and nacelles illuminated and clearly etched against the surrounding darkness, and the crouched figure of Harrison silhouetted in the front. Wumff-wumff-wumff, the explosions came again, the sky cascading with green flashes. In that moment of hell fire I saw Harrison release our bombs. I didn't need his thumbs-up to tell me to bank and dive away — anything to escape from that beam and those fearful explosions.

As we turned away a stream of red tracer spouted upwards just behind the aircraft, missing our tail by only a few feet. I could see Corporal Pilcher in the rear cockpit garishly illuminated in its light. In the turn, Harrison had crawled through from the front cockpit and came up beside me: 'Two-three-six,' he shouted, 'and watch out for fighters.'

I didn't need reminding that this was our course back to the lighthouse at Doullens, nor of the new hazard that faced us. As we were the last aircraft to bomb, the fighers would have had plenty of time to get off; we knew that if the ack-ack stopped there were fighters looking for us. We'd lost height in our diving turn, and as I brought the aircraft round on to its course away from the target I steadied its descent. We'd got down to 3,600 feet, which made us more vulnerable to fighters. There was only one thing to do now: gain more height as we headed for the lines.

I passed this decision to Harrison in a kind of semaphore, holding up my left arm at about forty-five degrees then dropping my hand on the throttles and opening them up, which he understood immediately. As I eased back the control wheel to take advantage of the engines' surge of power I glanced back over my left shoulder at Corporal Pilcher and gesticulated downwards. I think he realized what I meant: ack-ack he could do nothing about, but fighters he could. I wanted to climb as quickly as possible, but at the same time didn't want to stall the aircraft: I was watching the height grow to 4,000 feet again when there was a burst of tracer up into the sky from beneath us, and an almost instantaneous burst from Pilcher. I knew I had to elude our adversary by changing our heading or height, and did both by pushing the nose down again and heaving over the control column. Suddenly the Handley was in a giant corkscrew, going down into the night.

This didn't last long, however; it was only an evasive manoeuvre to throw off our adversary, and I decided to put the aircraft into a climbing turn, so that we wouldn't present a steady target and would also gain height. I heaved over the wheel again, but to the left this time, and brought it back, but keeping an eye on our airspeed, so that we wouldn't stall. Harrison was meanwhile looking round; there was nothing else he could do at the moment except act as another pair of eyes. It was my job to extricate us from this dangerous situation.

Suddenly there was a rat-tat-tat from the rear, followed by another burst. Just at that moment spurts of tracer came up — this time near our port wing. The fighter was climbing too: Pilcher had had his sight on him. I realized I had to turn the other way — a kind of upward corkscrew — so I heaved over the wheel again, just as another spurt of tracer came up — still on our port side, so it looked as if we were going to elude him.

As we climbed and turned, more tracer followed, but further away to the left and lower: we'd lost him, and the objective now was to get back on our course. What was it? I'd forgotten in those hectic few minutes.

'Two-three-six degrees?' I shouted to Harrison. My voice must have sounded a bit hysterical.

He gave me a big thumbs-up, as clearly as one could with a large pair of gauntlets, but I got the message and aimed to steady the aeroplane on the right course as we came round on our ponderous turn. At the same time I managed to glance back at Corporal Pilcher, who seemed to be checking the feed-belt to his guns, calmly as ever. He still had to keep a sharp look-out until we were over the lines. Harrison bent down to look at the compass, to steady me in the turn as we came on to the right heading.

Just then there was a 'wumff-wumff', followed by another 'wumff-wumff' on our right: 'Archie' was getting our range — the ack-ack we'd encountered on the way in to the target, determined to get us down as the fighters hadn't managed to do so. There was only one thing to do now: to get away from there as quickly as possible. I opened the throttles wide to increase our speed, and the big aircraft shuddered as it responded.

'How long to the lines?' I shouted to Harrison.

'About twenty-five minutes,' he replied, 'if you keep up this speed.'

I looked at the indicator: we were doing about 100 mph, the 0/400 rattling along. Behind us, a searchlight suddenly raked the sky; then it was joined by another one, probing around. But we were out of their area. We seemed to have left the defences of Valenciennes. Suddenly I felt very cold; the fear and exertions of a few minutes ago had made me oblivious to personal feelings, but now that tension was relaxed I became aware of them again, and above all of the freezing air.

'Let's go down a bit,' I yelled across to Harrison, at the same time making a downward motion with my left hand.

He gave me a laconic thumbs-up and shouted back: 'We should be over the lines soon.'

As I put pressure on the wheel to keep the aircraft in a gentle dive I looked down. Somewhere in that darkness thousands of men, living in utter discomfort and squalor, were trying to get some fitful sleep before the next attack — by themselves or the other side. Day after dreadful day, all they could hope for was just to survive, before death or disease claimed them.

We were lucky: at least we were going back to clean, dry tents. Suddenly down there, there was the flicker of an explosion, a burst of firing across the lines that we could see but couldn't hear, which meant some more poor fellows dead or another ugly pock-mark in the once fair face of France.

Our height was now 3,000 feet, but we could see less of the ground. As we crossed the lines, wisps of white cloud began to flick beneath our wings, gradually thickening as we flew westwards. Soon the ground was completely obscured from view. All I could do was to keep steadily on our course in the hope that the cloud would break up and we would see something which would enable us to identify our position.

'If we don't see a lighthouse or any landmark after ten miles we'll have to think about getting down somewhere,' Harrison shouted in my left ear. 'There's no point in going on indefinitely — we might find ourselves over the sea, out of fuel.'

I tried to adjust myself to this unexpected new situation. Just a short time ago we'd been in peril of being shot down by the Hun, or set on fire by his phosphorous shells. Now we were at the mercy of the weather, the mist and low cloud that had formed after the front had passed through our area. I'd just got to keep cool, as when we were over the target, in order to keep three airmen and a valuable machine intact to fight again another day.

There were no searchlights, and the mist drifting in from the sea had obscured the lines. It seemed sensible, to make sure we didn't come down on the wrong side of them, to fly on for a further ten miles and then try to get down. But by now we'd covered most of that distance and were down to about 1,000 feet. Almost subconsciously

I'd let the aircraft sink downwards as we peered over the sides looking for landmarks, but I knew there was no high ground in the direction we were flying.

'I'll drop a parachute flare,' Harrison shouted. As he released it I put the wheel over into a starboard turn to circle around the yellow glare.

The mist was thinning and we could see patches of ground. We dropped another flare and just ahead of us saw a large field. A third flare revealed ploughed furrows, and I judged that if I aimed the Handley along them we could make a reasonably safe, soft landing. The important thing was to keep that field in view. There was no time to lose.

I held the aircraft in a turn, losing height. When we were in the right direction for landing I yelled 'Wingtip flares!' to Harrison — there were four of them on the ends of our wings — and switched off the engines. We sank suddenly towards the ground and I heaved back on the control wheel as hard as I could. Earth flew up on either side of the cockpit as the wheels touched and then sank in the ground; our tail skid acted like an anchor and we didn't run very far.

For a moment we sat there in stunned silence. 'You all right, Pilcher?' I called back to the gunner. He gave me a thumbs-up. From the distance came a sound of gunfire, but from which direction? I looked at Harrison and he looked at the compass. North was ahead of us and the gunfire was coming from our right — the east. So we were safely on our side of the lines. The dark silence and stillness, after all that roaring of the engines and rushing of the slipstream, were deafening. For a few minutes it seemed as though we had just flown out of the war into some remote, peaceful place.

But this wasn't a time for philosophizing. Harrison crawled through into the front cockpit and dropped through the hatch on to the ground. It was a big drop from that high nose without a ladder, as I discovered shortly afterwards, flopping down heavily into the soft earth of the furrows. I picked myself up and went round to the rear of the aircraft to see Corporal Pilcher. It seemed incongruous, walking around in flying gear on strange territory, not on our own airfield.

'You all right, Pilcher?' I called up to him.

'Yessir,' he said, a blur of helmet in the darkness looking down at me. 'Are we on our side of the lines?'

'We think so,' was all I could offer. 'Mr Harrison and I are going to see what we can find, so we leave you in charge of the aircraft.

Somebody may have heard us coming down, and come over to investigate.'

Harrison and I stumbled off across the field, vaguely heading for the nearest boundary. When we got to it there was a grassy area, which we crossed, then by good luck stumbled upon a track which we followed. It was bound to lead somewhere, and eventually, after trudging along for what seemed like ages in Indian file, we came to a road. Fortunately, being summer time, it was by now just beginning to get light — at least the upper sky was brightening in the east — so there was some chance of being picked up if anything came along.

Although every minute felt like an age in those strange surroundings, we fortunately didn't have long to wait. A pair of headlights, belonging to a noisy truck, hove into view and we managed to stop it. I don't know what the driver must have thought, confronted by two lumbering figures without any badges of rank in the darkness of the early morning behind the lines. We might have just dropped in from Mars. The only proof of identity we could offer was verbal.

'Good morning', I said, believing that if one wants something from a stranger there's nothing like starting off on the right foot. 'Second Lieutenant Blacking, 207 Squadron. This is Mr Harrison, my observer. We've just forced-landed our 0/400 and want to get to the nearest airfield. May we have a lift, please?'

All I could see was a face under a cap.

'Climb in, sir,' said the driver, evidently (and fortunately) trusting us.

There was just about room for the three of us in the cab. Flying gear designed for open cockpits isn't tailor-made for road vehicles. As we sat there in our bulbous state, the truck grinding along with its headlights just picking out the road ahead (which the driver seemed to know), none of us said anything. I was too busy thinking of where we were going, and how we would have to establish our identity there, and no doubt Harrison's thought ran on much the same lines. The driver said nothing until, after about fifteen minutes and a good many bumpy kilometres of apparently unmade (or unrepaired) French roads, he suddenly pulled off to the right and ground to a halt. Almost simultaneously an armed sentry appeared.

'Corporal Bates, Service Corps, 2 Division,' our driver announced. 'I've got two airmen here, say they forced-landed a few miles back and want to contact their own airfield. I hope they're not English-speaking Huns.'

The last remark was half-muttered, as if not for our ears, but the sentry was taking no chances.

'Pull in over there,' he said brusquely, 'and don't get out of the truck.'

We sat there in the darkness and silence, wondering what was in store, until we saw a torch jogging towards us and two figures materialized: the sentry and a hatless officer, wearing a greatcoat flung over his pyjamas and apparently none too pleased at having been roused from his sleep.

'Who are you?' he demanded.

'Second Lieutenant Blacking, 207 Squadron,' I responded. 'This is my observer, Lieutenant Harrison. We had to force-land on our way back from a raid and want to contact Ligescourt airfield.'

The mention of this name seemed to act like a kind of password. Our interrogator then introduced himself.

'Captain Soames, Adjutant, 9th Wing. But I'm afraid, gentlemen, that until your identity is proved by contact with your squadron you'll have to remain under guard. There have been many breaches of security in this area recently, with German spies in British uniforms. Please remain here in your vehicle. We shall have to take you back to your aircraft.'

With that he left us, returning to the camp with the sentry. It was tiresome and frustrating, but we could see that he was quite right to act as he did. The only advantage of the delay was that the first high streaks of dawn were starting to appear in the eastern sky, and the increasing light would help us to find our way back to the aircraft. Thinking over our situation, I recalled what Captain Bishp had told me when joining the squadron, about the aircraft which forced-landed. Now the same thing had happened to me — c'est la guerre!

After what seemed an eternity to us, for we were now feeling the after-effects of the nervous strain of our night's adventures, we heard the sound of a tender which drew up and stopped beside us. A sergeant got out and saluted.

'We're to escort you to your aircraft, sir,' he said. 'Driver, go back to where you picked these officers up. We'll follow.'

Fortunately our driver's familiarity with the area paid off. He eventually stopped where he'd picked us up. Harrison and I then had the task of leading the sergeant and the four armed AMs who emerged from the back of his vehicle along the track we'd originally followed from the 0/400. By then, however, it was getting a bit light and the huge silhouette of the aircraft soon became visible, a dark shape against the sky. When we got to it, there was Corporal Pilcher, looking cold and drawn from his long solitary wait. The sergeant lost no time.

'My orders are to collect all the guns and ammunition, sir,' he said.

'All right,' I said, looking at Pilcher, 'the gunlayer will help you.'

The corporal, glad of something to do after his long lonely wait, quickly took off the rear guns and handed them down with the drums and the belts of unused ammunition. Then he clambered forward across the bomb-bay and over the fuel tanks into the front cockpit; without a ladder, there was no other means of getting up there. Then he disconnected the front guns and handed them down to one of the AMs, who could just reach up from down below, and then caught the drums and belts of ammunition.

'Right,' said the sergeant to two of the AMs. 'You two stay here and guard this aircraft. You come with me, sir,' he added to Harrison and myself collectively, 'and the corporal.'

So, in Indian file again, we made our way back to the tender, the AMs carrying our Lewis guns and ammunition. Daylight was beginning to appear when we got back to the airfield, and we could make out the shapes of huts and tents, the sergeant directing us into one of the latter where he left us under the eye of one of the armed AMs. Clearly this station was taking no chances about security until it had checked on our identities.

We were sitting there, feeling tired and hungry and disconsolate in an odd way, just wanting to get off again and back to the squadron, when a figure appeared in the tent opening and the AM sprang to attention.

'Oscar!' I said.

'Hello, Leslie, how are you?' Oscar Darke gripped my hand. Even in that half light, or perhaps because of it, he looked older. It seemed a long time since he'd visited the squadron. He greeted Harrison and explained how he'd found us.

'I'm doing the Orderly Officer turn, and I heard a Handley had come down nearby. I just wondered if it might be you. What an amazing coincidence. Would you like some breakfast or at least a cup of tea?'

'Either would be welcome,' I said, looking at George. Like me, he was beginning to feel the strain of our night's adventures, first the bombing operation and then the forced-landing. 'No doubt the squadron and Wing are being told where you are, then when it gets light we can see what the chances are of getting the aircraft off again.'

'Where exactly are we?' put in Harrison. 'When this thick mist came up it blanketed everything out completely.'

'This Beauvois airfield,' Oscar explained, 'north-west of Arras — DH4s and DH9s, day bombers. I'm on 27 Squadron.'

'Weren't you with 99 when you came to Ligescourt?' I asked.

'Yes,' he replied, 'and lucky to survive. Then 27 had some pretty heavy losses and wanted some people with a bit of experience rather than getting a lot of newcomers, so I was sent here.

'Come over to the Mess,' he added. 'We've an early start this morning so the cooks will be there and I can get you fixed up with something. You must be tired and famished.

'I'll look after these gentlemen,' he told the armed AM, 'but you stay here and if anyone comes and asks for them say they've gone to the Mess with the Orderly Officer.'

It was still too dark to see any details of the airfield buildings; we just followed Oscar and blinked when we got inside the lighted interior of the Mess, where he organized a meal for us. As always under quite unexpected circumstances, never had ham and eggs and cups of tea tasted quite so good.

Afterwards, relaxing in lounge chairs, I resisted the opportunity of a doze because our troubles were far from over and I knew that if I dropped off I'd feel much worse when I had to wake up again.

I was determined to make the best use of this unexpected opportunity of seeing Oscar; we might never meet each other again. In particular, I wondered, how was he faring on day bomber operations, which I thought were far more dangerous than ours. The DH9s often had to fight their way to the target and all the way back again.

'How are you getting on, Oscar?' I said. 'I think you have a harder time than we have under cover of darkness.'

'It's a matter of luck whether they spot us or not,' he explained.

'If they do, we stick together; it's the only thing we can do.'

'One of your famous defensive circles?' put in Harrison.

'Yes; if we keep it tight the Hun fighters find it very hard to break in.'

I looked at Oscar's young, pale face and thought how incongruous it was that someone who seemed little more than a schoolboy should be talking in professional terms about life and death in the air. Come to that, I already felt like a staid old night bomber pilot.

'What happens if you get caught by yourself?' I asked.

'Well, it depends how many Fokkers or Albatrosses are after you. If it's two or three, a Nine can give a good account of itself. It's very manoeuvrable. If half a dozen spot you there's really only one thing to do: get back to the ground as quickly as possible and head for home. But it depends on what height you're at whether you can get away with it, how long you can successfully twist and turn in your descent.'

'What height do you go over the lines at generally?' Harrison asked.

'About 14,000 feet, depending on how much cloud there is; we always take advantage of what cloud cover we can get.'

'Isn't it very cold?' I said, mindful of our own experiences at lower altitudes.

'Freezing. But that's soon forgotten when you get into action, either with the ack-ack coming up or if you get into a fight.'

Harrison looked at Oscar, then at me.

'It's a team game, isn't it, whether things go right or wrong? At any rate a better one than for the PBI. You can see the lines down below, in daylight. We can only see flashes.'

'If I were to choose,' Oscar put in, 'it's the air for me every time. At least we have this' — he waved his hands around the Mess, with its comparative comfort — 'to come back to.'

'Don't you wonder when it's all going to end —?' I began, when a figure appeared out of the dawning light. It was the captain who'd first met us and put us under guard until Oscar took us in charge.

'I've been in touch with your squadron and they're sending a party of AMs to look at your aircraft,' he said brusquely. 'Meanwhile I must ask you to remain here. I see you've met a friend. I'm sure Mr Darke will look after you.'

'Did the squadron give you any idea of how long they might be getting over here?' I asked.

'No,' responded the captain, in the same sharp manner, as if implying that it was entirely our fault that we were there at all, giving him all this administrative bother. Then he added, in a rather more helpful way:

'It isn't really very far, as the crow flies, from here to Ligescourt, but they've got to assemble a party, arrange a vehicle and get over here — and you know what the roads are like. It's hardly like driving about in England.'

I had a momentary vision of dusty, peaceful lanes in Sussex and the shattered landscape of Flanders, with its ruined trees, wrecked vehicles, dead horses, crosses marking temporary graves, constantly moving processions of men, vehicles, guns, motor-cycles and ambulances passing each other in an endless ghastly cavalcade of war . . .

'Well, now that Mr Blacking has been identified, can he and Mr Harrison stay here?' put in Oscar. 'I've got to get back to my duties.'

'Yes, all right,' said the captain, with a nod to us. 'But remain in here, please, gentlemen.'

Oscar winked at me as he got up and went out with the adjutant. 'See you later, Leslie.'

I must have dozed off then. The strain of the night had begun to tell.

I suddenly began to feel very alone and frightened. There were great masses of white cumulus cloud all around — hills and valleys, chasms and tunnels of it. Far, far down below I could just glimpse a small area of the Western Front, with all its horrors eradicated by our distance from it: it could have been any patch of peaceful earth, a 'corner of a foreign field' as Rupert Brooke had put it in that sonnet he wrote at the beginning of the war, 'that is for ever England'. I also felt extremely cold. The air rushing past the cockpit was icy. Of course, I was in the slipstream of the propeller — but what was I doing in a single-engined aircraft? Its wings seemed extremely short after those of the 0/400. Was I by myelf on some nightmare, suicide mission? I looked round towards the tailplane and there, in the cockpit behind me, was Oscar. He looked extremely cheerful and grinned at me, giving a thumbs-up sign. So we were in a DH9. I'd never flown one before, but somehow it didn't seem to matter. Suddenly I felt a tap on my right shoulder. It was Oscar, pointing downwards with excited gesticulations. I looked down and there were five red Fokkers, some 2,000 feet below but climbing up towards us. What did I do now? My only experience of air-to-air combat had been at night, in the Handleys. I realized I had to manoeuvre, somehow to escape these Hun attackers, or Oscar and I were dead ducks. But my mind seemed frozen with terror. Where were the other DH9s? They usually formed defensive circles when caught by the Huns on their daylight raids. That was the only way in which they could survive. But we were quite alone, a straggler.

Glancing back, I began to see that our pursuers were Fokker Triplanes. There was only one thing to do: try to out-climb them. I opened the throttle fully and pulled up the nose. The engine seemed to be shaking from its bearings and the aircraft just clawing the air, but still the Fokkers came on. I could now see their black crosses.

The Huns appeared to be gaining on us, so I had only one option — to get down through them in a spin, like a falling leaf, whirling its way to the ground. I pulled back on the stick until we were vertical, and despite the engine's power the propeller blades began to slip round meaninglessly, no longer biting the air. Then, full right rudder, throttle back; we did a 180 degree change of direction and were spinning, down and down, through the Fokkers, towards a patchwork quilt of ground and the zig-zag line of trenches.

Oscar was thumping me on the back: we'd got away from the Huns. None of them were trying to follow our spin.

'Wake up!' he cried. We were going straight on into the ground.

'Wake up, Leslie!'

I looked round. There was Oscar, still smiling.

'Wake up, Leslie!' he said again. 'Your aircraft's going to be towed in. I've arranged camp beds for yourself and Mr Harrison, so you can have a few hours' sleep. We'll call you when they're ready for you to go out to it, when they've got it in and checked it over.'

For a few moments — or it seemed like minutes — I tried to adjust my mind in that mental no-man's land between sleeping and waking. So vivid had been my dream that it was hard to accept reality — Oscar looking down on me instead of being behind me in an aeroplane spinning earthwards through that predatory gaggle of Huns.

'You and Mr Harrison might as well get some rest before you go back to your squadron,' he went on. 'I'll get my batman to wake you.'

I think Harrison dozed off almost at once on the camp beds set up for us in a corner of the Mess. He seemed mentally very calm, infinitely adjustable to any sort of situation.

I couldn't sleep. My mind was still on the day bomber boys, lugging over the lines the same 112-pound bombs that we carried (though not so many of them), but having only cloud cover or each other for protection from the swarms of Albatross, Fokker or Pfalz scouts which lay in wait and came up to engage them. Eventually I too must have dozed off, after what seemed like hours of turning these things over in my mind. Then only a few minutes' fitful sleep were interrupted by the voice of the batman:

'Tea, sir; it's half-past six. Mr Darke told me to tell you that your aircraft was being towed in. Tea, sir,' he went on, waking up George Harrison.

'Good morning, Leslie. Did you sleep?' Harrison looked across at me while he took a first sip of his tea. 'Did I hear the batman say something about the Handley?'

'Being towed in,' I said. 'Then the AMs will no doubt take a look at it before we can fly it back to the squadron.'

I felt I wanted to see the world again after that strange, long night, so eased myself rather achingly to the ground and went over to the door of the Mess tent. Harrison joined me there after a few moments.

Although it was a summer morning there was enough stratus cloud to make it still dark, though shapes were discernible — the drab tents, huts, vehicles and hangars of a Western Front airfield, with its pervasive aroma of petrol, dope and trodden grass. Harrison lit a cigarette and for a brief second the flaring match silhouetted his features against the background of the grey canvas, and I thought: how many hundreds of fellows will be lighting their last-ever cigarettes this morning; some just before they climbed into Camels or SE5As for a dawn patrol, or into DH4s or '9s for a daylight bombing operation, many more as they stirred in the muddy horror of dug-outs with the rats and the vermin, stiff and cold, scared at the thought of the daylight with its shells and mortars and machine-gun fire, its prospects of an advance across no-man's land and the shell holes and barbed wire, or of an enemy attack with Hun bodies leaping in on them with bayonets thrusting.

In the quiet darkness neither of us said a word for several minutes. Perhaps we realized how fortunate we were, after nearly four years of war, to be living in such comparatively civilized conditions, and all we had to do today was to fly our aircraft back to Ligescourt — at least, if we weren't required to do another operation tonight.

As if voicing my thoughts, Harrison said, 'How much longer do you think this is going to go on for?'

'I don't think the Hun is going to crack very easily,' I ventured.

As a second lieutenant in the RAF I didn't feel competent to express views on military strategy, but I think anybody of average intelligence understood the human factors involved. I went on, 'He's a tough nut militarily, but what's going to break him will be shortages and near-starvation on the home front. They surely can't keep going indefinitely. We're all right now the Americans have come in, with their endless resources — provided we can keep the U-boats at bay.'

Suddenly the sound of an engine starting up broke the silence, coming from the direction of the airfield. It fired, coughed and stopped, then fired and kept running.

'It's probably the weather flight,' said Harrison.

Then one or two figures became visible, moving between the tents and huts, hardly distinguishable as individuals, more like symbolic actors in a wordless play with a drab and colourless background. Behind us, in the Mess tent, there was a sudden and startling crash of crockery. The cooks were preparing breakfast.

Another day had begun on the Western Front.

'It's fit to fly, sir; we've been over everything.'

That was Flight Sergeant Arnett, with his honest face and his Geordie accent; and it was mid-morning at Beauvois, on a beautiful day, with a high ordered procession of fair-weather cumulus clouds, the sort of day when in civilian life we'd have looked up from our desks in our stuffy offices and wished we were at the seaside.

It had been about nine o'clock when they towed the Handley in. The wings were unfolded and the AMs under the Flight Sergeant's sharp eyes went over everything, until he was satisfied that no serious damage had been done in our forced landing. Holes were patched and the Eagles run up — they at least had been unaffected. The big wheels and the tailskid were cleaned of the mud which had encrusted them.

'Are you off then, Leslie? She looks all right.'

Oscar had just appeared, as had most of his squadron, it seemed; for the day bomber boys there was a bit of novelty in seeing an 0/400 on their airfield.

'Oscar, you ought to be in bed after your Orderly Officer duties.'

'So should you,' he said. 'You haven't had much sleep. How long will it take you to get to Ligescourt?'

I looked at Harrison: he was the expert on navigation. 'About twenty minutes, I should think,' he opined in his quiet yet firm way.

'Well, Oscar,' I said, 'thank you for looking after us. Come over and see us some time.'

He nodded as we shook hands, but I had the feeling I wouldn't see him again. Being on a DH9 squadron was a precarious existence.

I felt very much on view as we climbed up into the high cockpit. Behind us, Corporal Pilcher gave us his usual cheerful thumbs-up. The DH9s we could see looked quite diminutive. I realized then that this was the first time since coming to France and joining the squadron that I'd made a simple A to B flight in a Handley. All the others had been my conversion to the type, around the airfield at Ligescourt, or operational ones.

Our guns had been restored to their mountings and we'd been given sufficient fuel to get us back. It was a short distance and there didn't seem to be any weather problems. Harrison had set our course, 255 degrees on the compass on the floor. I glanced at him and he gave me a thumbs-up; then I looked at the AMs on the starboard wing and yelled, 'Contact.' The Eagle coughed and caught after a few moments — it had been run up previously — then we repeated the process with the port engine. When both were showing steady rpm I signalled for the chocks to be pulled away, and with a last wave to our friends at Beauvois — I subconsciously looked for Oscar, and thought I spotted him — pushed the throttles open until the tailskid unstuck and we rumbled forwards. With an eye on the windsock, though there wasn't much of a breeze anyway, I chose the longest run and opened up. The Handley responded. There was a blur of people watching, parked aircraft, hangars, huts and tents where we had spent the night. I felt the slipstream bite on the control surfaces and eased the wheel back; she came off and we were away.

We'd realized that a big, slow aircraft like ours was a sitting duck in daylight, so we had to hug the ground on the way back and pray that we wouldn't be spotted by any enemy scouts. Having taken off towards the north-west, and not wanting to fly too far in that direction, I put the Handley into a gentle turn to port to bring us back over or near the airfield as we turned on to our westerly course.

We were unfamiliar with that bit of the landscape of northern France, so kept our eyes peeled for the grass area with its aircraft, tents and huts which had been our refuge for the night. The harder it was to spot the better, of course, for our friends down there; it meant that their camouflage was reasonably successful in protecting them from prying enemy eyes.

Harrison thumped me on the back and pointed downwards: there it was, the green expanse of the airfield, the DH9s dotted round it, the huts and the tents and vehicles. We both waved, and Corporal Pilcher leaned over the side; he had the best view of all. I then straightened up on our course for Ligescourt and, far ahead, thought I caught the glitter of the Channel waters in the sunlight. What a difference between the world beyond them, the world of Blighty and the English countryside, and our world here!

We kept down to about 400 feet, and every road we crossed seemed to be full of military vehicles, going in both directions; tenders, limbers, ambulances, motor-cycles, tanks, London buses, staff cars. We had a bird's-eye view of the great war machine the Allies had created, on the move to and from the Western Front, an unceasing military procession.

It was quite a warm day, the air was bumpy and the big Handley was flung about much more than we were used to in the calmer air of night. With our short sleep, and the long wait in the morning while the aircraft was checked over, and having to clutch the wheel to compensate for the wings suddenly dropping in the unstable air currents, I began to feel quite sick. I looked across at Harrison and he too was looking pale, though like the good chap that he was, concentrating on his map-reading.

After about ten minutes of this uncomfortble wallowing, while I was still struggling to keep our heading on 255 degrees, Harrison thumped me on the shoulder and yelled: 'About ten degrees port. We're getting too far north.' So I pulled the Handley round to as near 245 degrees as I could; Harrison gave me a thumbs-up and continued staring at the ground ahead, then at his map. I'd got the aircraft settled again on course, and we'd passed over more roads, dusty and thick with military traffic, and many tented sites in the fields, and French farms going on about their immemorial business as if there were no war on at all, when I saw it: a sudden brief sparkle of water under the midday sun, which could, and must be, the River Authie.

I thumped Harrison on the shoulder and pointed: 'The river!' I yelled. It was half a statement, half a question.

Harrison, always careful, looked at his map; then he gave me a thumbs-up — another instant visual message — and pointed to port; I was to turn left when we got to the river.

As we got to the Authie I put the Handley into a gentle bank, until its waters appeared under the port wing. Keeping it on our left, we cruised along hopefully, until our expectations were rewarded by the sight of our own airfield, its huts, its tents, its Handleys and the road dividing the 'offices' from the aircraft, coming into view: a corner of a foreign field, but home to us.

I brought us across it in a slight dive, heaved the wheel over to port until we came on to the downwind leg for a landing and, noting that there was hardly any wind, took the longest run, turning on to the approach and steadying our speed to 70/75 mph. We crossed the river, the trees flashed under our wings, and in another minute our wheels rumbled on the grass, the skid slowing us down until we came to a stop — back again at Ligescourt. It had been a very long night.

7

Special Mission — The Tunnel

'Gentlemen,' said the CO, 'this is Major Murless from Wing who is going to describe the target for you.'

Behind the major, who was tall and had a languid air, was a large-scale map with various photographs pinned on it.

'This isn't a normal raid, gentlemen, let me hasten to explain,' he began. 'It's a fact-finding mission. The background to it' — he took up his pointer and held it between his hands — 'is the contribution you can make to slowing-down the Hun offensive. Up to now, you and the day bombers have concentrated on known vulnerable points along his lines of communication, within forty miles of the battle-front, with considerable success. The Hun, of course, has been doing the same to us.

'Now the High Command has decided that he is to be hit closer to his sources of supply, which means deeper penetration by the bomber squadrons. The DH4s and '9s have been spearheading this new offensive' — I thought of our unplanned visit to Beauvois, and of how that squadron there had been clobbered — 'and have discovered, photographed and bombed some important targets.

- 'This one in particular has attracted our attention.' He pointed to the map and the accompanying photographs. 'Here is the railway line between Maubeuge and Charleroi, and you can see here' — he tapped with his pointer to emphasise the exact location — 'how this single-track line branches off it to the east, then disappears at the edge of what looks like an area of waste land, on which some bombs have been dropped; though no craters are visible, which suggests that the surface might have been reinforced to protect something. Just what, we don't know, but it could be important and it's been entered on HQ's bombing-list.

'However, they decided to leave it alone for a while, and the day-bomber squadrons were told to keep away, so that the Hun, ignorant of what was cooking, might be caught napping.'

I looked at Harrison. Somehow, we knew just what was coming, knew the significance of the large-scale map and the photographs.

'HQ needs to know what this concreted surface — for that we believe it to be — conceals. We want a fact-finding mission, and to expose the cake,' he added picturesquely, 'the icing has to be broken.'

Here Major Folliott took over the briefing, and in his precise way said, 'In order to achieve this, gentlemen, one 1,650 lb bomb is to be dropped at the start of the operation. The other aircraft will follow with normal 112 lb bomb loads plus some incendiaries. All bombs will have delayed fuses to aid penetration. This will be a small operation, only 'B' Flight being involved.

Harrison and I again looked at each other: that was us. The only question was, who would be dropping the big one?

'Your Flight Commander will give you a detailed briefing, gentlemen. Thank you, and good luck.'

Captain Brinden, tall and quietly-spoken, then took over. I'd been impressed by him since our first meeting when I joined the squadron and that impression had been subsequently confirmed. What he had to say came as a surprise to me.

'Five aircraft are to fly on this special mission,' he said. 'They're being lined up in the usual way on the upwind edge of the airfield, one of them armed with the big bomb; that yours, Mr Blacking.'

This time, Harrison and I both looked at each other, than back at the flight commander. His information that we were to carry 'the big one' on this raid concentrated our minds wonderfully.

Captain Brinden went on: 'I'm to lead, taking the shortest route to the target area, where I shall drop flares. You are to follow, Mr Blacking, at 7,000 feet and start to descend when about a mile from the target. The bomb will be dropped at between 4,000 and 3,000 feet — no lower, because it's going to make a big bang. When you start your descent, fire a Very light. When you've bombed I will drop my 112-pounders, and the other three aircraft — Lts Brown, Farmer and Rochdale' — he looked at our fellow 'B' Flight crews at the briefing — 'will then bomb in turn. Mr Rochdale, as the last man, aim your two sticks at where the feeder track leaves the main railway line, to wreck the junction. Any questions, gentlemen?'

There were none. We were all experienced enough by now to grasp the implications of our instructions, and in a small operation like this one we could see clearly what we were meant to do. Brinden looked around the group of nine pilots and observers, including his own, and added:

'I'll leave you to brief your own gunners. For them, it's just like any other operation, but it's a very important one if we're going to slow up this Hun offensive. You'll find the target flagged on the wall map in the Map Room; I suggest you go there and study it, then check over your aircraft. It's now 4.15.' Everyone automatically checked their watches. 'Take-off will be at nine o'clock. Good luck, gentlemen.'

'What about the weather?' said Lt Farmer suddenly. He was a handsome, fair-haired chap with bright blue eyes, always extremely smart and well turned out; his appearance set us an example. He was quite right to ask. In the excitement of the briefing for the special mission, no-one seemed to have given a thought to the elements.

'We shall have a forecast for you at seven,' the CO intervened, 'but it looks as though there'll be no problems — little wind and clear skies.'

'Fine for the Hun night fighters,' said Lieutenant Brown half to himself, with his usual cheerful, sardonic grin.

I thought the cynicism of this aside was partly due to the fact that 'Tom' (which wasn't his real name but all Browns became 'Tom' because of *Tom Brown's Schooldays*), like other good pilots on the squadron, tended to be contemptuous of our non-flying CO.

'We can expect night-fighter activity,' put in Captain Brinden. 'The Huns may not know what we're up to. HQ have deliberately left this target alone for a bit — even the day squadrons have been told to keep away — but he's bound to react pretty quickly once he knows what we're after.'

We were all likely to be caught by the night fighters; Brinden because he had to hang around waiting for me to bomb, myself because I had the big bomb on board, and the other three because they would be bombing after 'the big one' had gone down, when the Hun had had plenty of time to realize what was going on.

'There's one compensation about this calm weather,' said Brinden above the buzz of conversation, obviously anxious to conclude the briefing on a cheerful note. 'You won't have any struggle against head winds in getting back, once you've done this job. I think you'd better take a look at the target in the Map Room, gentlemen, then check your aircraft. Let me remind you — take off from 9 p.m. Good luck!'

It seemed incongruous, coming out from that briefing into a beautiful afternoon, the sort of day when, in normal times, all one wanted to do was to laze about. Instead, here we were planning a war operation. But any idyllic thoughts were quickly succeeded by realistic ones. To the east, the Hun was engaged in a major offensive; our boys in the lines were taking the brunt of it and our job was to do anything we could to slow up the enemy's advance.

In the Map Room the target had been flagged on the large wall map: there was the junction, there the disappearing track, captured in a reconnaissance photograph. It would be 'marked' for us by the flight commander's flares. There was also a list of the 'lighthouses' we would be using, flashing stepping-stones from our 'home' one at Doullens, to and from the target, and the magnetic bearings we would follow. Harrison copied all these down, then we walked out into the sunlight, to go and look at our aircraft.

Above us there were streets of white cumulus clouds, hardly moving: the weather, good or bad, had been a common factor in battles down the ages — the sunshine or rain at Hastings, at Agincourt, at Blenheim, at Waterloo — except that in earlier wars they had picked the right season of the year for campaigning, but this Great War went on all the year round, in the rain, the mud, the cold, the winds, the heat and calm; or like today, when everything in the sky was beautiful.

'Penny for them?' asked Harrison as we crossed the road towards the line of Handleys. We'd not spoken a word since the briefing.

'I was just thinking,' I said, 'when our war might end and we could enjoy days like this; it's been going on for over four years now.'

'Well, if we can help to hold up this Hun advance and they run out of steam we ought to be able to knock them out, especially now the Americans have come in,' Harrison suggested. 'Surely they can't go on indefinitely. There have been much longer wars, like the Hundred Years' War and the Thirty Years' War, but not of this intensity; whole nations can't go on killing each other like this.'

'That's a matter for the politicians and our military leaders,' I countered. 'They've managed to go on doing so for all this time, and where are we? Neither side can score a decisive victory — it's just offensives and counter-offensives. What will happen when we've slowed the Hun up? Another stalemate?'

We'd reached the line of Handleys. There were three there so far and another was being towed across, its wings still folded back. Our aircraft, 1, was next to the end of the line, and the flight commander's machine, 2, was next to ours. When we got near to it we found a hive of activity. The AMs under Sergeant 'Taff' Jones, our voluble Welsh sergeant armourer, were attaching 'Bertha' — the big bomb — to a special metal housing beneath the bomb racks, between the undercarriage legs. Lt Westoby, one of the armament officers, was there supervising this operation and explained to us what we needed to know about the bomb and the release mechanism.

'You'll be responsible for letting it go, Harrison,' he said. 'It's wired to a release lever fastened to the side of the forward cockpit. Come on up, I'll show you.'

They climbed up the ladder, disappeared for a few seconds and then emerged in the front cockpit, Westoby showing Harrison the release lever and slapping the side of the aircraft in the enthusiasm of his explanation.

'Hello, Sergeant Jones,' I greeted the red-faced armourer as he and the AMs struggled to get the wire hawser round the bomb, a massive iron affair with a pointed nose, rows of bolts along its sides and four large fins. It had been wheeled out to the aircraft on a special low trolley, and on it had been chalked special messages for the Huns: on the top, 'A little Hell(p)' and on the bottom, 'From the RAF', a two-part but concise and meaningful message.

'Mr Blacking.' Sergeant Jones extricated himself and saluted. 'There you are, sir. All secure.'

'So long as it isn't too secure,' I said. 'We want to get rid of it, you know. I hope it'll go down all right.'

'You'll know when it does, Blacking.' Lt Westoby and Harrison had rejoined us. 'Your aircraft will go up about 200 feet. I've been explaining to Harrison. I've adjusted the bomb-sight for release at about 3,000 feet, to allow for a delay while the bomb slides clear of the hawser after he's pulled the handle. You'll know when it's gone.'

'What if it doesn't release?' put in Harrison, half jokingly, but I knew from the carefulness of his character that he liked to foresee all possible eventualities and decide how to deal with them.

'Then you'll have to take the matter up with Sergeant Jones on your return,' Westoby countered, looking me straight in the eye. But I knew, and he knew and Harrison knew that if the big bomb did hang up there was nothing anybody could do to help us.

'Let's hope it all works,' I concluded rather lamely, trying to show a jaunty confidence I didn't really feel. 'Hello, Corporal Pilcher.' I'd spotted our gunner's head in the rear cockpit, checking his Lewis guns.

'Make sure those are working properly: there may be a problem with night fighters, especially if the weather stays clear.'

'They'll be in good order, sir,' rejoined Pilcher, 'and the ones in the front,' — with a meaningful look at Harrison.

As we walked back to the Map Room, with four of the five Handleys now in position and the last one being towed across from the hangers, Harrison said, 'Westoby knows I wasn't joking. It's not like dropping a lot of 112-pounders, which are all neatly stowed in the bomb-bay. If this big one doesn't fall, we're stuck with it outside the aircraft and we'd have to bring it back and land with it — and you know what that means'.

I did indeed, for the bomb would be fused and the slightest impact would set it off. But these were hazards that any of the bomber crews faced. Mustering up some rather specious confidence, I said, 'Never mind, George. We'll either be one-night heroes on the squadron or our names will appear on a Roll of Honour somewhere after the war.'

Working out our compass courses in the Map Room, having copied the list of lighthouses and magnetic bearings to and from our base beacon, provided a useful antidote to speculating on what might happen that night; at least it gave us some constructive thinking to do.

'If there's going to be hardly any wind it looks as though we can fly these tracks,' said Harrison, speaking his thoughts aloud. 'We shall have to see what the met forecast is.'

I watched him drawing in the tracks and jotting down the compass courses with quick, neat precision and admired his professionalism. Strange, I thought, how just two or three years ago most of us were still schoolboys and many of us had never seen an aeroplane. Now here we were, flying these big machines through the night and making precision bombing attacks on the Hun, when we would have been occupying staid city offices in banks or insurance companies had this Great War not given us this strange opportunity.

'Right, Leslie.' Harrison interrupted my thoughts as he stowed his papers away. 'Let's go over to the Mess for a meal. Judging by that night when we had to force-land, you never know when you're going to get another one.'

Despite the lovely evening, the squadron had its usual preoperational look of quiet, purposeful activity with a certain tenseness in the air, and my thoughts were diverted from the beauties of Nature by thoughts of the bomb we were to deliver. What effect would it have on the Handley's aerodynamics? It was a big weight to carry in one lump, and we would start to feel the effect of this on take-off. I mentally advised myself to take extreme care with my flying that night, as if carrying a crate of eggs.

Perhaps there was a certain association of ideas in this, for we were offered ham and eggs as our pre-flight meal, and I thought fleetingly of Farmer Briand and his luscious daughter Jeanne, from whose farm they undoubtedly came. But such thoughts I kept to myself, for one couldn't say there was much sociability about the meal. It had as much jollity as a Last Supper and was also a trifle bizarre, for here were odd members of 'B' Flight sitting at the table in almost total silence, and there were members of 'A' Flight either lounging in the chairs reading old magazines or propping up the bar, looking at us curiously (or so I thought) from time to time. I wondered just what their thoughts were. Suddenly I felt a slap on my shoulder and there was tousle-haired Tex, the American I'd met when I first joined the squadron.

'Good luck, Leslie,' he said. 'I know you're going to do a great job tonight. Say, will you do something for me?' he added, in an earnest fashion. I thought he was going to make a particularly confidential request. 'Give 'em hell!' he roared, slapping my back. 'And tell 'em I'll be right over there myself.'

With that he took himself back to the bar.

I looked at Harrison, who grinned, saying nothing. There was a good atmosphere on the squadron, mainly twenty-two-year-olds who managed to get a bit of fun out of their lives, despite the grim business of their operational missions.

Harrison glanced at me. 'Time to go and get changed,' he said quietly.

As we left the Mess I looked round. It was odd how such strange surroundings had suddenly become so familiar and comfortable, that one longed to be there, or to get back to them. How lucky we were, I thought, to have this civilized accommodation when thousands of chaps of our age — or younger, or older — were living in the lines.

'There's one thing about it,' remarked Harrison as we strode across the grass. 'It shouldn't be too cold tonight. Although we've passed the middle of the year the air's still warm.'

By now, I'd got pretty used to wearing flying clothing, but I always felt a sense of apprehension when I put it on: the Sidcot suit seemed to be our working dress; it had replaced the leather jacket, which I preferred, but it gave better all-round protection for the sort of flying we had to do, though it seemed strange to be getting into it on a beautiful evening. The whole procedure was so automatic that my thoughts wandered a bit. What could I be doing on a day like this, at a time like this, at home? Going out to play tennis, perhaps, or for a ride on my bicycle.

'Any earwigs, Leslie?' asked Harrison, as we pulled on our suits.

'I hope not,' I said, but I did a double check on the fur, something which, in my temporary abstraction, I'd forgotten to do. In fact I found one of the little menaces. They used to crawl into the fur during the day, while our suits were hanging up, then crawl out on to our necks while we were flying, a disconcerting and uncomfortable experience. Still, we were lucky to be in tents, rather than in the awful squalor of dug-outs, so we couldn't complain about the local wildlife.

I picked up my helmet with its black felt cat emblem, which I gave an affectionate rub, as I always did, for good luck; then I looked round the tent. In a few hours' time we'd either be back there, our minds freshly filled with some new and perhaps rather terrible experiences, or someone else would come in to sort out our things and send them home.

'Ready?' asked Harrison quietly, with a glance at his watch. He'd already changed into the efficient observer. We were now once again an operational team, and as we trudged across the grass in our Sidcots, to collect the maps and go out to the aircraft, I felt almost out of place on the ground.

The evening was now disappearing into the West; there was cloud, but conditions were still and calm. There was a pale moon, which in an hour or so would light us — and the Hun night fighters — on our way.

The line-up of five aircraft looked a small force when there could be as many as ten for a night's operation, but it still seemed a long way to reach ours, which was at the end next to the flight commander's. The Handleys had their backs to the road which divided the airfield and the hangars and offices. One way, it led to Ligescourt; the other way (guarded by a gate and a sentry) to Crécy.

'Do you realize,' I said to Harrison, 'that down there the English won a great victory nearly six centuries ago, and that their successors have been at war on the Continent in every century since, only this time the enemy is a different one — the Germans — for the first time?'

'Well, let's hope we can do something tonight to help to bring this one to an end,' Harrison responded philosophically. He seemed to have a calmness and determination of spirit which I didn't feel, but it gave me confidence to have him flying with me.

Sergeant Pilcher — his promotion had come through — likewise, with his cheeriness and conscientiousness. There he was, up in the rear cockpit, checking his Lewis guns. And there, slung underneath the aircraft, was the big bomb. Next to our Handley was the flight commander's and there seemed to be quite a crowd of AMs swarming round both of them. Torch lights were flashing like glow-worms in the gathering darkness as they checked the bomb, the wheels, the tailskid, the control surfaces, the bracing wires, the pitot head, the wingtip flares (which we'd had to use when we did our forced-landing), the propellers and the engines.

I went round with Flight Sergeant Arnett, and was glad of his cheerful experience and keen eyes. He knew far more about the Handleys than I ever would.

One thing I noticed which was quite irrelevant to the night's operation: the dew already on the bruised grass we were tramping around on. It made me realize that, whatever awful things man did to man, Nature never changed her ways. Undoubtedly the dew was falling on the other side of the lines, at the beginning of another autumn night.

'I've checked all the guns, sir, and the ammunition.' Sergeant Pilcher's voice broke in on my reverie. 'I think the big bomb's all right. It's not like carrying 112-pounders. Still, easier to check than all those,' he added cheerfully. 'It'll either go or it won't; I shan't have to do any checking with my flashlight to see if we've got any hang-ups.'

'We'll know when it's gone all right, Pilcher,' I assured him. 'You'll see; you'll feel it leave.'

What concerned me more at that moment was getting the Handley into the air with that load slung underneath it. Undoubtedly the flying characteristics would be affected, especially when we had a full load of fuel and ammunition on take-off. But there wasn't time for reflection. I'd been all round the aircraft, checked everything I could see and got to the front again. Harrison was there — we'd got into the habit of doing our outside checks independently, as a duplicated safeguard — and Flight Sergeant Arnett was standing by the step-ladder.

'Good luck, sir,' he said. 'We don't want to see this again.' He indicated the big bomb. 'Just deposit it where it'll do most harm.'

'We'll do our best, chiefy,' I assured him, putting my foot on the ladder. I'd noticed Harrison's impatient look; in his quiet way he anticipated every situation.

It's 8.45,' he reminded me. 'Time to get aboard.'

I got up the ladder, ducked when I got inside on to the slats and heaved myself into the right-hand cockpit seat. Two AMs were already on the wing waiting to start the starboard engine; both powerplants had already been warmed up, so there shouldn't be any trouble about starting. I realized once again, when I got up there, what a commanding view there was from the Handley's 'office' of the four other aircraft lined up, one on our right and three on our left, and of the control tower on the right-hand side of the field, which would give us our signal for take-off.

I checked the controls for full movement, pulling the wheel right back then pushing it forward, heaving it over to the left and the right, being careful not to bang Harrison's knees. He'd climbed in after me, and was busy setting the compass and arranging his maps.

Just then the starboard engine of Brinden's aircraft fired, then his port engine. It was time for us to start and I gave a thumbs-up to the two AMs crouched on the starboard wing. The Eagles had already been run so our starboard engine caught within a second or two, the great wooden propeller began to turn, then the revs increased, the AMs slid down off the wing with their starting-handle and we repeated the process on the port side. Soon the whole line of Handleys had their engines roaring as the pilots opened them up to check the rpm and the magnetos, then throttled back, satisfied with the synchronization of their powerplants. Harrison looked at his watch by the light of his torch: it was just coming up to nine o'clock.

I glanced across at the flight commander's aircraft and saw him wave, then he opened up to full power and started to move forward, rumbling across the grass, leaving only slipstream behind in the darkness. It was our turn to go; I looked round to Pilcher, gave him a thumbs-up, then across at Harrison, and saw the torches at either ends of the wing where the AMs were standing ready to remove the chocks. Control signalled my cypher, the chocks were pulled away and I opened-up, putting on power as quickly as I could while keeping the Handley straight.

We seemed to gather speed very, very slowly, rumbling on towards the boundary and the river. Harrison held the throttles wide open (we'd long regularized our take-off drill) while I pressed forward on the control wheel to bring the tail up. Despite the warmth of the night and of my Sidcot suit, I broke out into a cold sweat. Would we never get off? Then the airflow began to bite over the control surfaces and I eased back on the wheel; but our landing wheels were still rumbling on the grass. Then suddenly their rumbling ceased — we were off into the darkness with our big bomb.

Almost subconsciously (though I must have had some sort of tactic like it in mind) I'd veered on our take-off run towards the far corner of the airfield, because of the wide, deep valley beyond it. We seemed to hang over this once we were airborne and I banked to starboard to remain within it. Also, this would take us towards our 'home' lighthouse —'Q', near Doullens, the starting and finishing point for all our operations.

I banked rather gingerly, watching the airspeed, trying to climb a little at the same time: we aimed to be at 6,000 feet before we got to Arras and at 7,000 feet before we crossed the lines. Night had closed in all around us, there was a clear sky and three-quarters moon — good conditions for our special type of operation but suitable also for the Hun night fighters.

Harrison banged me on the shoulder and pointed: there was the Doullens lighthouse, ahead but over to the right (my starboard bank had been a bit too cautious and gentle — not surprising, under the circumstances). I spotted the dash-dash-dot-dash and steered towards it, easing the Handley up towards 2,000 feet. With an introductory thump on my left shoulder (another one — it's a wonder I wasn't black and blue on that side, but this was our quickest and least ambigious means of communication), Harrison shouted: 'Your course to Arras is oh-seven-five degrees,' and bent down to put it on the compass.

I responded with a thumbs-up, kept the aircraft in its climb and when over Doullens eased it into a port turn, heading for Arras — from where, suddenly, a thin pencil-like searchlight beam shot up and began probing the night sky. I realized that we must identify ourselves if that beam wasn't to be followed up by something much more lethal, so reached down and grabbed the Very pistol, already loaded (I hoped correctly) with the colours of the night, and fired it off. The coloured stars soared into the sky above us. The searchlight beam was extinguished as quickly as it had appeared, seeming to ripple down to the ground: those clots below had got the message. We were at 6,000 feet over Arras, still climbing; on up to 7,000 feet, the height we wanted for crossing the Hun lines.

'Oh-seven-eight,' Harrison yelled.

I gave him the usual thumbs-up and eased the wheel over. He bent down to set the new course on the grid ring, with the aid of his torch; and I was just thinking that Captain Brinden couldn't be far ahead, and the others not far behind, when it happened: a Hun searchlight came up, found and held us.

In seconds all hell broke loose, for it was followed by bursting shells, the shrapnel spattering and clattering around us; one burst came close enough to hurl splinters through the cockpit.

Instinctively I'd pulled the Handley into a diving turn; perhaps because of this quick reaction, the barrage missed us. Then I thought, 'Oh God, the bomb!' — its weight might twist our fuselage in a steep turn; so I straightened up again. But if a shell hit us, that was it. I was in a cold sweat.

Suddenly the barrage ceased; we'd flown through it. We'd also gone down about 300 feet and veered to starboard.

Harrison, cool as ever, thumped me on the shoulder and gestured with his hand: up-up and back on course. It was amazing how expressive our sign language had become. He looked at his watch. 'About twenty minutes to the target,' he shouted in my left ear.

There was a 'crump-crump', a dull, sinister sound — no searchlight, but I could imagine the German gunners' excited voices down below; the message had been passed along the line. We were over Hunland all right, but the defences' range was short; the bursts were below us.

Harrison's torch was on his map: 'Start descending,' he instructed, in the usual megaphone voice we had to use in the air. 'We've got to get down to 4,000 feet. Steer oh-six-eight — we're too far south.'

I pulled the Handley over to port and put her nose down. At the same time I had a quick glance towards the rear; Pilcher was busy scanning the sky. I didn't think he'd be caught out if there were any Hun night fighters around. I adjusted the knob between the throttles to bring the engines into synchronization after reducing power. At least there seemed to be no problems there; they were running as smoothly as could be.

Although Brinden's aircraft should be only a mile or so ahead and we were being followed closely behind, there seemed to be only ourselves in the whole dark world at that moment — until a searchlight flicked up, over to our left, and probed about. These were city defences, for we were now well over enemy-held territory. A moment later there was the crump-crump of bursting shells. The enemy's defences must have been alerted by Brinden's aircraft, but they hadn't got our range. I continued our descent, trying to keep as cool as possible but at the same time sweating with fear.

'About ten miles to go,' Harrison shouted. 'Don't go below three thousand eight hundred. I'll go forward when we're three miles from the target; we should see Brinden's flares when he drops them.'

I was grateful for his coolness and experience; he'd dropped one of these blockbusters before. This time we had to align ourselves on the railway track, to be heading for the tunnel when we released it. There was enough moonlight for us to be able to pick out the lines.

By now we were down to 3,800 feet. I levelled off and opened the throttles again to cruising power. A searchlight, probably alerted by Brinden's appearance in the area, shot up ahead of us and over to the right, probing for its target; then another came up to our left and flak followed — flaming onions, which arched over above us, and a rattle of light gunfire. Things were hotting up; the defences had been thoroughly aroused, but we had to concentrate on finding that railway line and watching for Brinden's flares.

There was no sign of lights below — the civilian populace had got used to our raids by now — but the towns showed up as dark masses and there was enough moonlight to illuminate the parallel gleam of railway tracks. I felt sorry that our target was in Belgium. It was to help the poor Belgians that we had originally gone to war, when the Huns invaded them, but this area was crucial to the Huns' latest offensive, which we had to try to stop or slow up. This was where they built up their supplies, bringing up troops and guns and ammunition.

'That's Maubeuge,' yelled Harrison. How he knew I wasn't sure, but he sounded confident, and he'd had a lot of experience of this area. 'Follow the railway line going north-east.'

We were over the centre of the town, but as we crossed it and the buildings thinned out I could see the tracks going purposefully out into the countryside.

'Watch for the single track going eastwards. When you see it, turn and follow it. I'm going into the nose, so watch for the lights.'

With these shouted instructions, Harrison disappeared through the tunnel; then I saw his head and shoulders come up in the forward cockpit. At the same moment a searchlight beamed up into the sky ahead and started probing: the defences had been alerted, presumably by Brinden's arrival. Because we were now so low — I had got down to 2,500 feet — the area of attack had been identified, though the Huns wouldn't know we were aiming for a tunnel.

Suddenly I spotted that junction and a single track going eastwards. As I banked to the right to follow it, Harrison gave me a thumbs-up: What we had to do in the next few moments was to spot where it disappeared into the tunnel.

Harrison was now in control. All I had to do was to follow the dashboard signals he gave, those winking lights telling me to adjust our heading — 'left, left' or 'right, right' — to keep us straight above the railway line. Suddenly the sky ahead lit up; not the searchlights which were probing around, but a steady incandescent light illuminating the countryside below as it descended — Brinden's flares!

I felt quite naked and unprotected as we flew into this glow, but it was imperative that I concentrated on keeping our course until 'Bertha' had gone — I was in Harrison's hands.

One shell, then another, burst to our right; the guns were getting our range. They had our height now; next time they would have our exact position.

Suddenly we shot up like a lift: we must have been hit underneath. They'd got our range!

But the burst was below us — a great flash of fire, followed by an explosion which shook the aircraft, then another and another. 'Bertha' had gone, I realized. There was only one thing to do now: to get my Handley and crew back safely to Ligescourt.

As I banked to port and put on maximum power to get us into a climb, Harrison crawled through from the front cockpit and took his seat again beside me. He looked elated and gave me a thumbs-up.

'Steer two-seven-five and let's get out of here,' he shouted. As he bent down to put the new course on the compass and gather up a map which had fallen on the duck-board flooring, there was a sudden rat-tat-tat on our right.

'Night fighter!' he yelled.

I instinctively tightened our turn and glanced round at Pilcher. He was standing up, staring intently into the darkness, his guns pointing downwards. I knew he wouldn't miss anything if he saw it within range.

The ack-ack had stopped, but there might be more than one fighter. The searchlights were still probing around, and if they coned us we were a sitting duck. They'd also be looking for the three aircraft behind us. I decided to keep in the climb; we might outdistance the fighter — the Handley, freed of its bomb and now with only half-full petrol tanks, had plenty of power.

'Keep on two-seven-five,' Harrison shouted. In looking round, and thinking about our adversary, I'd drifted leftwards on to 270 degrees. I pulled the aircraft to starboard, keeping in the climb; we were up to 3,500 feet now.

Suddenly the moon was revealed as the clouds moved away from its face. We were in a moonlit arena; we were slow and big, and terribly vulnerable. I couldn't have imagined a more dramatic mixture of beauty and terror. There was only one thing to do: keep climbing, heading for any bit of cloud protection there might be. The moonlight, which had been a help in finding the railway line, might be our doom now.

Rat-tat-tat-tat-tat: the rattle of our Lewis gun came from the rear. Harrison dropped his maps and disappeared through the tunnel to man the front gun. I was amazed that, with his Sidcot suit on, he got through there so quickly and appeared standing up in front of me, swinging the Lewis round on its Scarff ring.

Rat-tat-tat-tat-tat: he fired and I was showered with a hail of spent cartridge cases. I didn't know what he saw and I couldn't take evasive action because I didn't know where the Hun fighter was. I realized, though, that the moon had disappeared; there was some cloud ahead, then, and we must be almost over the lines again, back on our side and heading for Arras and safety.

Just then the cloud moved, the moon came out once more and I saw the Hun fighter, on our starboard side and slightly above us: a two-seater Halberstadt or Hannover with a front gun and a gunner in the rear cockpit. Harrison and Pilcher saw it too and both fired. Then, as they said in the New Testament, 'a cloud received him out of our sight,' and a moment later we were in cloud too. It swathed us in a kind of damp cotton wool, making the engines and the wings seem closer to us as it flicked past.

I concentrated on my instrument flying, keeping the aircraft straight and level, watching the altimeter and airspeed indicator.

Harrison had sat down in the front cockpit — we might at any moment burst through into clear air again. However, apart from one momentary clearance we stayed in cloud for several minutes, though it seemed much longer than that. Then it began to thin out and we came into plain darkness, cloudless but with no moon. We couldn't be far from Arras now. Harrison evidently decided that we'd lost the Hun fighter, which wouldn't go far from its defensive area, and crawled back through the tunnel.

'Steer two-seven-zero,' he shouted. 'I'm not sure where we are after that. There's a lighthouse north-west of Arras — number five — so if we spot that we'll know where we are.'

I realized I'd gone very cold; after sweating through the bombing operation and the night-fighter incident, this was probably a delayed reaction. But I didn't mind; all we had to do now was to find a friendly lighthouse, get from there to Doullens, and from there to base.

I wondered what had happened to the other aircraft behind us, whether they had been intercepted by the fighters.

The night was partly clouded, partly moonlit, the moon riding high and serene, visible for a few moments then completely obscured. I looked at our altimeter in one of the flashes of moonlight, when for a few moments it was as bright as day: we were nearly 4,000 feet.

'I'm going to start going down,' I shouted to Harrison, who responded with a thumbs-up.

The Eagles seemed to purr as I throttled them back. Most of our worries of the night were over; Harrison would steer us back via the lighthouses and I would get the aircraft down. There would be no repetition of that forced-landing we had on a former occasion. Nevertheless I was getting a bit tense, and worried that the clouds seemed to be getting a bit lower; what if we missed the Arras lighthouse? Where was it? What if we were caught by our own searchlights and ack-ack? They might still be on the lookout for Hun bombers. 'I'm going down a bit more, in case we get in cloud,' I yelled. Harrison responded with a thumbs-up, and I saw him take a quick glance at his watch.

I worked the throttle knob back to reduce power, using it at the same time to keep the engines synchronized. A blanket of cloud enveloped us and the aircraft shuddered as it went through it, then we were in the clear.

Almost at that moment Harrison thumped me on the shoulder and pointed over to our port side. There, about ten miles away, were the five flashes of the lighthouse north-west of Arras; we'd got well to the north of our track in evading the Hun fighter. I swung the Handley's control wheel over in an immediate reaction, and that line of a hymn I remembered singing came into my mind: 'Lead, kindly light, amid the encircling gloom.' Curious what odd things one recalls in moments of stress. As we got nearer, so the flashes got clearer.

'Steer two-five-eight when you get over it,' Harrison shouted. 'That should bring us to Doullens. Magnetic is two-six-six.'

I took the Handley over the top of the lighthouse, descending to about 2,000 feet, then turned for Doullens. Harrison had re-set the compass ring and I aimed to undershoot on the turn: there was always a 'delayed reaction' effect, tempting one ot put on more bank than was necessary. I'd levelled up and we were droning along, peering ahead for a first sight of 'Q', when Harrison thumped me on the shoulder and pointed over on our port side. There, down below, a series of vivid yellow flashes lit up the ground: it was our artillery, responding angrily to some enemy fire. Day and night, week after week and month after month, the fighting on the ground went on. I thought of that line about 'where ignorant armies clash by night' in Matthew Arnold's poem about Dover beach. Every now and then our Allied Armies advanced a few yards, then might be driven back again, thousands of men being trapped in an obscene and mindless struggle. Would this counter-offensive succeed in really driving the Huns back for good? Our attack tonight had been designed to block up some of their supplies: had it been successful? We wouldn't know until some reconnaissance photographs had been taken. Perhaps we would have to do it again . . .

'Q!' shouted Harrison. He pointed ahead and to the right. Sure enough, a steady dash-dash-dot-dash was just visible. I steered towards it, but then its message changed: it signalled in Morse code, 'Wait; enemy aircraft.'

As we had to get our clearance to land from 'Q', there was nothing we could do but wait, orbiting the lighthouse. We were now at about 1,800 feet and I tried to keep this height steady in our turn. I glanced back at Sergeant Pilcher. He was standing up, his hands on his gun triggers, ready for anything which might appear out of the darkness. How long would we have to wait?

Just as we completed a second circuit the light changed to green; we were cleared to go to the airfield to land.

'Two-eighty!' shouted Harrison and I eased the Handley round on to this heading, starting a descent to our circuit height.

'There's the river,' he added a few minutes later. We were more or less above it; Ligescourt was in a bend of it, but where was the landing tee? Fortunately I knew the layout well enough, and sufficient features became discernible in the darkness, for me to make an approach, then, as we were steady on our final descent, the tee came on again.

I could see the huts and tents, and moonlight shining on the river. We were down to about 100 feet when the lights of the tee went out.

By then we were committed to our approach, with the engines just ticking over. I could see the landing field but needed the lights to judge how high we were above the ground for rounding-out. It was too late to open-up and go round again; our touch-down would have to be pure guess-work — which it was.

As I didn't want to hold off too high, we hit the ground hard and bounced. I juggled with the throttles, the Handley hung there for a moment then came down with a thump, ran along and tipped up on its nose. We were back, not very gracefully, but safely, from our special mission.

I found myself tremblng, with a kind of delayed shock I suppose, as we sat there in a daze — poor Pilcher right up in the air behind us. I had the presence of mind to turn the switches and fuel off; there was a sudden dreadful silence after the roaring of the engines. Harrison had been flung against the cockpit coaming and looked pretty dazed. I glanced back — and up — at Pilcher: he was clinging to his guns. All this took seconds, but we had to get out of that aircraft and acted instinctively to escape from it. Harrison and I clambered over the nose, feeling clumsy and bulky in our flying kit, and dropped on to the grass. Pilcher had much farther to come but came with remarkable quickness and agility — over his cockpit coaming, across the bomb-bay then into and out of our cockpit and so over the nose and on to the ground. I involuntarily shook him by the hand.

There was a lethal smell of oil and petrol from the tipped-up Handley as we ran clear of it; at any moment it might burst into flames and the remaining ammunition start to go off. What a way to end our night's operation! But nothing happened, and in a few moments we saw the lights of a tender coming towards the aircraft, looking for us. Then the tee came on again and we heard the sound of another machine approaching to land. Perhaps he was heading for our stranded Hamdley, nose down, tail up in the air, and there would be an awful crash. We felt quite helpless standing there, not only on our own account, for we could foresee an almost inevitable accident, but for the sake of the other crew who couldn't.

By now the tender had come up. Flight Sergeant Arnett and two AMs were in it. They put down some red warning lights by the Handley just as the other one swished in, fortunately avoiding our machine, and us, and running on down the field.

We climbed aboard the tender and as we drove up to where we should have parked, had we been able to taxy in, the flight sergeant remarked:

'I see you got rid of the bomb, sir.'

I'd almost forgotten about it, in this untoward ending to our night's operation. 'Otherwise you mightn't have been so quick coming out to us,' I rejoined, adding, 'Why did they switch the tee off, sergeant?'

'There's been a Gotha about, sir, they found the airfield and were trying to bomb us. Must have followed Captain Brinden in from the lighthouse.'

'There's one more aircraft to return, isn't there, sergeant?' put in Harrison.

'Yes, sir; four are back now.'

We could see the shapes of two of them as we drove up.

'That means Captain Brinden's back,' I said.

'Yes, sir, landed about ten minutes ago.'

I peered at the aircraft. There were figures moving about them; their wings had already been folded back ready for towing them away and one of them seemed already to have a tractor attached to it, to tow it back to the hangars.

When we stopped and climbed out of the Crossley the last of the 0/400s swept over to its landing, disappearing down the field. In the darkness, everything seemed rather confused, but Captain Brinden's voice came into aural focus:

'Well done, Blacking. Well done, Harrison. But we'll have to wait until we get some reconnaissance photographs to see how successful we were. In the meantime, the Mess has been opened up, if you want a drink or a meal when you've taken your kit off. We can give you a lift across — there's a tender here.'

'What about the landing tee being switched off?' I asked. I felt more concerned about that recent shaking experience than about the success or otherwise of the raid.

'The CO's orders,' said Brinden. 'There were enemy aircraft around. You got the warning from Doullens.'

'Doullens gave us a clear to land signal,' Harrison put in. 'Then when we were on our approach the lights went out. We were very lucky to get down safely.'

'I think you'll have to discuss this with the CO in the morning,' Brinden said curtly. 'I don't know what the situation was on the ground — I only landed a few minutes before you did.'

I walked back down to our aircraft, to get rid of some of my feelings of anger and frustration over that landing business, and found Sergeant Pilcher. He had already taken off his guns and was superintending the unloading of the spare live ammunition, the belts glinting like snakes in the darkness as they fed down sinuously from the rear cockpit.

'Thank you, Sergeant Pilcher,' I said. 'That was a near thing with that Hun fighter; we were lucky to get away with it. It was fortunate for us there was some cloud about.'

'Well done, sir; we've lived to tell the tale.' Pilcher had taken his helmet off and the outline of it and his goggles could be seen on his face, which looked streaked and dirty. 'We'll know tomorrow, I suppose, if our raid was successful.'

'As soon as Wing get some photographs. In the meantime, Pilcher, get some well deserved rest.'

He still had a lot to do, dismantling all the guns and packing up the ammunition, so I left him there and walked back to the flight lines, where Harrison was still waiting for me.

'Come on, Leslie,' he said impatiently, 'the tender will take us across.'

I put on the light when we got to the tent so we could take off our kit and in the sudden illumination, which made us blink after the world of darkness in which we'd been flying, I noticed something white on my bed. It was a letter addressed '2/Lt Blacking' and I took off my gloves and opened it.

Inside was a folded sheet of paper on which was written: 'Message from 27 Squadron. 2/Lt O Darke missing. Believe KIA.'

I sat down on the bed. Oscar. I think he'd known that he was going to go down one day.

'Bad news, Leslie?' Harrison was getting out of his flying kit.

I felt too numbed to reply.

'I'm afraid so,' I said. 'A friend of mine — the observer you met at

Beauvois, after our forced landing — Oscar Darke. He seemed to have a premonition about this, that he wouldn't survive. His squadron had already had a lot of casualties when we saw him. Their survival rate is pretty low.'

'Well, it happens every day on every squadron,' said Harrison quietly, 'though it hits you hard when it's someone you know. Come on, let's go over to the Mess; you need a drink.'

8
Interlude in an Orchard

When we got back to the tent and rolled into bed, I couldn't sleep, though I was overwhelmingly tired. My mind kept on whirring away, going over the operation again, the big bomb, the Hun night fighter and the bizarre business of the landing tee (still to be explained), then the message about Oscar which I'd found in the tent. Poor Oscar; he must have asked his squadron to let me know if anything happened to him. When the daylight began to creep through a gap in the tent flap and various little holes in the canvas, and I still couldn't sleep, I pulled on a cardigan, my trousers, greatcoat and flying boots and eased my way out into the dawn of that summer morning. Harrison never stirred; he was fast asleep.

It was absolutely still and quiet; the war might have been a thousand miles away.

I knew that at the back of our tented area there was an orchard, part of Monsieur Briand's farm (from where we got our vegetables), and that although there was a fence or barbed wire, the sort of wire which in recent years had become such a terrible symbol of war on the Western Front, it was quite easy to get through, so I walked over in that direction.

The grass was wet with dew and by the time I got there my boots were soaked; it's amazing how Nature supplies this nightly refreshment to our vegetation, something that never fails, like the seasons. It was easy enough to get through and there I was among the apple trees, with their gnarled trunks; they'd seen many campaigning seasons before the present armies came to this part of Picardy.

The red-roofed farmhouse was some distance away, and although I didn't consciously make for it, somehow I was drawn towards it. It, too, seemed to have been there a very long time — indeed, before the apple trees, which had presumably been planted by its original owner.

Their trunks were knotted and mossy, and the fruit they bore looked very green and hard. Nobody seemed to have done any pruning on the trees. I thought that the farmers would have always been too busy with their animals and crops; the apples came regularly every year — nobody bothered about them.

Then, in this arboreal stillness, I saw a movement, a brown flickering in the grass, then another, and heard an excited clucking. Monsieur Briand's hens were rushing towards some objective, which I couldn't see but which they, from daily habit, knew was there and which always began their day. Then I too saw it: a brown slim figure, no less beautiful than Nature itself and perfectly part of this rural scene, Jeanne the farmer's daughter dispensing the chicken-feed to the hens, scattering it with her right hand in a timeless, universal gesture.

She didn't see me, and I rather hoped she wouldn't, so I could watch her. She had bare feet and a plain, slightly ragged white dress which showed off the brownness and beauty of her limbs. To me, at nineteen (how old was she? seventeen or eighteen, I suppose), she seemed to epitomize an ideal of womanhood, and the whole scene a thousand miles away from any war; although had it not been for the war I wouldn't have been there. I hadn't even been to 'the Continent' when I was a schoolboy, and the same probably went for thousands of other young fellows in the British Army and the RAF.

Jeanne didn't waste much time over feeding her brown, clucking brood, though she obviously enjoyed being out there in the fresh morning air. I remembered a song which used to be sung on Sunday evenings when my father and mother had friends in:

> I've been roaming, I've been roaming,
> Where the meadow dew is sweet,
> And I'm coming, and I'm coming
> With its kisses on my feet —

Funny, I thought, how things come back to you at the most unexpected times from the recesses of the mind.

Should I try to speak to Jeanne? She obviously hadn't seen me; there was never anyone else in the orchard at that hour, so far as I knew. The chickens must have been one of her duties on the farm, like taking eggs and vegetables to the 'Tommies'.

The trouble was that, having only schoolboy French, I had to work out in advance what I was going to say — not only the opening sentence, but a response to whatever might be said in reply, so it took a few moments to prepare myself; and by the time I'd worked out my opening gambit, Jeanne had given a final shake to the bowl she'd carried and disappeared, as swiftly and silently as she'd appeared, like a beautiful rural ghost, although she was certainly rounded and substantial.

Ah well, I thought, no doubt she'd have been surprised at the sight of this tousled young officer in the orchard in the dawn. Perhaps she'd have laughed at me or, more likely, given me a mouthful of the vernacular; I'd heard she'd picked up some choice phrases from the boys in the Mess kitchen, though she didn't know their meaning. After all, I was trespassing.

I ducked under the barbed wire and between the posts of the fencing, avoiding the brambles which seemed to flourish there. The huts and tents came into view and I made my way to ours, opening the flap carefully. Harrison was still asleep and I took off my flying boots, greatcoat and trousers carefully so as not to disturb him and rolled on to my bed. That vision in the orchard, like a frieze or a painting of another, quite natural and simple world, of Nature herself, had erased the memories of the night and the news of Oscar. Within a few minutes I too was asleep.

9
Farewell to the Front

I was in the 0/400 cockpit again. We were cruising along in the darkness, looking for a lighthouse, when suddenly Harrison began shaking me by the shoulder. I couldn't make out what he was saying: was it a Hun fighter on our tail, or was it Doullens or the landing tee? Gradually his words penetrated my consciousness:

'Wake up, Leslie,' he was saying, over and over again. 'Wake up, the CO wants to see you.'

I was looking up at the brown canvas of the tent; Harrison was leaning over me.

'Wake up,' he repeated. 'I thought you'd never come round.'

'What time is it?' I said.

'It's 8.30 and a lovely morning, and the CO's sent a message over: he wants to see you.'

'Is it about the landing tee going out?' I said. 'If so, I hope he's going to apologize to us.'

'I just don't know — only that he sent a message over. So you'd better get yourself spruced-up, old chap. You know what the Major's like for appearances. I'll get you some hot water for shaving.'

George Harrison, practical and helpful as ever, I ruminated as I quickly got myself smartened up to see the CO who, whatever his shortcomings as an operational commander, was a stickler for spit and polish. He always 'looked the part' himself and expected his men to do so, which probably wasn't a bad thing. We'd have quickly got slack on the ground if someone hadn't set an example.

But what could he want to see me for? We hadn't committed any breach of flying discipline last night: when the lights of the tee went out so suddenly we hadn't any option but to land.

Had our operation been a failure? Surely he wouldn't know yet whether or not it had succeeded, unless there had been a dawn reconnaissance and Wing HQ already had photographs. When I was ready to go across, all spruced-up, Harrison said quietly:

'Don't worry, Leslie, I'll support you to the hilt if there's any inquiry. You had no option but to land when you did — it was too late to do anything else.'

On my way over to the CO's office I dwelt upon my first meeting with him, so many weeks ago, before my first operation: how long ago it now seemed!

His clerk, Corporal Coombe, was sitting in an outer office where he had a desk and a typewriter. A likeable young chap (though there probably wasn't much difference in age between us, he always seemed young — perhaps we felt ourselves to be older than we were) with dark short hair, pale cheeks and a plummy voice, he seemed to have been born to be a CO's clerk; it was his military destiny, just as Napoleon's was to be a general. He was tidy, neat and courteous, though not subservient — there was nothing of the Uriah Heep about him — and always unflurried.

'Ah, good morning, Mr Blacking,' he said. That was another thing; he always remembered everyone's name. I felt as if I'd come to apply for a job.

'The CO's asked to see me, Corporal,' I told him, as if he didn't know. 'Is he in?'

Corporal Coombe nodded, sprang up and tapped on the Major's door: 'Second Lieutenant Blacking, sir.'

I went in and saluted. Major Folliott was a small man. He looked more impressive sitting behind a desk than when standing up, and I think he felt more comfortable, more authoritative, in that position. He had a soft, rather precise mouth with a carefully trimmed moustache and his uniform was immaculate; I could see his cavalry boots shining underneath his desk. I'd always felt that smartness of appearance went a long way towards making a man's character acceptable, even though it might be lacking in other respects. The Major didn't fly on operations, and therefore couldn't share our experiences, but in other respects he was a good CO and a conscientious administrator — a paper tiger, you might say. Had he called me in because of last night's unfortunate incident?

I stood to attention while he went through the motions of tidying some papers, as if other affairs were of more importance. Then he looked up and said:

'Good morning, Blacking. You put on a good show last night. We should have some reconnaissance photographs from Wing shortly, to show us how successful the raid was. It was unfortunate that the landing tee had to be switched off suddenly when you came back. We had to protect the airfield from discovery by the Gothas.'

That was all. Was this what he'd called me in for? Then he went on, in his dry, meticulous tones: 'What I have to say now concerns your future.'

This is it, I thought. I'm to be grounded, or posted to another squadron, or sent home for further training.

'Plans are being made, now that we have an independent RAF and a strategic bombing force able to attack targets well behind Hun lines, for bombing attacks on German cities — including Berlin — by the new four-engined Handleys, the V/1500s. Pilots who've already had operational experience on twin-engined bombers are required for training on this bigger aircraft, which I hear has been referred to as "a bloody paralyser". The idea, of course, is to try to bring Germany to her knees by this new blow — and to do to their capital city what their Zeppelins and Gothas have done to London.'

I recalled, from what my parents had told me in Beckenham, the horror of those raids; the searchlights probing the night skies, the anti-aircraft fire, the bombs whistling down — and what happened when the Gothas came over London in the day time.

These thoughts passed through my mind in a flash. I didn't say anything. Major Folliott leaned back in his chair, put his fingertips together, looked me straight in the eyes and went on:

'As you're one of the squadron's youngest pilots, Blacking, I propose to submit your name to Wing for training on the V/1500s. Pilots are required for this very quickly, so you will be prepared to leave at eight ack emma tomorrow, with orders to report to the Air Ministry in London.'

Tomorrow morning — that was pretty quick! I couldn't help feeling, in view of last night's incident and the possibility of a Wing inquiry into it, that the CO wished to get rid of me as a potentially hostile witness in case the inquiry sympathized with the pilots, and that the request he'd had to nominate trainees for the big new Handleys had proved a godsend.

As I hadn't said anything, and he must have realized I was cogitating, he said somewhat sharply:

'Any comments, Blacking?'

What could I say. One always thinks, afterwards, of things one might have said at such important interviews, but they never come to one's mind or spring to one's lips at the time. All I could manage was, 'No, sir. Only that I shall be sorry to leave 207; it's a happy squadron, and I shall miss my crew, Mr Harrison and Sergeant Pilcher. Presumably Wing have only asked for pilots, not crews.'

'Only pilots,' the Major said dryly, 'with suitable operational experience. I shall confirm with Wing that your name has been submitted, that your orders will be prepared and transport arranged to Boulogne. Good luck, Blacking, and thank you for your contribution to this squadron.'

So that was that. I saluted and went out. Corporal Coombe gave me a little wink — he'd obviously known all the time what I was going to be told — and said as I passed: 'I'll have the papers ready for you this afternoon, sir.'

When I got out into the open air again, and realising that it was a beautiful, calm early autumn morning and Wing would undoubtedly call on the squadron for a raid that night — we were on a kind of operational treadmill — I suddenly felt quite hungry, after the events of the night and the shock of what I'd just heard. I decided to head for the Mess.

After a raid night there were generally a few late breakfasters and normally things were quiet; people avoided conversation, perhaps ostensibly absorbing themselves in an old copy of the *Illustrated London News* or *Punch*: but as soon as I got through the door I heard the sound of an animated discussion.

Most of the pilots and observers who'd taken part in last night's do were there: Tex, the tousled-haired American, a big and cheerful character; the youthful-looking Semple, who had such an intense glance; Brinden, the flight commander; and Harrison.

'Hiya, Blacking,' drawled Tex, 'we're rootin' for ya: what's the noos?'

I pulled out a chair and joined them. One of the Mess waiters came up and I ordered some breakfast. I looked at Harrison and then at Brinden, then said quietly:

'I'm posted back to Blighty.'

'What, because of last night's misadventure?' asked Semple, looking at me in his direct manner.

'By the way, they've examined your wheel tracks and it looks as though your tailskid hit a bump while you still had some speed and caused you to nose over,' put in Brinden. 'You seem to have touched down on a rough bit of ground when the landing Tee was off.'

I was relieved to hear this and went on:

'No, the CO hardly mentioned that — he explained that he had to prevent the airfield being located and bombed by Gothas, that was all. He went on to tell me that pilots were wanted for training on the new heavies — the V/1500s — and he'd nominated me.'

'Wow!' exclaimed Tex. 'That sure gets you out of the way if there's any inquiry' — he put the emphasis on the first syllable — 'about last night. When d'ya have to go?'

'Tomorrow; eight ack-emma,' I said.

'Tomorrow!' put in Harrison, with unusual excitement for him. 'That's pretty quick.'

'Well, they want to get these 1500s over Hunland as soon as they can to try to help finish off the war — so the Major told me. They're aiming to attack Berlin.'

'Berlin! That's a long haul.' Semple gave a low whistle of surprise. 'You'll be over Hunland for hours.'

Looking around at their faces, I suddenly realized how much I was going to miss these chaps when I left the squadron; Harrison's calmness in difficult situations, Brinden's authority (he seemed much older than the rest of us because of his seniority, but he couldn't have been more than twenty-three), Tex's transatlantic buoyancy which gave us a fresh perspective on nearly everything, Semple's boyish directness, and many others who contributed their different qualities.

'Well, I must get over to HQ,' said Brinden abruptly. 'There may be another show on tonight. If I don't see you again before you go, Blacking, good luck. You've done well on the squadron, I'm sure you'll do well on the bigger crates.'

He gave me a pat on the shoulder and Tex and Semple went out with him, Tex saying, 'Remember me to Piccadilly,' and Semple adding, 'Want a pilot, Harrison? You'll have to train another one now.'

Harrison sat with me while I finished my breakfast and had another cup of tea, then he said, 'I'll go over to HQ and see if there are any recce photos yet.'

We parted at the entrance to the Mess; already our ways were beginning to diverge now that I'd been posted.

'I'll see you back at the tent or here at lunch time,' I said.

As I was making my way towards the 'tented lines in the brightness of that early autumn morning, full of thoughts as to what I had to do before leaving the squadron, I spotted the back of a familiar figure going towards the armoury.

'Sergeant Pilcher!' I yelled.

He turned round and, as I got up to him, revealed an enormous black eye. It had obviously come up overnight after our accident. When the Handley had tipped over he'd had the worst of it, being in the rear cockpit; he was lucky not to have been thrown out.

'You poor chap,' I said. 'How are you? Any other bruises or cuts? You must feel pretty shaken.'

'Well, I'm here to tell the tale, sir, and we live to fight again.'

His face had been spoiled by the black eye, but it still had that honest, open look. 'How about you, Mr Blacking? Ready for operations tonight? I've heard rumours about a maximum-effort raid.'

'I'm afraid I shan't be on it, Pilcher. I've been posted away from the squadron for a training course at home and have to leave tomorrow morning.'

'Training, Mr Blacking? I shouldn't have thought you needed that. And why so soon?'

'Well, not exactly training,' I explained. 'It's a conversion on to V/1500s, the bigger, four-engined Handley; and it seems that pilots are needed urgently to fly them.'

'And crews?' put in Pilcher. 'Are Mr Harrison and I to come?'

'I'm afraid not. I suppose that your jobs would be much the same except over greater distances. The idea is to bomb Berlin, to help to persuade the Huns to surrender and so bring this terrible war to a close.'

'Berlin, eh?' observed Pilcher. 'That would bring up the night fighters — going and coming back.'

'If it does, Pilcher, I'd like to have you in my crew. Thanks for what you've done; I've known I could always rely on you.'

I shook him warmly by the hand, and with a 'Good luck, Mr Blacking' he went on his way to the armoury and I to the tent.

I thought I should possibly never see him again; or Harrison, or Captain Brinden or the CO or Flight Sergeant Arnett or any other of the good fellows on 207. It depended whether the Air Ministry had decided to form a new squadaron of V/1500s or re-equip one of the existing ones. I might never go back to Ligescourt, where a few months' experience of the bombing war had changed my life.

When I got to our tent the batman was there, cleaning up. He was a small, fresh-complexioned fellow with a shock of dark hair; his movements were quick, almost jerky, as if he always had a lot more energy in store.

'I'm off in the morning, Peters,' I said.

'Yessir, I'd heard that.' News certainly travelled fast around the squadron. 'Any special time, sir?'

'No, the transport's coming for me at eight ack emma, so if you call me at 6.45 that'll be fine. Don't disturb Mr Harrison — he might have to be on operations again tonight.'

When he'd disappeared through the open flap I looked round the tent, at our camp beds, flying gear hanging up and the odd personal possessions — photographs, book, pocket diary, coins, all the little things that make a man into an individual and which, if he goes missing on operations, are swept up, listed and returned to his next of kin. Strange, I thought, how a temporary dwelling like this could become one's home; but how fortunate we were, compared with the PBI in their dreadful conditions!

Harrison suddenly appeared in the tent entrance.

'Good show last night,' he said laconically. 'The recce photos show that the tunnel was bombed successfully.'

He came in and sat down on the bed, then changed his mind and lay on it, his hands behind his head.

'I expect to be flying with one of our new pilots tonight,' he observed. 'A chap called Reddaye.'

'Well, best of luck,' I said. 'I shall miss not having you with me.'

I realised this was something any pilot might say to any observer, but in Harrison's case I meant it; he was not only accurate and skilful in his navigation, but was also utterly reliable, cool, forward-thinking, helpful, tactful — almost any epithet you could apply to a valued flying colleague would fit Harrison.

I realized, too, that after tonight I might never see him again. The military machine had already found a replacement for me; as far as the squadron was concerned, I had gone, and any personal relationships established by me on the squadron were in the process of being broken. Rather embarrassed, I made out that I was sorting some of my things prior to packing them up. I wasn't really, but Harrison took the point and decided that he had to go back to squadron HQ. Standing up suddenly and tapping the tent pole with his fingers in a kind of nervous gesture, he said:

'Well, see you in the Mess at lunchtime, Leslie.'

'Yes,' I replied. The tent flap darkened for a moment and he'd gone.

There was a deep silence, then I gradually became aware of a whirring noise. I looked out, down towards the airfield, and in the top corner of it could see Farmer Briand, Jeanne's father, mowing the grass with two horses. There, I thought, was a timeless sight: the immemorial, international farmer figure harnessing his skill to the Allied war effort. No doubt he got well paid for it (M. Briand would see to that, after endless bargaining with our Adjutant), but wasn't this an ideal example of ploughshares being turned into swords?

I had to 'check out' at various offices on the squadron, getting signatures to confirm that I wasn't carrying away any equipment on loan. I went to the armoury to hand in my revolver to Lieutenant Westoby and found Sergeant Pilcher giving instruction on the Lewis guns to a newly-arrived gunlayer. I went to the clothing stores to hand in my Sidcot suit (retaining my helmet with its lucky 207 black cat badge) and there saw — the operative word because of his usual elusiveness — Sergeant McTavish, who after some calling emerged darkly from behind his shelves, with a quizzical 'Sirr?'

'Mac,' I said, 'I have to leave the squadron. I've been posted on a training course, so I must return this Sidcot.'

The dark, lined face regarded me questioningly.

'Are ye no going tae fly any more, then, sirr?'

'Oh yes,' I said, 'but back in Blighty. I can't take any of this kit with me — except for my helmet.'

Already, with an instinctive reaction, Mac had pulled a pad of forms from under the counter. He put two carbons in and without a word started filling the top one in. I admired the professionalism with which he filled in the columns and drew lines across the blank spaces, then reversed the pad and pushed it across the counter for me to sign, all without a word. I really felt I was being 'signed off' the squadron.

I had rolled up my suit and put it on the counter. Mac, who seemed to have an automatic distrust of any mere Second Lieutenant, checked it as if it were the Crown Jewels and put it on a shelf behind him.

Then he said: 'Right, sirr, taes all in order.'

That was all. So with a 'Thank you, Mac' I walked out of the store. But just as I got to the door he added:

'If ye come back, sirr, I'll no doubt still be here. Wish ye good luck, then.'

'And to you, Mac. We'll try to finish this war off for you. It can't go on much longer.'

When I stepped out of the stores I reflected that this Great War on the Western Front was being fought on two levels: there were the infantrymen and the airmen — chaps in the lines and chaps like ourselves flying over them, both liable to get killed at any time; then there were the backers-up, the long tail of stores, signals, transport, maintenance, armament, messenger and messing people, down to those Chinese labour corps coolies who'd been 'buzzed' recently by that visiting Bristol Fighter pilot and whom it took days to round up again after they'd scattered in a panic.

For Sergeant McTavish and tail-enders like him, the war had become a routine business. Unless there was a Hun attack on our airfield, or one of the Handleys crashed on the camp, or bombs blew up, they would survive the war and come safely home. Well, good luck to them.

I had one more call to make to get cleared from the squadron, on Corporal Coombe, the CO's clerk, to collect my orders. As usual, he was quite unperturbable, handing them to me with a smile — of course he had them ready, with his customary efficiency. They said I was to report to the Air Ministry in London and would be given further orders when I got there.

I told Coombe I'd cleared all the sections so was ready to leave. 'There'll be transport for you outside here at eight ack emma tomorrow, Mr Blacking,' he said. 'Good luck, sir.'

'Thank you, Coombe; good luck to you. This war will be over one of these days.'

'I hope so, sir; it's gone on long enough.'

I looked up at the sky when I got outside; cloud was moving over from the west. It looked as though another front was coming in and I wondered whether there would be any operations that night. One of the Handleys was being towed across the road, perhaps for an air test or familiarization flight; it was too early for the aircraft to be lined up yet.

'Hello, Blacking,' said a voice behind me as I was making my way back to the tent. 'The weather's beginning to look a bit uncertain. However, the aircraft will be ready. You can rely on the old firm. Are you flying tonight? We've been asked for a maximum effort.' Bishop, the engineering officer, was one of my favourite characters on the squadron — a tall, alert chap, always cheerful and extremely good at his job.

'I'm afraid not,' I said. 'I've been posted to Blighty.'

'Posted, eh?' his face wore a quizzical look. 'Surely this isn't as a result of your little contretemps last night? No serious damage was done; the aircraft will be back in service.'

'No, I don't think so.' Whatever my private feelings about the CO's character, and his action in sending for me, I felt I ought to give him the benefit of the doubt. 'It's just that the Major's been asked to provide a pilot for training on V/1500s, so he picked on his youngest. I'm on my way to Blighty in the morning, to report to the Air Ministry.'

'Tomorrow morning! That's quick.' Bishop gave a whistle of surprise. 'They must be keen to get you trained. Presumably all the other Handley squadrons are sending pilots.'

'I expect so. I shall miss it here; they're a good bunch of chaps — even the engineering officer.'

'Careful,' said Bishop. 'We do our best for you pilots, patching-up your aeroplanes, helping to keep them in the air. Where will you train?'

'I don't know, yet, but there've been rumours about a new squadron being formed somewhere in Norfolk. Maybe they'll tell me all about it when I get to Bolo House.'

'Maybe not,' Bishop observed. 'They're more likely to ask you what you're doing there — nobody had told them you were coming. Anyway, good luck, Blacking. If you can win the war for us on the new bombers perhaps we'll all be home for Christmas.'

'I'll do my best; cheerio, and thanks. Perhaps we shall meet again.'

Perhaps not, I thought, as we parted. One of life's ironies was that one met and liked people, then never saw them again, especially in the RAF.

That afternoon was going to be one of the slowest days in my life. I was still at Ligescourt but no longer on the squadron. The crews — my friends — were preparing for their raid that night; another attack on Valenciennes marshalling.yards, with the aim of slowing up the Hun offensive. But I wasn't among them. I had nothing to do but watch the preparations, as I did when I first arrived there.

There was little jollity in the Mess at lunch time. Under those circumstances, the aircrew drank very sparingly, mostly grenadine. I had a beer or two but felt out on a limb.

In the afternoon the BE12 was due to go up to check on the weather, which I thought was going to be marginal; there were showers and moving cloud. The Major usually flew this weather sortie. He liked to 'take to the skies' to demonstrate his leadership of the squadron, although he never flew on operations.

I picked up an old *Illustrated London News* in the Mess and read its articles on the war. At least we were advancing in Palestine, I noticed, unlike the ghastly stalemate on the Western Front, and made a mental note of some of the long-running shows I might see if I got any spare time in London: *Chu Chin Chow*, perhaps, or *The Maid of the Mountains*.

I must have dozed off in one of the wicker chairs, because the next thing I realized was that someone was shaking me by the shoulder.

'Wake up, Blacking. I've got a job for you.'

I blinked and recognized Captain Brinden, my flight commander — ex-flight commander, now I'd been posted.

'Yes,' he went on, 'I know you've more or less left the squadron, but that's no reason for you to take things easy, you know. The war must go on.'

I wondered what he was going to say next.

He sat in a chair opposite mine and, giving me time to take in his words, said, 'You know the Major usually does the met flight?'

I nodded.

'Well, he's been called to Wing HQ at short notice. All the pilots available here are on tonight's raid, so busy with their preparations. You are the only one who could do it.'

'But I've never flown a BE12,' I protested.

'You won't have any difficulty.' Brinden was a very determined man, used to getting his own way when he'd made up his mind. 'I'll brief you on the cockpit and tell you how she handles; she's a very stable aeroplane. Then you can do one take-off and landing, then take off again on your weather check. Fowler will tell you what information he requires.'

Fowler was the met officer, a bespectacled second lieutenant who enjoyed sending up balloons to check on the wind strength; it was the high spot of his day to watch them rise up into the sky. He had a geography degree, and to him the war seemed to be a kind of outdoor academic activity. He had a perpetual smile and was the butt of many jokes, but he added to the general happiness of the squadron.

On the way over to see him, Brinden suggested that I should take off at about four o'clock, so as to be back with some weather information in time for the crews' briefing at five o'clock. As we strode across the grass to where the map and briefing rooms were, I caught sight of Harrison and his new pilot — a tall, gentle-looking chap with fair hair and a vague but kindly expression. It was going to be a big night for him, I thought. So the war went on — the individual hardly counted, but each one had to bear the strain of it.

Brinden flung open the door of one of the huts and looked around. Fowler wasn't there so we tried a second one. There he was, chatting with Tex, the American.

'Fowler,' said Brinden, without preliminaries, but with a nod towards Tex. 'Mr Blacking is going to test the air for us. Will you tell him what information you require?'

Fowler cogitated for a moment, looked at Brinden and then at me. 'The CO usually offers a general impression of conditions around the airfield and likely ones en route,' he said carefully. 'Height of cloud base, visibility, approximate wind speed and direction and the future trend — whether things are likely to change over the next few hours. I then put all this with my own observations and produce a forecast.'

'Well, Blacking knows what's needed. He'll let you have this information by half-past four. Thank you, Fowler.'

With that, we were off again to look at the aeroplane I was to fly, the single-seater which had been used as a fighter, then as a bomber, but had been unsuccessful in both roles and was withdrawn from active service. No 207 Squadron happened to have this one at Ligescourt. Most of the others were back in England on home defence duties and some had found their way to the Middle East.

Our BE12 had been pulled out to the top of the field, two AMs carrying the tail on their shoulders, and Flight Sergeant Arnett was there to give me advice on the engine and superintend starting. It looked small by comparison with the Handleys but was actually quite a large single-seater, with a thirty-seven-foot span upper wing and a thirty-and-a-half-foot span lower wing, with a six-foot three-and-a-quarter inch gap between them and a two-foot stagger, so there was a lot of space and air around the cockpit. I didn't know those detailed measurements at the time, of course, but looked them up afterwards because the flight I was about to make remained so vividly in my memory. Most of the young pilots on the Western Front knew only about the aircraft with which they operated or on which they had trained. Indeed, had it not been for the war, most of us would never have flown at all.

I climbed into the cockpit and Captain Brinden showed me the controls and instruments. It seemed strange to be sitting behind an engine, instead of between two of them.

'Now, about the instruments; they're pretty standard,' he said. He pointed out the airspeed indicator, rev counter, altimeter and fuel gauge. That seemed to be about all there was, plus the throttle and control column, which I waggled about a bit. It felt very heavy, yet this was supposed to be a fighter.

'Would you like to try a start?' he said.

I indicated that I would. He reached down to put the fuel cock on and Flight Sergeant Arnett instructed one of the AMs to stand by to swing the propeller. With Captain Brinden pointing them out, I put the ignition switches down and called 'Contact!' As the propeller turned, slowly at first, he clung to the side of the fuselage, then when the engine fired we were hit by a blast of slipstream, though I had the shelter of the little windscreen. The powerplant was a 150 hp Royal Aircraft Factory 4a, not nearly as big as our 375 hp Rolls-Royce Eagles, but it seemed quite impressive. I got it to settle down at about 500 rpm, so as not to blow Captain Brinden off the wing. Then he gave me a pat on the shoulder and jumped down. The AMs were sitting on the tail so I opened up fully for a few moments, then shut it down suddenly; it ticked over quite smoothly and I switched off.

'There's one other thing,' Brinden's face appeared by the side of the cockpit. 'Remember that you've got a fairly long nose in front of you — this was originally a two-seater. So, on take-off get the tail up as quickly as you can so you can keep straight. And remember, no diving or stunting — just plain flying. Your job is to bring us back a weather report.'

When I climbed out he added, 'You won't need a Sidcot suit because you won't be up for long or going very high. You have your own flying jacket and helmet, haven't you?'

'Yes,' I said.

'All right. Take off at about half-past three' — this as much to Flight Sergeant Arnett as to me — 'and do your check circuit, then fly around for half an hour or thirty-five minutes looking at the local weather and report to Mr Fowler when you get down.'

I felt wanted again. Life had a small purpose for me after all, and when I got back to the BE12 with my helmet and flying jacket, I'd not had time to worry about the prospect of flying a new type of aeroplane. If I'd had more time to think about it I might have worried a lot. As it was, the engine started almost first time, I gave it a chance to settle down and run smoothly before trying full power — just over 1000 rpm — once again, and gave Flight Sergeant Arnett a thumbs-up. He responded, the AMs pulled the chocks away, I opened up until the tailskid unstuck then started to roll forward. The airfield looked much bigger than it did when one was in a Handley, and with the throttle fully forward the old BE12 started to gain speed. I pushed on the stick with its spade-grip top to get the tail up, and before I realized it we were sedately in the air — the first time since I came to Ligescourt that I'd been alone in an aircraft, without fellow crew members and courses to fly and a bombing mission to fulfil. I had an extraordinary impression of freedom and pleasure in sheer flying as the field fell away and I soared up across the river.

The BE12 had come off quite smoothly. Once the tail was up, it steered easily, but I had to pull back on the stick to get it into the air. It felt heavy for a fighter, which was probably why it had never been successful as one; there was no design genius behind it. Once in the air, too, it was stable, not giving the impression that it wanted to be flung around the sky, like a true scout aeroplane. Its engine chugged noisily, rather than purred along. Still, so long as it kept going I didn't mind that.

Having got up to 500 feet I banked around to the left: banking wasn't so sluggish a process as in the Handley with its long wings, but the BE12 gave me the impression that it was quite happy as long as it went on flying along in a straight line, doing nothing else. It would never have made a fighter, as the RFC had soon discovered.

I could see the river down on my left, then the field and our tents and huts and aircraft beyond it, so kept on turning to keep them in view. I hadn't throttled back yet, and kept on climbing to about 700 feet. There was cloud above me but it was of broken, cumulus type. I estimated the local visibility to be about three miles.

It was time to throttle back a bit and prepare for my landing. It seemed strange to have the whole field in view and not to be aiming just for a landing tee. The engine still chugged away so I throttled back further, then right back, until I was in a steady gliding, descending turn with the ASI on about 70 mph. It began to look as though I'd got it right as I straightened up and glided over the huts, tents, aircraft, vehicles and people down below; but I was a bit disconcerted that, once I was straight, I couldn't really see ahead because of the engine and the nose in front of me — not like our clear view in the Handleys. I had to 'feel' for the ground and at the same time try to watch lest my airspeed fell off and we stalled. I was still feeling for the ground when the wheels touched and we bounced into the air again. I gave the engine a quick burst of throttle and we sank down again, quite heavily and not very elegantly, but safely. My first landing in the old BE12 was over successfully; now I could go and 'test the air' for the squadron.

Turning the aircraft on the ground was a bit more tricky than with the twin-engined Handley, which you could bring round with a burst of throttle on one side or the other, and the grass seemed to be longer and thicker in a smaller machine. But I got it round with a harsh use of rudder and bursts of throttle, and taxied up to the top of the field again for my second take-off and 'testing the air' sortie.

This time I was more confident and the BE12 felt like an old friend. I soared over the river, banked round, and the airfield with its Handleys, its huts and tents and its scurrying figures fell away behind me as I climbed up. What was that course to our lighthouse at Doullens? I thought I'd better go over the track our boys were to fly in a few hours' time, to see what the weather was like on their route. I almost turned to ask the faithful Harrison, then realized he wasn't there: I was all alone. What was it? — 080 degrees, I thought; better remember that because of steering the reciprocal to come back to Ligescourt. It was a typical autumn day, with broken white cumulus around me. By about 400 feet I was getting into the base of it. I'd better report that.

There seemed to be about three or four miles' visibility as I looked over to the right, down towards St Quentin where the British and French armies linked. The patchwork of fields and hedges and buildings below looked peaceful from that height. One wouldn't think that there was a terrible war going on down there, ignorant armies clashing both by day and by night.

I suddenly remembered the war, and realized that I had better keep a sharp look-out, all around me. I twisted my head like one of the scout pilots and heaved the stick from side to side, but the BE12 was heavy on the controls. She just wanted to go flying along steadily, solidly like a bomber, which was why she'd never made a good fighter.

At that moment I saw I was not alone in that patch of sky: an aircraft dived past me, pulled up into a stall turn to port and started to dive back again. I reacted by going into a steep diving turn, a kind of corkscrew — the bomber pilot's escape manoeuvre. But whatever I did, he followed. It flashed into my mind how ironic it was that, having survived bomber operations and being posted to Blighty to learn to fly an even bigger type of Handley, I should be shot down on a weather sortie. The old BE12 was just a sitting duck, whatever I tried to do.

Then, as swiftly as he'd come, my adversary left me, with a wave from the rear cockpit. In that moment I recognized him — a two-seat Bristol Fighter, from one of the squadrons that patrolled that area trying to draw the Huns into the air. It was the gunner who gave me a wave of recognition; they'd had to satisfy themselves as to what I was: BE12s were pretty rare birds on the Western Front, having been withdrawn from squadron service there and put on Home Defence duties.

As the fighter flew away — a really purposeful-looking war machine, I thought, with its distinctive big tailskid and rounded, low-set rudder, and a white number on its fuselage — I realized I was sweating. I felt a kind of delayed shock, sensing what a near miss that had been: had he been a Hun I would have been a goner, a flamer, another heap of smashed wreckage and a broken body in a Flanders field. Watch out! I told myself. Meanwhile, I had to finish off my weather observations. But where was I? All that twisting and turning had disorientated me. As an 0/400 pilot I was used to flying around with an observer who told me what courses to steer, and as it was usually in the dark we had those friendly lighthouses scattered over northern France. All we had to do was to fly towards one and identify it. But there were no such signposts now, only the clouds and sky and a patchwork of landscape down below. I was in a pretty pickle, and if I ran out of fuel and had to force-land, what a sorry ending that would make to my time on the squadron! How long had I been flying? I glanced at my watch: only twenty minutes; but in that time the whole world seemed to have changed. So much could happen in such a short space.

There were only two things to do: not to panic and to fly westwards, towards the coast, and look out for, say, Abbeville. That was logical, too, because if we had any bad weather it would come from there and I could try to assess the trend.

I pulled the BE12 round on to 270 degrees and descended further so as to be able to recognize any landmarks; I'd lost altitude during that encounter with the Bristol Fighter. I had to remind myself, too, to continue to keep a sharp lookout for other aircraft; the RAF must have thousands of them on the Western Front by now.

A long way ahead, there was a sudden sparkle, one of those flashes you get from sunlight reflecting off the sea. It could be the Channel, so I kept on towards it, hoping I would recognize something below me or the shape of the coastline. There were one or two distinctive indentations and the coast swung north towards Berck Plage, where we sometimes went if the PMC had a special permit to buy supplies there, though it was normally out of bounds. I noticed quite a large town coming up on the port side: could it be Abbeville? If so, the bay of the Somme lay ahead and I was south of Ligescourt. Sure enough, there was the river, whose name was now etched for ever in British military history, flowing towards its outlet into the sea; and there was the road going north from Abbeville which would take me to Ligescourt.

I pulled the BE12 round to follow it and in a few minutes saw our own familiar river, the Authie, curving round in the valley which formed the northern boundary of the airfield. Now that I felt comfortable again, having dispelled that awful feeling of being lost, I thought I'd better sum up my impressions of the weather and enjoy the last few minutes of my final flight on the squadron. I banked over in a wide sweep to port, looking down on the airfield where I'd had so many experiences in that summer/autumn of 1918, and where I seemed to have grown old in a few months.

Despite being intercepted by a (fortunately friendly) fighter, and temporarily losing myself, I'd enjoyed my final flight and collected some weather observations for the raid that night. I made a rounded circuit, keeping the airfield well in sight, and glided-in across the tents and huts, the roads and the growing line of parked Handleys; another, with its wings still folded back, was being towed out as I came in.

The old BE12 rumbled down comfortably on to the grass — an inoffensive aeroplane, I thought — and I taxyed her back to the top of the field, where two AMs caught hold of the wingtips and I switched off. It was just after half-past four. I'd been longer than I should have been, so I jumped out quickly with a word of thanks to the AMs (I never forgot the chaps who kept our aircraft in good flying condition) and hurried across to find Second Lieutenant Fowler.

He was, in fact, compiling his weather briefing in a corner of the map room.

'Hello, Blacking. We thought you'd gone off, perhaps flown across the Channel in your eagerness to get to your new posting.'

'I'm sorry, Fowler,' I said, 'to be back later than I should have been; I got intercepted by a Bristol Fighter then lost my bearings for a while.'

'Good thing it wasn't a Pfalz or Halberstadt, otherwise you wouldn't be here to tell the tale. What's the weather like?'

'Well, there's broken cloud, base about 4,000 feet. The tops I don't know — I was going on up when this fighter found me; I thought at first he was a Hun, so had to evade him and lost altitude.'

'Never mind,' said Fowler. 'What about the visibility?'

'I should think three or four miles.'

'And the wind speed and direction? What impression of drift did you get?'

'Well, when I was heading westwards after getting disorientated I got the impression of a drift to port, and a quite strong wind — say, fifteen or twenty miles an hour from a north-west quarter.'

'Good,' said Fowler. 'That confirms my balloon observations. It's a wind which will help the boys along tonight but give them an extra struggle getting back.'

'Always the case,' I observed. 'Our aircraft get carried easily over the Hun lines but then have to fight against the prevailing winds.'

'Well, I must do my report for the briefing,' Fowler adjusted his glasses with one hand and squinted over the top of them at me. 'Thank you, Blacking, and good luck when you get to Blighty. Remember me to Leicester Square — and don't get lost when you go to Bolo House. It's a big place, I understand; full of staff officers, like a rabbit warren.'

Then he added, ruminatively, as if talking to himself, 'I wonder if they really realize the problems of airmen out here; the enemy and the weather? It's bad enough that the squadron has to operate nightly, and sometimes twice a night, in helping to blunt the Hun offensive; the unstable climate is always an additional hazard. Look at tonight: it's all right now, but in a few hours may change dramatically, just when the Handleys are coming back. Still, you don't have to worry about that now — it's farewell to the front for you, at least for the time being. All the best, Blacking; and by the way, if you go to Ternhill give my love to that cuddly bit of stuff in the Post Office.'

'I didn't know you were interested in such things, Fowler,' I said as I went out of the door. 'You concentrate on your cold fronts and depressions — they're much safer.'

I wandered across to the Mess but it was deserted. All the flying people were doing their briefing ready for tonight; Bishop and his engineers were getting the aircraft ready. I felt quite out of it all. Then, just as I was going out again, I literally bumped into Lieutenant Pinnett. He had an enormous moustache and wore the oldest looking peaked cap I'd ever seen.

'Hello, Blacking,' he said. 'You not flying tonight?'

'No, I've been posted — back to Blighty for a course.'

'Lucky sod. Are you being taken off flying then?'

'No, it's a course on the bigger Handleys — the V/1500s.'

'Phew!' Pinnett whistled through his teeth. 'Wish I were coming too. Want a job for tonight then, Blacking?'

'Yes, of course,' I said. 'I've nothing to do. What is it?'

'It's control — seeing the aircraft off. When I came in here I was looking for the CO to tell him I couldn't do it tonight. It would be damned convenient if you could take it over for me.'

I knew the job: it involved sitting in our control tower, which was a small sandbagged structure on the south side of the airfield, and looking towards the aircraft lined-up for take-off. Each of them had a letter and an order of take-off was drawn up for the night's operation. What the man in the control tower had to do was to flash the Morse code letter by Aldis lamp to each aircraft in turn, with an interval of about five minutes between them, which was their signal for take-off. I'd been on the receiving end of this signal so many times, the green light flashing in the darkness, telling you to go off on your bombing mission.

'All right, Pinnett,' I said. 'I'll take over the duty if it will help you.'

'Good, I'm very grateful. Pick up the list at briefing, where you'll also learn the time of the first take-off. Get down to control in plenty of time; the tender will take you. There's a field telephone in there in case of any last-minute messages, like an aircraft not being able to get off. But if you don't hear anything, flash their letter on time and watch them go. It's a full house tonight — ten are operating.'

'Where are you off to?' I asked him as we crossed over to the briefing room.

'To Abbeville, to see one of our observers in hospital there — Lieutenant Trelling. You remember him; he was injured in that show against Valenciennes a week ago.'

I did: he was a dark-haired Scotsman with a quiet sense of humour, got hit by shrapnel when they were on the way back. Our medical NCO, Sergeant Gentey, and two AMs had to lift him out of the front cockpit after the Handley landed. The poor fellow couldn't move from there; he'd just slumped on to the floor. His pilot, Lieutenant Kimber, did well to find his way back to Ligescourt.

'How's he getting on?' I asked.

'They think he'll pull through,' said Pinnett as we got to the briefing room. 'The trouble is, the poor fellow got so weak through loss of blood, when he's fit enough to travel they're sending him back to hospital in Blighty.'

I sat at the back during the briefing. It seemed odd to be there and not really part of it, as far as the target and weather information was concerned. The only thing I had to do was to collect my list of the order of take-off, and to make sure I had the correct Morse code signals for the aircraft letters, so there would be no hesitation in flashing them.

The target for that night was again the railway marshalling yards at Valenciennes, and when the CO announced it he pointed out that within a small area were the main lines themselves, warehouses alongside them and sidings filled with rolling-stock. In other words, a concentrated centre of supplies for the Hun offensive. The squadron was to raid it in force — all ten Handleys — and the first aircraft would take off at eight o'clock. Main altitude would be 4,000 feet and the CO warned of flak and fighters: the Hun was sure to defend the target fiercely.

From force of habit, I almost made notes of this information. Even though I stopped myself from doing so, I took it all in as intently as if I were going on the raid myself.

When Second Lieutenant Fowler stood up to give his met briefing he used the information I had given him about the local cloud base and visibility, and approximate wind strength, plus his own observations. He deduced that the weather was changing, that there was rain coming from the west and a cold front was approaching, but that it wouldn't affect the Ligescourt area until the early hours of the morning, after the aircraft had returned. Winds, of course, would strengthen gradually, but should not affect the return flight too seriously. I hoped not; I didn't like the thought of the boys battling their way back into a rising gale, the first of the autumn ones, sweeping up the Channel and across northern France.

As the briefing broke up a voice hailed me — Harrison's. 'Leslie,' he said. 'I'd like you to meet my new pilot; Second Lieutenant Norman Reddaye.'

I'd seen Reddaye about, and he'd done an 'operational experience' trip as a gunner, like I did. He was tall, fair-haired, with blue eyes and very quietly spoken.

'How do you do?' I said, shaking him by the hand. 'You're very fortunate to have one of the best navigators on the squadron. Good luck on your first raid.'

'Thank you, Blacking,' he said. 'I gather you're off to Blighty to do a course on the big new Handleys. Good luck to you too.'

'We'd better check our courses,' interposed Harrison, always the efficient organiser. 'I gather you've got yourself a job in the control tower, Leslie, seeing us off.'

News certainly travelled fast around the squadron.

'Pinnett said he couldn't do it and asked me to do it,' I explained. 'I suppose that as everybody's flying tonight I was the only spare body he could find. I'll be wishing you good luck when I signal you off.'

'Thanks, Leslie. I'll see you again before you go.'

I hoped I would see Harrison again, back in our tent before I left for London in the morning. But who could tell? He had an inexperienced pilot; they would encounter flak and also Hun fighters, which were getting daily more active; there was the weather — what if it changed before Fowler predicted it would, and the crews had to fly back into a gale, with the rain lashing into them out of the darkness, getting soaked to the skin in their open cockpits? I hoped they would get back without this additional hazard, but as the autumn came on it became daily more of a possibility.

There was nothing more I could do until I went down to the control tower in good time for the take-off. I had my list, with the Morse code signals clearly written on it. What about a torch, and what about checking that the Aldis lamp was working properly? As if in answer to my thoughts, Pinnett appeared.

'I've been looking for you,' he said. 'Come on, there's a tender outside; I'll take you down to the control tower, make sure everything is working and that you know what to do.'

As we drove over the road, past the parked Handleys and bumped across the grass I realized I hadn't been down to that side of the airfield since my first day on the squadron when Harrison had shown me round. What a lot had happened since then! I noticed that the sandbags round the control tower were frayed and weathered, their contents starting to spill out. They must have been there since the airfield was opened, perhaps in 1916 or '17. How many more months of winter, spring and summer would they have to withstand before falling into disuse for ever? How much longer would this war — now in its dreadful fifth year — go on? The structure looked like a bit of the trenches, preserved as a museum piece in the middle of a French field.

We climbed out of the tender and Pinnett showed me the inside. Looking up the airfield, there was a clear view of the aircraft lined up side-by-side on the starting-line, with AMs climbing over and ducking under them, checking everything for tonight's operation. In the draughty interior was a chair, a pair of binoculars, a field telephone for emergency instructions, an Aldis lamp and a chronometer, a reminder of the days when No 207 was a Naval air squadron, No 7: so there was no excuse for not knowing exactly what the time was.

'It's a quite simple procedure,' Pinnett explained. 'You know from your list exactly which aircraft is which. You'll see and hear them start up, and at the designated take-off time — tonight it's eight o'clock, as you know — flash his letter at the first one due to go. Watch him get away, then exactly five minutes later signal to the second, and so on. You're in control — the pilots look to you for their starting signal. They should all be away within an hour.'

'What about when they come back?' I said.

'Well, be back here for the estimated time of arrival of the first one, say ten-thirty: you can base that on the predicted duration of the sortie. I think it will be two-and-a-half hours tonight. If there's no difficulty, like a Hun raid, switch the landing tee on and give the boys a green light. Don't forget that they will have asked for, and got, permission to land from the Doullens lighthouse, so there should be no problems. If there are, you'll be told about them on the field telephone.

'One other thing,' he concluded. 'Don't forget to wrap up well; this is a draughty place. Now I'll run you back to the Mess — I must be on my way.'

When we got up to the road we had to wait for one of the Handleys being towed out, its wings still folded. I'd counted eight already lined up, so there was one more to come.

Pinnett dropped me at the Mess tent, and with the engine ticking-over, grasped me by the hand. 'Good luck, Blacking. Give Berlin hell in your V.1500s; I've heard about them. Help to bring this bloody war to an end.'

I slammed the door shut, waved, and he accelerated away. Inside the Mess was quite deserted: everybody was busy preparing for tonight's operation. I decided to walk across to the briefing room and check on the order of take-off.

There, the scene was just the reverse — crowded, noisy, an orderly scrum of pilots, observers and gunners, checking on compass courses, magnetic bearings of lighthouses, times of take-off, the weather situation, target photographs. All ten crews seemed to be there in that confined space, all seeming to know exactly what they wanted. I spotted Harrison and his new pilot, Second Lieutenant Reddaye, with a map spread out in front of them, as I pushed my way to the board where the order of take-off was displayed. I noticed that 'A' Flight's commander, Captain Halfer, was to lead; his letter, as it happened, was 'A'. Reddaye and Harrison were in 'J', I noticed.

'Hiya,' said a voice behind me. It could only be Tex. 'I thought you were on your way to London,' he went on.

'Not yet — in the morning, Tex. I've been asked to do the controlling tonight, so I'm checking on your letters and times of take-off.'

'I'm in "K" — the good ship K for King. Don't you fail to give me a good clear signal.'

'I will, Tex. Good luck to you.'

'Don't forget to give those Huns hell in your big new bombers,' he said. 'With you and the Yanks we'll win this goddam war soon, and all go back home. Remember me to Leicester Square,' he added, grasping my hand, as if we would never meet again (which we probably wouldn't), 'and to —'

'That little cuddly bit of stuff in the Post Office at Ternhill?' I suggested.

'Could be. Good luck, Leslie.'

'And to you, Tex. Get back home safely.'

Looking at the crews milling around me, making their final preparations for tonight's raid, I couldn't help thinking what a motley crowd they were; some in Naval uniform, some in Army/RFC get-up, some sporting RAF insignia. The new Service, now nearly six months old, hadn't yet had time to standardize its ranks and emblems; it had been too busy fighting the air war to worry about such peacetime stuff as the blue and the buttons and the badges of its new uniform, distinguishing it from the former RNAS and RFC. Old traditions from those two battle-hardened air services died hard — especially as they had distinguished themselves from 1914 onwards, long before the RAF was ever thought of. And what did it seem to matter on a squadron like ours? Its number had been changed to 207 from the former Naval 7, but that didn't seem to make any real difference. Everybody knew what he was doing and did it in a cheerful, professional way. We were a young, happy lot, and I, at nineteen, was one of the youngest.

'All set, Blacking?'

Captain Brinden's voice brought me out of my brief reverie.

'Yes, I think so,' I said. 'I've got my list. Good luck tonight, especially with the weather.'

'Thank you; it could be a bit unsettled, but we should be back before there's any real trouble.'

The flight commander's voice had the ring of experience, but so far the squadron had operated in the summer months — the more unpredictable conditions of autumn were only just beginning.

When I stepped out of the flight offices I looked up at the darkening sky. The cloud had thickened from the west, although it was still reasonably high, its base about 6,000 feet, I reckoned. A light wind had sprung up. It was getting near time to go out to the control tower, so I decided to make my way across via our tent to pick up my great-coat. Inside there, everything was quiet and orderly: my own things, apart from those I needed overnight and in the morning, had been packed; Harrison's as usual, were tidy. If anybody had to come and sort through them, as they did when someone was killed or went missing, I was sure everything would be found in order — he was a most methodical man. But I hoped that that sad eventuality would never occur; we had our casualties, but not as many as the day-bomber or scout squadrons did. I put on my greatcoat, remembered to pick up my torch, without which I'd be sunk if the light failed in the control tower, and set off.

Across the road, all ten aircraft had been lined up, their wings unfolded, ready to go. Their fuel and bomb loads were being checked. I went from one end of the row to the other, noting their individual letters, making sure I had them in the right order so I could point the Aldis lamp at each one when it was time to go. That done, I walked out to the control post across the grass, which smelt fresh as I trod on it, by contrast with the oil and petrol fumes around the Handleys. It was half-past seven: still plenty of time to get myself organized before the take-off.

Inside my lonely 'office' I checked the light, tried out the Aldis lamp by shining it on the floor, where it made a green or red glow on the duck-boarding, and gave the handle on the field telephone a good whirr. A voice answered curtly: 'Flight Offices.' 'Second Lieutenant Blacking here,' I said, 'reporting on duty in the control tower.'

'Right, Mr Blacking,' the voice said. 'We will call you if there are any changes. Meanwhile, assume that all aircraft will go off as planned.'

He rang off, and I felt like a conductor on his rostrum, waiting to lift his baton for the orchestra to begin: I'd never realized, on all the occasions when I'd taken off on raids, how lonely it was for the chap in the control tower waiting to flash his letter.

I checked the time — 7.40; then I picked up the binoculars. Through their powerful lenses I could see every detail of the crews getting aboard, though it was impossible to recognize anyone personally because of their flying helmets and the bulkiness of their gear, and the AMs around each aircraft ready for the start. I picked out Captain Bishop, the engineer officer, and Sergeant Arnett. Fifteen minutes to go: it was extraordinary, I thought, how slowly time seemed to pass when one is measuring it in minutes or seconds but how quickly it goes by at times when one isn't particularly noticing it.

Then, at ten minutes before take-off time, with a burst of exhaust smoke the first propellers started turning: first one, then another down the line, then the original starter got both going, and so on until all twenty Eagles or Sunbeams (some of our Handleys had one type of engine, some another) were roaring away as if eager to go. I knew what the aircrew felt when they heard that roar, and first experienced that vibration and rush of air which was to accompany them for the next two-and-a-half hours.

Five minutes to go, all engines started, and I knew all the pilots were looking towards me. I checked my list for Captain Brinden's position in the line: he was fourth from the left-hand side. I glanced at the chronometer again: how slowly the minutes seemed to creep round when they were being watched! Two minutes to go — one. I raised the Aldis lamp, made sure it was selected to green and on the stroke of eight flashed a steady 'A' — dit-dah. I suddenly remembered Pinnett saying I should repeat it, as confirmation, so I did that, slowly and deliberately: dit-dah, holding on to the second syllable.

'A's propellers began to whirr faster, then he started to move, slowly at first, then gaining speed as he disappeared into the darkness. I glanced round to see that he had taken off and the field was clear, then I looked again at the chronometer, creeping up to five-past eight.

'J' was the next one on my list and I checked on his position — fourth up the line. With one eye upon the clock I focussed on him: as the time came up to five-past eight I flashed his signal: dit-dah-dah-dah.

'K', scheduled to be the third to go, was dear old Tex from the USA. As I aimed the Aldis lamp towards his aircraft I could feel him looking at me and saying impatiently, 'C'mon Leslie, let's go; let's get this goddam war over.'

I checked over my shoulder that 'J' had gone, then aimed my signal towards Tex: dah-dit-dah, then repeated it, but before I'd got to the repetition his engines had opened up and the Handley had begun to trundle over the grass in its typically slow but deliberate take-off. Tex and his crew merged into the darkness, the exhaust pipes of their engines glowing for a while then begin swallowed up. I wished them well.

A quarter-past eight and the fourth aircraft ready to go: this was 'B' and I signalled dash-dot-dot-dot twice, very deliberately, and in my heart wished them luck, for this was Second Lieutenant Reddaye taking off on his first operation and Harrison was with him. The Handley's engines revved-up and the aircraft moved slowly forward; the tail seemed to be ages coming up. In fact they were a third of the way down the field. Young Reddaye appeared to be a bit slow in his reactions and I watched him apprehensively. But there was no crash, which I'd dreaded I might hear, so they must have got airborne successfully. I turned my attention to my list, to the next man to go, and to the chronometer: nearly twenty-past eight. At the precise moment I flashed 'C' — dash-dot-dash-dot — twice, slowly, and held the lamp on the green: the two propellers whirred round faster, the Handley crept forward, gained speed and was away.

So on until all ten had gone, giving time for each one to get clear, lumbering off to the Doullens lighthouse to set their first course. With a five-minute interval between each, it was after nine o'clock when I put the Aldis lamp down.

Everything had gone very quiet: there was a sort of soundless echo of the engines. Through the binoculars, I could see the last of the AMs going back across the road to the camp area. When I stepped out of the control tower the wind was gusting up, the cloud had thickened and the first drops of rain began to fall. I pulled up my greatcoat collar and walked across the grass, speculating on how my friends were getting on as they flew through the darkness. When I got nearer the road which divided the airfield from the HQ area, still absorbed in my thoughts, I heard the cheerful chug-chug behind me of one of the squadron's Ford light tenders. It stopped beside me and a voice said, 'Jump in. I'm going to the Mess.'

In the darkness I recognized Bishop, our cheerful engineer officer. Having seen all his aircraft off successfully he was no doubt on his way to some well-earned refreshment. He knew where I'd come from.

'How did you get on?' he asked as he changed gear noisily and we bumped towards the Mess.

'All right, I think; there were no kind of snags; all the boys seemed to get away without trouble. Must be something to do with good maintenance,' I added, giving him a sideways glance.

'You know it is,' Bishop asserted. 'That's what keeps you boys flying. Come on, I'll buy you a drink on that, young Blacking.'

He pulled up with a flourish outside the Mess and we went in; the place was deserted.

'Cheerio,' he said, 'and I mean that — you're leaving us in the morning. They're certainly making you work up to the last minute.'

My 'Cheerio' when I responded must have sounded somewhat half-hearted, and Bishop, whom I always liked for his cheerful manner, must have realized I was sorry to be leaving the squadron, having to leave a familiar set of circumstances and people for something unknown. He went on, 'I hear those big Handleys will make ours look like scouts. You're facing an interesting challenge, young man; it's fortunate you've been trained on a good squadron.'

'It's chaps like you who help to make it one,' I put in, 'keeping our aircraft serviceable and repairing them when they get damaged.'

'I hope they don't run into trouble tonight,' said Bishop, looking round at the empty Mess, 'because we've no reserves.' He was thinking of the Handleys, but I was thinking of their crews, especially of Reddaye and Harrison. As if reading my thoughts, Bishop then said, 'I feel quite helpless when the boys have disappeared into the darkness. We can prepare their aircraft and see them off, then there's nothing more we can do except hope they'll all get back. Like sending them over the top with polished-up rifles.'

'But there the comparison ends,' I suggested. 'At least we come back to a reasonably civilized way of life — not like those poor devils in the lines.'

'Then that's an argument for our kind of warfare,' Bishop countered. 'If we can bomb the Huns into defeat — and I hear your new Handleys are going to attack Berlin, which will shake them — the sooner those boys on the ground will be able to get back home.'

'I'll drink to that,' I said. 'Here's to the end of this terrible war.'

We were silent for a while. I glanced round over the empty chairs and tables, whose usual occupants were now battling it out somewhere beyond the German lines, and thought I could hear the noise and laughter and see the smoke which usually filled the Mess, especially on our party nights, when there wasn't a 'show' on. Having stood by until midnight on these 'washout nights' we usually had a binge, when 'Murphy's Band' performed: its tinselled cardboard-covered and paper-covered comb instruments, blown with vigour and directed with genial enthusiasm by Lieutenant Horace Semper, made a distinctive sound, sometimes to the astonishment of small French towns when members of the band happened to be 'on tour' locally.

All these thoughts would have taken only a few seconds, but Bishop must have noticed I was looking rather pensive.

'Drink up,' he said, 'we've time for another one. It'll be an hour or so before any of the boys start to come back. I'd have thought you'd be happy at the prospect of returning to Blighty.'

'I am, in some ways.' I took a long swig of my beer as if to lubricate my thoughts, then went on, 'but in many ways I shall miss the squadron life; they're a good bunch of chaps. When you're in these conditions you really discover what a man is worth. You know nothing of his background — his family, his religion, his politics. You value him for what he is: his character, his ability, his reliability under pressure.'

'Come on, young Blacking,' Bishop put in, 'now you're getting psychological, and it doesn't do, you know. What about the other things you'll miss, like when we were 'at home' that Sunday to the citizenry of Ligescourt and all those pretty girls just had to be shown round the aircraft? Didn't it take a long time to explain all the gadgets in the cockpit to them? Or that occasion when we had some neutral newspaper correspondents to see us and you took them for a flight, going as near the lines as you dared.'

'Yes, I remember those specks from the east diving down on us,' I suddenly recalled. 'Fortunately they turned out to be Camels. It doesn't really do to fly a Handley round in daylight — too big and conspicuous a target.'

'Your next Handley will be even bigger.'

'Yes, like the 0/400 was bigger than the 0/100.'

'Maybe this war will be over before the RAF can get the new ones into operation,' suggested Bishop hopefully. 'It's been going on for over four years now. Surely if we push the Boches back now they'll give in.'

'That's the object of our operations,' I said, 'to disrupt his supplies so he can't maintain his offensive.'

'Well, young Blacking, no use getting morbid. It'll all come to an end one day. All these thousands of men in France and Belgium will go back home when victory is won; hundreds of aeroplanes will be flown to England and broken up, hundreds of guns will be melted down; tanks will be dismantled or rust away — you can't do anything else with 'em; and the French and Belgians will be left to restore their devastated countryside.'

I thought of Farmer Briand and his daughter Jeanne. Some of the French had done quite well out of the war — they would miss us.

'What are you going to do when you get back to Blighty?' I asked as we went towards the door of the Mess tent. 'Still be an engineer?'

'Good Lord, no. There'll be hundreds of us. I might as well ask you if you're going to be a pilot. No. Try something quite different, I think, like farming or boat-building. How about you?'

'Well, I think I'll go back into banking — perhaps try to go out to China; there are good prospects there.'

'Watch out for Chu Chin Chow, then,' said Bishop cheerfully, 'there are millions more like him at home. Good heavens, it's blowing up.'

The wind caught our faces as we stepped into the darkness; there was rain on it and we pulled up our collars.

'You going back to the control tower?' asked Bishop. 'I can give you a lift over.'

It was still quiet and deserted as we drove out of the camp area, across the road and on to the airfield, but at any time the Handleys would start to return.

'If I don't see you in the morning,' said Bishop as he drove off, 'good luck. We may meet again one day.'

'I hope so; we've been lucky to have you on the squadron.'

With a wave he was gone. I switched on the light in the control tower and glanced at the chronometer — nearly ten o'clock. Any time now I should hear the first aircraft returning. They must be having a rough trip with this worsening weather; obviously a front was moving in. Hopefully they would get down before the worst of it came over.

I rang the Flight offices on the field telephone, reported my position in the control tower and asked if there were any difficulty about switching the landing tee on when our aircraft started to come back. No, I was told, there should be no difficulty, except for the weather, which was blowing up to be stormy. There had been no reports of any Hun fighter activity, and when the Handleys made their Aldis lamp recognition signal over Doullens on return they should be given an 'all clear' to come on in and land. All I could do was wait for them to arrive and give them an encouraging green light. I sat there patiently in my sandbagged enclosure, listening. There was no sound except for the occasional flurry of wind, but at any moment ten big aircraft would appear out of the night one by one, their crews desperate to land.

I looked at the chronometer: five past ten. The first machine had been away over two hours.

The field telephone rang — I nearly jumped out of my skin. 'We've had a report from Doullens,' the voice said. 'The first Handley has checked in. Be ready to switch on the landing tee.' I listened; it would arrive in the next few minutes and — hopefully — identify itself by flashing its letter with the Aldis lamp.

There was the sound of one of our MT vehicles, probably a Crossley tender, being driven out to the airfield with a grinding of gears. Then that stopped abruptly. There was silence again for a few minutes; then I thought I heard the noise of aircraft engines, coming from the south-east, the direction of Doullens. As the sound grew louder and came overhead, an Aldis lamp signal flashed out of the darkness, a deliberate dit-dah followed by another one. Captain Brinden was back. I picked up my Aldis lamp and gave him a steady green, then switched on the landing tee. The Handley whirred over and disappeared into the darkness, making his landing circuit. He seemed to be gone for a long time, then reappeared over our camp area, making his approach. In seconds he had rumbled on to the grass then disappeared down into the bottom end of the airfield. I switched off the tee — it was only put on for landings and we had to taxy back up the field in darkness — and waited for the next arrival, the sound of his engines or the sight of his identification letter.

I knew Brinden had got up to the parking area because I could see the AMs' torches flashing about there, directing him in. Who would be next?

Again the sound of engines, from an easterly direction; again the deliberate signal when they came overhead — dit-dah-dah-dah. 'J' was back and I aimed a deliberate green at him and switched on the landing tee. So far, so good; another one ticked off my list. I was hoping they would keep up this steady procession; the reason for having a five-minute interval between each take-off was to give the Handleys a safe separation on their return. 'J' had disappeared into the darkness. He reappeared out of it over the tents and huts, rumbled safely on to the grass and I switched off the tee.

The wind had freshened and the rain came in lashing flurries as one by one the Handleys returned, struggling through the stormy darkness. I gave them the green signal, switched on the tee, they landed and disappeared down the field, then taxyed up to the waiting torches.

I was worried that I hadn't seen 'B', with Reddaye, Harrison and Pilcher aboard. Then at last I saw their dash-dot-dot-dot and gave them a steady green, switching on the tee. The Handley disappeared and seemed to be gone for a long time. I could imagine young Reddaye feeling his way round the circuit as the rain lashed on his face and goggles, then steadying his aircraft on its final approach.

At last they appeared over the HQ area: they seemed a bit low and there was a big burst of throttle; then the Handley hit the ground and bounced. It seemed to hang there for a moment, then come down with a thwack. There was no further burst of throttle to catch it on the point of stall. What had happened? I expected to see a tender rush down the airfield, for Captain Bishop, Flight Sergeant Arnett and the AMs were watching too, but nothing happened. Then, after what seemed an unconscionable time, the big dark shape reappeared, seeming to be picking its way up to the parking area where torches were waving for it, after that awful landing: but at least they had survived.

'B' was the last aircraft in. What had happened to them?

Having checked my list that all ten had arrived back I gathered up my things, pulled up my greatcoat collar and jammed on my cap against the wind, then set off to walk up towards the line of parked aircraft, most with their wings already folded back. The rain and wind came out of the darkness in stinging bursts. When I got up to 'B' there was a great deal of activity around the rear cockpit. They seemed to be lifting somebody out, though I could see nothing in detail.

I spotted Harrison. His face was blackened and his helmet and Sidcot suit soaked with the rain. When he caught sight of me he said, 'Pilcher's dead — we got hit. We were lucky to get back. It was shrapnel, I think, up through the bottom of the aircraft. Poor Pilcher didn't have a chance.'

There was nothing I could do. Our medical NCO, Sergeant Gentey, a big bluff Irish 'old sweat' who looked after any casualties, dressing wounds and sending them to hospital for treatment if necessary, was there, as he always was when the aircraft came back, going to each one to see if any of the crew were wounded. He looked after everyone with extraordinary gentleness for such a big man, displaying an almost womanly tenderness, and I saw him caring for Sergeant Pilcher — though poor Pilcher was by then beyond human aid. He must have been killed instantly when the aircraft was hit. I hoped he didn't have a slow, agonizing death on the flight back and had to suffer the crunch of that heavy landing.

As I could do nothing — they were all around him, doing what was necessary — and as Harrison and Reddaye would be going to their debriefing, I went off in the darkness towards our tent, across that familiar road which divided the airfield from the HQ area and which I would see no more after tomorrow.

Poor Pilcher would be buried at Hesdin. I remembered the funeral I attended there, of another gunner, Sergeant Ellis; my first duty on the squadron. How long ago that now seemed, like a lifetime, in which I'd had a whole set of new experiences, many of them terrifying, but had made many good and firm friends. Now, there was nothing more for me to do; 207 was coming to an end as far as I was concerned and in the morning I would begin a different set of experiences.

It had turned cold with the rain; an autumn chill was in the air, a kind of sad epilogue with a moaning wind. I was glad to get back to the tent: Harrison wouldn't be back for some time as they had a meal after debriefing. I got into bed and fell into a troubled sleep, thinking of my crew — now broken up by death — and my posting to Blighty, of the faithful Harrison and the ever-cheerful Pilcher. They were good, brave fellows, like hundreds more whose war was in the air.

'Tea, sir, six-thirty.'

I became conscious of a figure coming and going through the tent flap, as on my first day on the squadron, months — it seemed like years — ago. Behind him there was a bright, low dazzle of sunlight; clearly last night's front had passed through, leaving behind a beautiful, calm autumn day.

I sipped my tea — it was more of psychological benefit than

anything else, hardly the finest ever brewed — and looked round the tent. Strange, I thought, how somewhere like this could come to seem a home, a familiar place, so when the time came to leave it, to go to somewhere else unknown, it was quite a wrench to have to do so.

Harrison was still fast asleep and I was careful not to wake him while I had a quick shave with the mug of hot water the batman had brought, then dressed and tidied up my bed. I was ready to go, once I'd had breakfast. It was odd how, in military life, one did things quickly and almost automatically, hardly thinking about them. That was what one's training was all about, I suppose.

It really was a beautiful morning. Some mist hung over the valley where the River Authie wound round the airfield, swathing the distant trees in a mantle of whiteness. The air was absolutely still and the war might have been a thousand miles away. In any case, Nature still proceeded with her changes of seasons in a majestic way, whatever man did, and here in northern France she had produced one of her best autumn scenes.

There was nobody about when I walked across to the Mess tent and only one solitary figure there, the orderly on duty to serve breakfast. I said 'Good morning' to him and asked him what was available. I had mentally decided that, having a long day's travelling ahead of me, I had better make the best possible start, so I ordered bacon and egg, bread and butter, jam and tea.

The orderly was a cheerful-looking lad whom I didn't think I'd seen before, a real youngster who perhaps had only just arrived at Ligescourt to begin his war service. He disappeared to give my order to the cook and re-appeared a few moments later with a mug of tea.

I was just sipping this meditatively, as a prelude to my bacon and egg, when there was a slight squeaking behind me, the sound made by highly polished leather being walked in. I looked round, recognized the Major in full fig — Army uniform with breeches and leggings — and made to stand as we always did when the CO appeared.

'Sit down, Blacking,' said Major Folliott, putting his cap on the table. 'Good morning to you. Ah, tea, bacon and egg, I think.' The orderly had appeared at his side — no wonder I'd got such quick service. They were ready for the CO to come in for breakfast.

'An early hour for a night bomber squadron,' the Major observed.

'I'm off to Home Establishment this morning,' I reminded him, 'on my posting to fly the big Handleys.'

'I know,' the Major put in dryly. 'You're coming with me on the first part of your journey. I have an appointment at GHQ. The car will then take you on to Boulogne for your Channel crossing and then return for me.'

He gave me this information with an air of well-organized superiority, his little moustache bristling slightly. I was taken by surprise but decided not to show it. I wondered how I might survive a car journey in the Major's company, and decided I had better act carefully, not saying too little, nor too much.

Since breakfast is the Englishman's silent hour, I judged that this part of our time together might pass without embarrassment. As it happened, the Major broke the silence, sipping his tea.

'We had a bad time of it last night,' he observed. 'One killed and three injured. Sergeant Pilcher was in your crew, was he not?'

'He was,' I said. 'A splendid fellow. Always cheerful, always reliable. He kept his guns in good condition and was very alert in the air. It was ironic that he should have caught it from ack-ack fire, which he could do nothing about.'

The Major was silent. He took another sip of tea, ruminatively, in that careful way which characterized everything he did. He was a sound, efficient staff officer rather than an inspiring commander.

'Who were the injured?' I asked.

'One was Tex, the American. He got shrapnel in his right arm; did very well to bring his aircraft back.'

'Poor old Tex,' I said. 'Maybe it's a Blighty one and he'll see Leicester Square again before he expected to.'

The CO made no comment about our ebullient American. He went on, 'Captain Brinden's observer, Lieutenant Tring, also got hit when he was in the nose of the aircraft on their bombing run. He lost a lot of blood on the way back, and it was fortunate he was with a pilot of such experience, for he was so weak that Brinden had to take over the navigating.'

Our breakfasts arrived just then and the Major didn't come up with a third name. I think he was more preoccupied with what he had to do at GHQ so we ate in silence: perhaps he would tell me during our journey.

'More tea, sir?' The orderly appeared at the CO's elbow and filled his cup.

'For you, sir?' I was similarly replenished.

'Thank you, Bates,' the Major called out as he finished and stood up. I stood up too.

'Be outside my office at five minutes to eight,' he said. 'We leave at eight sharp.'

As I walked across to the tent to pick up my greatcoat and bag I thought of the irony of the weather — the beautiful, calm autumn morning after the rain and wind of the night before. Where would the squadron be operating tonight and what conditions would they have? What about the day bomber boys in their DH9As? If they operated this morning there wouldn't be much cloud cover; the Hun fighters would soon be up among them. They would form a defensive circle and a terrible battle would begin. How much longer would this slaughter in the air, and on the ground, go on for: yet another winter? Or would the Huns give in before then?

Harrison was still asleep. Should I wake him or let him rest after last night's bad experience? I patted his shoulder gently.

'Cheerio, George. Thanks for all your help to me on the squadron.'

Harrison groaned slightly under his blanket. Then he seemed to change gear from sub-consciousness to consciousness. He groaned again, his eyes opened, and he became aware of me, saying, 'Oh, it's you, Leslie; you off then?'

'Yes, George; about to hit the road with the CO. He's going to GHQ and the car will take me on from there.'

'Well, good luck, Leslie. Give those Huns hell and we might be home for Christmas.'

'You too, George; I was sorry about poor Pilcher.'

'Damned bad luck, that. Still, if we'd been hit further forward and the bombs had gone off we'd all have been finished.'

'How did young Reddaye get on?' I asked.

'He managed very well, though we had a rough arrival here, as you saw — he was pretty shocked, I think.'

'Well, he's had his baptism of fire, and he couldn't have had anyone better than you to fly with. All the best, George.'

'And to you, Leslie.'

I picked up my bag, pushed open the tent flap and set off across the grass for the CO's office. The car was there, within two or three minutes he emerged, smart and shining, and we were away.

It felt odd to be going out where I'd come in in the early summer, ages ago it seemed, and I took a last backward glance at the huts and tents and hangars. So much had happened since then. What would happen to my friends on the squadron while the war went on? What would happen to Jeanne and her farmer father, and all the other

French people, when peace returned? None of our lives would ever be the same again after these experiences.

During our thirty-five minute drive to GHQ I had two preoccupations. One was to look out at the countryside and see how it was being affected by the great war, now in its fifth year. The other was to converse with the Major, for in the back of a car one is in such close proximity that conversation is unavoidable. I quickly discovered one thing: that even if one may have disliked another person, talking with him may bring out attributes in his favour, things one had never realized before.

I had only seen the CO in his office or at briefings or in the Mess, and had never had any sustained conversation with him on a social level. Although he cut an impressive figure because of his sartorial smartness, he was regarded with some contempt by the officers — up to the rank of captain — who actually flew on operations. But I was to form a different impression of him on that drive to GHQ, the last time, no doubt, I should ever encounter him in the whirligig of military life.

'You asked me who else was injured last night,' he said as we got on to the road leading towards Crecy. Ahead of us was the barrier, guarded by a sentry, and over to the left the sandbagged control tower where I had been during last night's operations.

'Captain Brinden got badly hit in his right arm; he might have to lose it. We hope not. He has been recommended for the DFC for his work as a Flight Commander, and his leadership of that raid on the tunnel off the Maubege-Charleroi railway line, in which you carried the 1,650 pound bomb.'

I remembered the special mission, my most exciting experience on the squadron.

The Major talked in a rather clipped and self-conscious way. It was a form of self-protection with him, like his immaculate uniform and spruce appearance. I learnt as we went along that he had been in France with the Royal Flying Corps since its earliest days there and knew some of its leading figures, like General Trenchard and Brigadier Newall; that he himself was thirty-five (very middle-aged to youngsters like us) and had always been in the Army; that his wife had been killed in one of the Zeppelin raids of 1917 and that when he got home leave he spent it with his parents, who lived in Sussex.

'Do you know Sussex, Blacking?' he asked suddenly, with what I almost thought was a touch of wistfulness in his voice.

I had to confess that I did not, that I'd been brought up in Kent, at Bromley, south-east of London. Our holidays had usually been spent at Herne Bay or Margate.

'It's a beautiful county,' the Major went on, reflectively, almost as if thinking aloud, 'with a long coastline that gets a lot of sunshine, the lovely Downs inland, small towns which are full of character, like Petworth, Midhurst and Arundel, attractive villages and a fine cathedral city, Chichester. You should go and tour around there after the war.'

After the war, I thought: where would we be when it ended, and when was it going to end?

During the Major's discourse I'd been keeping an eye on the countryside, still green and unspoiled with its foliage turning to autumnal colours, unlike the terrible wasteland of the battlefields where there was no foliage and the only colour was that of the obscenely scarred black earth. We were passing through the back areas of the lines, areas of supply dumps, field hospitals, spares depots and HQs. I saw crashed aircraft being transported to repair units, occasionally a tank lumbering slowly up the road, troops on the march towards the Front, casualties returning from it and hordes of dejected German prisoners.

I was just reflecting on the massive organization of warfare — thousands and thousands of men engaged in supporting and supplying the Front — when we turned in sharply through the black iron gates of a white château. It was like entering another world, a France of pre-Revolutionary days, never mind pre-Great War. I wondered how many *vicomtes, monseigneurs,* Duchesses and Cardinals had been driven through those stone gates in centuries past. It seemed to me incongruous that there should have been a British Army sentry on duty there, but he was real enough and checked our papers.

Once inside the gates the reminiscing Major, who had briefly lifted aside the curtain which normally hid his private life, his personal tragedy and loneliness and his devotion to RFC/RAF service, at once became the punctilious CO again.

'Goodbye, Blacking,' he said as he got out at the entrance to the château, adding, 'when you pull out of the gate, look across to the field opposite — there is a monument there which marks the deepest penetration by the Uhlans in 1914. Good luck.'

'Goodbye, sir; good luck to the squadron.'

We saluted and he disappeared up the steps, a dapper figure.

As the car pulled out of the gates and turned right I glanced across at the memorial. How the war had changed since then, particularly in the air. No longer was it just a matter of aerial reconnaissance; aircraft now made their own contribution, as fighters or bombers, in a two-dimensional conflict. 1914-style warfare seemed like something as old-fashioned as the Middle Ages.

I missed the Major's company on the journey to Boulogne; it had been interesting to discover something about his personality, to find out why he was like he was. I felt sympathetic towards him in a way I never did when I was on the squadron, but such feelings were of academic interest now. A new life, new experiences, lay ahead.

The driver, a young corporal with a solid expression whom I'd seen occasionally driving vehicles around Ligescourt, threaded his way through the military traffic and marching soldiers. Troops in their thousands were still being sent across to stem the Huns' advance and, hopefully, to mount a big Allied offensive to push them back before the winter. Now the Americans were in the war, and pouring men and material into Europe, the tide would surely turn in the Allies favour.

It was very moving to catch a first glimpse of the sea — the English Channel that had saved us from the fate of the French and the Belgians, whose countries had become battlefields. I could understand the reaction of those Greeks we'd read about at school in Xenophon's *Anabasis*, calling out 'thalassa, thalassa!' — 'the sea, the sea!' — after their long march across the arid mountains.

Although I did my best to talk with the driver en route — about how long he had been serving, whether he liked being on the squadron, what he would be going back to when the war ended, etc. — he was a taciturn young fellow and I couldn't get anything more than monosyllabic replies out of him. Perhaps, rightly, he felt he ought to reserve his whole concentration for his driving.

The hills above Boulogne reminded me of where Napoleon pitched his camp, on the last projected invasion of England. Now such military movement was mainly the other way, of fresh troops, supplies of ammunition, stocks of food, guns, vehicles and tanks being unloaded to reinforce the Allied offensive; but there was movement my way too, of a lighter kind, mainly personnel: troops going on leave, walking wounded with 'Blighty ones' and terribly shattered bodies on stretchers — young fellows who, perhaps only a few weeks or months before, had marched confidently from their troopships. Now, their lives had been changed for ever, and in the cases of those who had been gassed it was 'another shall lead thee', for they could not see.

I felt a fraud, fit and riding in a staff car. What evidence was there that I had done any fighting?

The young driver threaded his way carefully through the mass of moving figures and vehicles, stationary loads and other obstructions towards the dockside, where there was a notice about embarkation. I said cheerio to him, wished him a safe journey back and good luck on the squadron, then joined a queue with my bag to have my papers checked. I felt very much alone; at Ligescourt one had been among friends, part of a small society. Here one was among strangers, an anonymous part of the vast war effort. All one could do was shuffle forward patiently and go through the checks required. I was glad to get aboard the ship.

She was a typical cross-Channel steamer and I went up to the top deck, where I could look down on the mass of activity below and out towards the harbour mouth and open sea, where various grey-camouflaged warships were dotted about. It was a drab scene, compared with the colour and variety of pre-war days; when would such peacetime scenes return?

I relished the thought of the next couple of hours and the feeling of detachment that one gets even on a short sea voyage: nothing to do but watch the waves creaming and receding down below, marvel at the non-stop accompanying flight of seagulls, so graceful until they dived and screamed after anything thrown from the ship, listen to the steady throb of the engines and gaze at the endless vista of water stretching to the far horizon.

I was prepared to settle for the monotony of my own thoughts, speculating vaguely on what lay ahead and hardly taking any notice of my fellow-passengers as the ship eased away from the dockside and made her way slowly towards the open sea — it seemed at first as if the buildings on shore were moving and not us, as they faded from view — when I became aware of a tall figure by me with his coat collar turned up against the freshening breeze. Where had I seen that face before? It struck a strange chord in my memory, of some occasion in which I had been involved and which had made a deep impression on me.

We were both looking, in a casual way, at the receding harbour mole and then at the coastline of France, the view that so many thousands of our fellow-countrymen had seen for the first and the last time over the past few years.

My neighbour at the ship's rail was a captain and seemed to want to talk. He had an interesting face; he was a kind of man for all seasons, able to adapt himself to any kind of company.

'You going on home leave?' he asked.

'No,' I said, 'on a course.' I thought it wiser not to be any more specific.

My neighbour persisted. 'Been over here long?'

'I came across in the early summer — June.' There didn't seem to be any harm in telling him that.

'RAF?' he queried. He was certainly determined. But as I was wearing my greatcoat it was a fair question, since he couldn't see my flying badge. In any case, there was a fair old mix of uniforms in the RAF at that time — some still Navy (especially on our squadron), some still Army and some in the new style, which wasn't very popular. Nobody really wanted to be bothered with it; the important thing was getting on with the job.

'Yes,' I said, not wishing to enlighten him as to whether I was on scouts or bombers, or whether I flew at all.

'It always seems to me that the RAF people have a special attitude,' he went on. 'they don't have the terrible fatalism of the soldiers in the lines, living in squalor and any day expected to go "over the top" in some dreadful "push" that will gain a few yards of devastated landscape and cost thousands of lives. They have a different kind of fatalism — expecting to get killed every time they go into the air, so developing a carefree reaction when they're on the ground. At least they have reasonable living conditions, compared with the soldiers.'

I thought back to Ligescourt, to our neat bell tents, our batmen, the Mess and the stewards. Life on the ground was pretty comfortable in the midst of a great war.

'I suppose there are differences too between fighter and bomber pilots, and between the night bombers and the day bombers — the latter have had some terrible casualties. At least at night there's some protection, operating under cover of darkness. I recall that verse of the Psalm which goes:

If I say, Peradventure the darkness shall cover me:
then shall my night be turned to day.'

Here was a turn-up for the book. It wasn't often one heard the Psalms quoted on a troopship in mid-Channel, although I knew there were some war poets who might have done so, like Siegfried Sassoon or Wilfred Owen — but out of bitterness rather than for comfort.

'Are you a poet?' I asked him, feeling I ought to take the initiative in the questioning. 'You seem to have a philosophical outlook.'

'No,' he said, 'a padre; it's my job — or part of it — to be philosophical.'

I hadn't, of course, noticed his dog-collar because his greatcoat collar had been turned up. Although it was a fine autumn day there was a fresh breeze up there on the top deck, and smoke from the funnel billowed out behind us, snaking into the distance above the ship's creamy wake. This revelation as to my fellow voyager's profession narrowed my field of thought as to where I might have seen him before. We hadn't had a padre at Ligescourt: we only encountered 'men of the cloth' usually on special occasions, like funerals.

That was it! That funeral at Hesdin I went to on my very first day on the squadron, of Sergeant Ellis, who'd died during the night before. I thought about this for a while, then I said, 'I've been wondering whether I'd seen you somewhere before. Were you ever in the Hesdin area?'

He looked at me thoughtfully for a moment. The ship's engine throbbed away and her smoke billowed out behind us, towards France.

'I was. I used to have to take funerals there — always a melancholy duty. What upset me most was that the people observing the rites were all strangers, not relatives and friends. But of course that's been the fate of war casualties over the centuries.'

'When is this one going to end, padre?' I asked.

'It cannot go on much longer,' he said. 'It's now entering its fifth year and I can't see the Germans lasting through another winter. The economic strain is too great, and the weight of the Americans' inexhaustible resources will soon begin to tell. It's that which will defeat Germany; the military machines are pretty evenly matched, and the main difference the American participation will make will be in manpower. Perhaps it will all end before you complete your course and get back.'

'I'm not sure what "going back" will mean in my case,' I said. 'It depends on where the new squadron I'm to join will be based. How about you, padre, are you going back soon?'

'Yes, after one week's leave. It'll be good to get home for a while, to renew one's perspectives. The Western Front is an unreal world — there's a different set of values there. In some ways it brings out the best in us. Certainly right and wrong are sharply clarified.'

I was just pondering this when he said suddenly, with a change of tone and pointing; '"Westward, look, the land is bright". That's not very accurate, compass-wise, but it's a suitable quotation.'

A shaft of sunlight from the autumn sky had lit up the white cliffs of Dover and they stood out sharply, a landmark to friend and foe for nearly two thousand years. Every moment that our troopship ploughed on in her steady course they grew larger and more distinct.

We were heading to the west of them for Folkestone, of which I had boyhood memories from school outings there; of the graceful high green sweep of its Leas, which commanded a view across the Channel towards France; of its ever-swirling, crying seagulls; of its fish market down by the old harbour; of its great hotels like the Grand and the Metropole (which was even bigger than the Grand), and which I used to wonder that people could afford to stay in for their holidays; of Sandgate, Sandbanks and Hythe along the coast towards Romney Marsh; and of Shorncliffe Camp, where so many hundreds of young men, waiting to be shipped to the Western Front, had had their last view of England.

The harbour gradually came into perspective and, with that dignified slow motion proper to ships, which war would never change, we berthed alongside the harbour wall, a procedure which the padre and I watched with fascination, looking down on the dockside scene below. Then, as the ship's engines fell silent, our brief acquaintance was over; like many another shipboard ffiendship, it ended with our arrival in harbour.

In the mêlée that followed our docking — orders being shouted, stretcher cases carried off, 'walking wounded', bandaged, gassed, armless or eyeless men feeling their way down the gangway, supported by medical orderlies, horses and vehicles being lifted off — I lost sight of the padre. Of course, like all others returning to home establishment for one reason or another and being still able-bodied, each of us had his own business to do, offices to report at, passes and forms to be checked, instructions to be given and train tickets to be received.

I felt very much alone and missed the company at Ligescourt. However, I was heading for the Air Ministry and to a posting to another squadron, and had best get there as quickly as possible. Having gone through all the formalities and collected my ticket, I made my way to the train; how lucky I was, I thought, to be an officer (albeit a very junior one) and therefore entitled to a first-class seat! I was lucky, too, to find one in a corner and I settled down with that comfortable feeling that I could do nothing for the next two hours except think about the future.

I didn't ponder for very long, however. As the compartment filled up, with a major, a couple of captains and three very young-looking lieutenants (what had they all been through, I wondered), we nodded to each other, but the only ones who had anything in common were one of the captains and one of the lieutenants, who seemed to have emerged unscathed from some bitter fighting. No-one asked me about the war in the air; perhaps they had seen quite enough of it on the ground.

As we pulled our way out of the harbour station and gradually puffed along into the Kentish countryside I looked through the window and couldn't believe my eyes: no devastation, no shell-holes, no damaged buildings or shattered trees! Everything was quiet and orderly, peaceful and beautiful, as it had been for centuries, turning gradually into another autumn on this lovely October afternoon.

I'm afraid that the combined effects of the beauty of the view, the rhythmic dit-dit-dah dit-dit-dah of the train, the sea air I had imbibed on the way over, and the low-toned conversation of my fellow officers caused me to drop off after about ten minutes or so.

In my sleep I dreamt that I was in an aeroplane again — by myself. It was an unpowered machine, one that was unfamiliar to me, that skimmed silently over the countryside, made up of flat lands interspersed with lakes, with an unchanging, ever-receding horizon, so that it seemed as though I would never get where I was going. There were no trees, and no birds flying up before me, to be swept aside as the aeroplane passed over and swirled away in its slipstream. How long could I fly on thus, I wondered. Would I run out of fuel or was I gliding? I was too close to the ground, too parallel to its surface, to be gliding; yet there was no sign or sound of any engine: perhaps my aeroplane was a vision of the future, something that would be developed after the war. Certainly I felt very calm and comfortable sitting there. Suddenly someting seemed to go wrong with my epic flight: things started shaking, my machine appeared to be turning and I heard voices. Where could they come from? I thought I was by myself.

Apparently not, for someone was patting me on the shoulder and one of the voices sounded in my ear, 'Wake up, old chap, we're here!'

Here? Where? Had I landed? Involuntarily I said, 'Oh, what a lovely flight.'

'Not a bad journey,' one of the captains opined brusquely, giving me an odd look as he got his bag down from the rack. 'You got far to go?'

The train had finished its rattling across the points and was drawing into the platform with a hissing of steam, a clanking and a jerking as the brakes went on. We were in Victoria.

'No,' I said. 'I've got to find a hotel and stay overnight, then go on to the Air Ministry in the morning.'

'Well, good luck,' put in the Major. 'If it's anything like going to the War Office you'll need it. You have to fight your way through the red tape to get to see anyone. Goodness knows whose side they're on — ours or the Boche's.'

I bade farewell to the Army types as they struggled out with their bags. Then it was my turn, and I had a bit more than the normal military type because of my flying jacket and helmet, which wouldn't go into my valise. However, I managed to manoeuvre myself along the platform and out into the crowded concourse, and eventually got a cab.

How noisy London seemed! I had asked the driver to take me to the end of the Strand, near Waterloo Bridge, where I would look for a small hotel for the night. There, I would be conveniently situated to report to 'Bolo House', as it was called — Air Ministry Headquarters in the Hotel Cecil, half-way along the Strand from Charing Cross. The Ministry had got this nickname from Bolo Pasha, a Turkish spy, because it was considered — at least by those at the 'sharp end' of the new Air Force, on its operational squadrons — to be a nest of intrigue and the abode of staff officers who 'fixed' things.

Goodness knows, one was used to the noise of war, across the Channel: the aircraft, machine-gun fire, ack-ack, mortars, motor transports, the shouts of men and the screams of terrified horses. But London's noise was different; there seemed to be a perpetual hum, with many sounds rising and falling from it, the buses, the taxis, the cars which all seemed to be carrying red-tabbed staff officers, the newspaper vendors' and the flower-sellers' cries, the clanging of trams, the perpetual bustle of hundreds of people weaving past one another on the pavements (where were they all coming from and where were they all going?); or maybe I just wasn't used to all this big city din. My ears and senses had become accustomed to other sounds.

'This all right, guv?' The driver's sharp question brought me back suddenly to the business in hand. We had passed the top end of Waterloo Bridge and were near St Mary-le-Strand Church.

'Yes, this'll do,' I said, assuming a confidence I didn't really feel and struggling out of the cab with my luggage. (In the Air Force, everything was arranged for one; temporarily outside its administrative umbrella, one had to think for oneself.) I paid for my taxi ride and gave the driver a tip. 'Thanks, guv,' he said with a quick little half salute, before his cab disappeared into the traffic. Then I took stock of my bearings.

Across the Strand, in the corner leading to Waterloo Bridge, was the magnificent Somerset House, along the river (surely it should have had formal gardens at the back, between it and the Embankment); behind me, the noble sweep of the Aldwych, leading into Kingsway, where some of the Air Ministry offices were. Anywhere around here would do, if I could find a modest hotel.

By luck I happened to spot one on the south side of the Strand, its upper windows looking out on to the Aldwych. I made a quick dash across the road — not a wise thing to do, with my baggage, but the traffic never seemed to stop. One had to take a chance (though how ironic it would be, having survived the Western Front, to get knocked down in London!). I found myself in an unpretentious hallway, clean but plain, except for a potted palm by way of decoration.

It was quiet in there after the noise of the Strand. The reception desk was untenanted but there was a brass bell on it and when I brought my fist down on this, the 'ping' seemed to resound through the corridor in a most embarrassing way. In response a woman appeared, as plain and unpretentious as her surroundings, though whether she took after them or they after her, I didn't know. She seemed perfectly camouflaged for her job: her hair drawn back in a bun, a pale face, neat white lace collar and a black dress.

'Yes?' she said interrogatively, without any noticeable sign of interest, as if she had seen my kind before, many times during four years of war.

'Good afternoon,' I responded, determined to act like an officer and a gentleman. 'I was wondering if you had a room for the night.'

With a glance at me but without further comment, she consulted the register. Looking at it upside down, I could see several empty spaces.

'Number twenty-three,' she said, 'second floor,' handing me a key. 'Will you be requiring dinner?'

Would I be requiring dinner, or should I go out and see what I could find? I tossed up mentally between these alternatives, then said, quite untruthfully, 'No, I have an engagement this evening, but I'd like to have breakfast in the morning.'

She gave me a curious, half-suspicious look then picked up the key. 'If you would like to follow me I'll show you to your room,' she volunteered in a flat, disinterested voice.

Number twenty-three had a bed, a wardrobe, a wash-stand and a chair; it looked out on to the Strand.

'The toilet's along the corridor,' the plain lady informed me as she shut the door.

I stood looking out of the window for a few minutes, gazing ruminatively at the bustle down there; then I took off my shoes and lay down on the bed. It was a bit soft and narrow, but what a change to be in an English bed at all after France! Simple though it was, it seemed to me like a paradisal couch as I lay there speculating the future. What would the V/1500 Handley be like to fly? It had double the power of the 0/400. Where would we operate from? As to the immediate future, I would go out and find a modest restaurant, take a stroll along the Strand then turn in early to be ready for the morrow.

I must have dozed off, however, because when I woke up it was getting dark and I could see the reflection of street lights in the window. I had a quick 'wash and brush up', went downstairs and dropped my key on the desk, then walked out into the Strand. Which way? West towards Charing Cross and Trafalgar Square, north into Kingsway, or eastwards past the Law Courts and the Temple and into Fleet Street?

I thought it might be more useful, in view of my appointment there the following morning, to go past the Hotel Cecil where the Air Ministry had its headquarters. I passed Savoy Hill, where the beautiful little chapel of the Savoy was tucked away, protected somewhat by the slope of the hill from the noise and bustle of the Strand. I passed the Savoy Theatre, built for the performance of Gilbert and Sullivan operas, and several shops; then I came upon the Hotel Cecil — or should I say the Air Ministry — where I felt my future destiny lay, in one of its many offices. It seemed to be a huge place; there was a guard on its main entrance and lights were burning in many of its windows. So this was where the fate of so many young fellows — over 300,000 — fighting the war in the air on the Western Front and elsewhere was ultimately controlled! I hurried on. Tomorrow would be soon enough to storm its ramparts and find out what lay in store for me. Nelson's Column looked secure enough; so did St Martin-in-the-Fields and the Admiralty Arch and the fountains with Landseer's lions guarding them. Nothing would change these national landmarks, not even a great war.

I found an ABC teashop, always the refuge of the lonely and strangers in London, and ordered a simple meal: poached egg on haddock, bread and butter, a pot of tea. The waitress who served me was a middle-aged, homely soul. 'Here you are, luv, this'll cheer you up,' she said when she brought my tea. 'Going or coming back?' she asked when she returned with my meal.

I was nonplussed for a moment, then realized she was referring to France.

'Oh,' I said, 'just come back.'

'Well, good luck, dear,' she added. 'I hear it may all be over soon.'

She left me, with this parting shot, to munch my lonely way through my meal and to reflect on her comment. Would it be over soon? Would I do my course on the V/1500 and get back on operations? When I left the café I decided to stroll back along the Strand and get an early night.

When I got to Waterloo Bridge, however, something made me turn on to it and walk a little way across. An autumn fog had started to come down and settle over the city. As I looked along the dark river towards Westminster Bridge and the noble outlines of the Houses of Parliament and Big Ben, the silhouette of the buildings along the Embankment were etched and softened in the gloom. The Thames had been a waterway since before Roman times; whatever the tides of history and their effect on Britain, its own tides rose and fell continually, its waters perpetually flowed towards the sea.

Looking down into their darkness and absorbed in these thoughts, I failed to notice a figure beside me, until a voice said, 'Hello, soldier: you on leave then? Want to have a good time?'

I looked round, suddenly remembering Waterloo Bridge's dubious reputation, and found myself looking into a pair of beautiful dark eyes.

They belonged to a girl who was nearly as tall as I was and whose features seemed vaguely familiar, with a mass of chestnut-brown hair. She wasn't — she couldn't be — Jeanne, the farmer's daughter, the vegetable seller, from our neighbouring farm at Ligescourt? Not here in London, standing beside me! However, the illusion persisted for a few seconds while I looked at her; perhaps my imagination was in a very heightened state. But her next words dispelled the illusion.

'Come on, luv: come back with me and I'll give you a good time. It isn't far.'

Just then a London bobby loomed up out of the fog now shrouding the bridge; he was walking towards the Strand. He looked at us incuriously and marched on. He had presumably seen the same little scene enacted hundreds of times before. I tried to appear as if in nonchalant conversation, leaning against the parapet of the bridge. Truth to tell, I didn't know what to say to the girl. She certainly looked attractive, but this was a situation with which I'd never been confronted before, in all my nineteen years. Finally resolved after a few moments' cogitation, I said, 'No, I'm sorry; I've got to get back.'

I didn't know whether she was going to disappear, or curse me, or try to persuade me; she was obviously a professional.

'Get back?' she asked. 'Where to — your hotel? I can come there, you know; there's no difficulty about getting in. Just tell me your room number.'

This was an approach I hadn't bargained for. I had to make some excuse to get rid of her. 'No,' I lied, 'to the Air Ministry — I'm working late.' Certainly the lights had been burning in Bolo House. 'I — I just came out for a breath of fresh air. Cheerio.'

Remembering I had a pound in my pocket I pushed it into her hand, which she had raised towards me — I knew that once she had touched me, with the scent that she was wearing, I was done for, and pushed her away from me. Then I turned on my heel and hurried off towards the Strand. At the corner I groped my way across the bridge and along towards my hotel. She didn't seem to be following and I got inside the hallway. There was no-one there so I picked my key off the hook and went upstairs.

It was a delicious feeling, modest though my room was, to lie in bed in clean white sheets after months of living in France in a bell tent on an airfield. I could get up when I liked, have a comfortable breakfast and walk along to the Air Ministry to find out what was in store for me. With these thoughts in mind, and with the traffic sounds conveniently muffled by the fog, I soon fell asleep.

10
The Air Ministry

It has always struck me how drastically a great city may change its character within a few hours: by night it may be eerie, mysterious, full of potential danger; then a few hours later, when the light returns, bright, bustling and uncomplicated. When the office workers leave for home in the evening, and the lights come on with their concomitant shadows, it begins to change again.

I noticed this when I set out for the Air Ministry in the morning, after a breakfast as modest and simple as the hotel itself, hardly enough to keep a young airman's body and soul together for the day.

As I walked along the Strand, the fog of the night before had gone; and perhaps the figures in it had been phantoms too. But the guard at the entrance to the Air Ministry/Hotel Cecil/Bolo House premises was real enough. Having checked my identity he directed me to a reception desk in the hall.

'You want to see Postings,' the large man behind it informed me in a stentorian voice, when he'd scrutinized my papers, addressing me as if I'd come to the wrong place. I wished he didn't speak so loudly; it rather reminded me of the old song:

> The waiter roared, right down the hall,
> You'll get no bread with one fish ba-a-ll.

'Yes, I suppose I do,' I said. 'Can you direct me?'

He consulted a well-thumbed directory of names which lay on the desk in front of him, found an appropriate page then ran his finger down it. Then he picked up the telephone and said, 'Give me 342, miss.'

When he'd explained the situation, however, that here was a 2/Lt Blacking, sent by 207 Squadron to go for training on V/1500s, No 342 retorted that I wasn't his pigeon. They should try 339 and 341 — preferably the latter.

There was no answer from 341, so after allowing it a long ring, my large friend clicked his receiver rest impatiently and said, 'Try 339, dear.'

By happy chance, even if he wasn't the right man, 339 said he would see me, so reception — whom by now I was beginning to regard as an old friend, indeed my only friend — summoned a messenger to escort me up.

'Room 280, dear,' he said, handing her a pass he'd made out for me.

We went to the lift which in former (hotel) days had raised princes, dukes, counts, princesses, duchesses and countesses to their rooms. Now everything had a well-worn look, stripped down to the bare Governmental essentials. The messenger, a pleasant little woman wearing glasses and her hair done up in a neat bun, escorted me past numerous office doors. Each one had a white card on it, bearing the name of lieutenant-colonel this or major that or captain the other and his position described in hieroglyphic letters and numbers. Occasionally one of these doors opened and a civil servant emerged, clutching a file, and rushed off down the corridor to another office. So the war was being won: this was one front, here in London; the other was in France and Belgium.

The numbers on the doors we were passing started to decrease: 288, 287, 286. When we got to 280, however, there was a further complication: the card on the door said 'No Entry — Enter by Room 279'. Clearly there was an important officer inside, with an outer office housing a deputy or a personal assistant. The messenger knocked on 279. There was an immediate 'Come in' and she ushered me inside, handed over my pass and disappeared with a faint but encouraging smile. I felt I had lost another friend.

A figure rose from behind a plain deal table which served as a desk; in another corner was a typist. There was a filing cabinet and, from the window, a view across the Thames.

'Second Lieutenant Blacking?' queried the figure, the personification of an immaculate captain, perhaps unused to war's alarms. I felt the lowest of the low.

'Yes,' I said, putting a brave face on it. '207 Squadron.'

'Ah,' he said, 'Yes. You have been posted to Home Establishment for a specific purpose, which Lt-Col Warriss will explain to you. Just one moment, please; I will see if he can see you now.'

I was glad that my name seemed to be known to somebody in the Air Ministry, and I recognized the terminology of military protocol: the senior officer concerned might be sitting with his feet up on the desk, or writing a letter to his wife, or trimming his nails, or admiring the view through the window. His subordinate had to give the impression that he was so intensely busy he might just be able to spare a moment to see you about your business.

Through the communicating door I could hear some muttered conversation, while the typist's machine clattered away. I was glancing out of the window — it was a beautiful autumn morning and the Thames sparkled in the sunshine — when the immaculate captain reappeared.

'Lt-Col Warriss will see you now, Mr Blacking.'

As I went into the office a tall figure with a monocle unwound itself from behind the desk. 'Ah, Second Lieutenant Blacking. Do sit down, please.'

I found myself facing a kindly, lined face with penetrating eyes and receding hair. The features were angular and furrowed, seeming to reflect a good deal of experience. I got the impression that he knew what he was talking about.

'Whatever you may have heard on your squadron, Mr Blacking,' he began, 'I must ask you to regard what I am about to tell you as Secret, if not Top Secret.'

I realized from the way he pronounced it that his reference to Secret was with a capital 'S'. Sometimes one sees spoken words as if they were written down: this was one of them.

'I understand that, sir,' I replied.

'Well then,' he went on, 'the Air Ministry has been impressed by the results achieved by the 0/400 squadrons — your own and those in the Independent Force — and has decided to extend these operations with larger aircraft, in fact to hit the Hun in his very nerve-centre: Berlin.'

'Berlin?' I queried as if to make sure I'd heard right, although rumours of such an operation had been going round the squadron for some time.

'Berlin,' he repeated, looking at me steadily, 'will be the primary target. It will be a great psychological blow to the Hun to have his capital city bombed. The new four-engined bomber developed by

Handley Page, the V/1500, can do this, and we are training crews to fly it. That is why you have been posted from your squadron, as a potential V/1500 pilot.

I nodded; there didn't seem to be anything I could usefully say.

He allowed a moment for his information to sink in, then went on; 'Of course, this will be a hazardous operation because of the long flight involved over enemy territory — much longer than the ones made by the Zeppelins and Gothas, which was principally across the North Sea, when they bombed London; so you may decline if you wish.'

Another pause for me to react.

'No sir,' I said. 'I'd like to have a go at this.' 'Good,' he went on. 'Your record shows you to have been a reliable and cool pilot on 0/400s. But I cannot promise that you will be selected to fly the bigger aircraft. First there will be a routine medical check-up, then you will be interviewed by a senior officer and then given a choice of one of four night-flying aerodromes. There you will keep in practice, with circuits and landings and the occasional cross-country, and await your next instructions. So far only one very experienced crew is under training on V/1500s. The selection of further aircrew depends on the finalization of Air Ministry policy on the use of these aircraft, because problems of range and bomb load are involved: if the bomb load is to be significant the fuel would be correspondingly limited, and this might involve a landing in Holland on the way back, the crew being interned.'

I felt he had told me rather more than he had meant to, so I simply said, 'I understand, sir.'

'Well,' he went on, looking at me very hard, 'let's get you given a quick medical and then you will see Brigadier Oldall.'

He rang the bell on his desk and the immaculate captain appeared.

'Arrange a medical examination for Mr Blacking, Captain Starton,' he said crisply, 'then he is to see Brigadier Oldall. I will arrange a time, so he can return here first.'

'Very good, sir,' said the captain.

'Good luck, Blacking.' The lieutenant-colonel extended his hand. 'Don't forget to give 'em hell when you get over Berlin.'

'I will sir — if I ever do.'

Captain Starton rang for a messenger and another little woman appeared: she wore glasses and had a cheerful expression. Nothing, apparently, took her by surprise.

'Ah,' said the captain when she appeared in the office, 'Take Mr Blacking to Room eighty-four please — Captain Brisson.'

Again the lifts, the long corridors, endless doors with names on them, figures appearing and locking doors behind them, other figures carrying files and papers, messengers escorting visitors, tea trolleys — all the bureaucratic paraphernalia of a new Ministry conducting the air war.

'Back from the Front, are you sir?' asked my guide as I followed her quick footsteps.

'Yes,' I said.

'I've got two brothers out there,' she went on; 'been there since 1915 — in the Army. It's a terrible war, isn't it? When's it all going to end?' 'I don't know,' I answered. 'Soon, I hope.'

The numbers were decreasing in the corridor we were in — ninety-two, ninety-one, ninety; they had all been bedrooms in the hotel days. Suddenly eighty-four came up. My messenger tapped on the door, put her head round it and announced, 'Second Lieutenant Blacking, doctor.'

'Thank you, miss,' I said, and found myself inside.

'Strip down to your underclothes, Mr Blacking, and call me when you're ready.'

Here, I thought, as I undressed behind the screen, is where a man can offer no excuses; he is just himself, for good or ill, for better for worse, when he removes the façade of uniform. No outward appearances can save him now; he is stripped down to his essential parts — those he was given at birth and those (less any lost en route through illness or accident or warfare) he will take with him to the grave.

'Ready, doctor,' I said, trying to sound confident.

Captain Brisson, a big man, dark-haired, white-coated, wearing his spectacles on his nose, sounded me with his stethoscope, tapped me on the chest, examined my stomach and my groin, made me stand up and sit down quickly, had me standing on one leg (first the right and then the left) and balancing with my eyes shut, checked my blood pressure, looked at my throat, my teeth, my eyes and ears, tested my reflexes by tapping my legs below the knee or running a pointer across my bare soles and made me read out some letters on a board in one corner of his room — letters which diminished in size towards the bottom — with first one eye and then the other covered.

He made no comments or conversation, simply jotting down figures or notes on a form on his desk. I admired his professionalism.

'Right-ho,' he said suddenly, 'ye can get dressed again, Mr Blacking.'

When I'd struggled back as quickly as I could into my uniform and made myself reasonably presentable (fortunately there was a little mirror on the wall so I could get my tie straight and comb my hair), I pushed aside the curtain. He'd just signed the form and was blotting it.

'I'll get the messenger.' He picked up the telephone and passed a brief instruction; the procedure was obviously a familiar one.

'D'ye ken it'll be over this year?' he asked me suddenly.

'I don't know,' I said. 'I've been posted to Home Establishment to train for some long-range bomber operations. The Hun's not beaten yet.'

'Aye, but he will be.' Captain Brisson leaned back in his chair, putting his fingertips together. 'Wi' the Yankees in, it's only a matter of time.'

Just then the messenger appeared — a plump little blonde woman this time — and I thanked the dour Scots doctor, who wished me luck. When I went through the door and glanced back, he was putting my form into a buff envelope.

Blondie said nothing on our way back to Captain Starton's office, silently leading the way along all those corridors, past all those offices with names and titles on them. At last we got to No 279; she knocked, ushered me inside and disappeared.

'Ah, Mr Blacking. Would you mind waiting here please until the Brigadier can see you:' The gallant captain motioned me to a chair squeezed into one corner of the office.

His typist, a dark-haired, round-faced girl with a neat fringe of hair, wearing spectacles, looked at me and said, 'Would you like a cup of tea, sir?'

It was such a surprise to me to be called 'sir', as a mere second lieutenant amongst all this military hierarchy, that I responded at once to this generous invitation. 'Yes,' I said, 'I would.'

Obviously I'd have to wait a while for my medical report to be checked; the brigadier wouldn't interview me unless it was satisfactory. She brought me some pale-looking tea in a thick white china cup, with a plain biscuit in the saucer. I sipped and nibbled, listening to the clatter of her typewriter and watching the captain leafing over papers in his neat folders (or popping into the lieutenant-colonel's office for a quick consultation). How many other lives would be affected, I wondered, by decisions made here and in the other Air Ministry offices today?

I'd just taken a last sip and found somewhere to put my cup down when the 'phone rang.

'Ah, yes. Yes, I'll send him along.' Captain Starton put the receiver down and looked at me. 'Brigadier Oldall will see you now,' he said, ringing for a messenger.

Another neat little woman came to escort me up in the lift — this time to the sixth floor — and along more corridors. Another outer officer with a typist in the corner, but this time with a Personal Staff Officer, a Major Duncan. Tall, keen-eyed, with crinkly hair and the red tabs of a Staff Officer, he greeted me perfunctorily but not unkindly and asked me to 'take a seat'.

Again the wait, the cogitation. Just how many people — Staff officers, clerks, Civil Servants, messengers, typists etc. — did they employ in this new Ministry to run the air war, not only in the Hotel Cecil, a big hotel, but in all the offshoot offices in Kingsway? I was just doing some mental totting-up — if you have an Air Force of 30,000 officers and 300,000 men, how many Civil Servants do you need to administer and supply it? — when a buzzer went on the Major's desk and he disappeared into the inner office. A few moments later he re-appeared with some files under his arm and summoned me into the presence.

The brigadier's wide desk was completely clear of any papers. Across it I saw a thin-faced man with a well-trimmed moustache, carefully brushed hair and remarkably alert eyes. The crown and three pips rank badges on his shoulder epaulettes, the red tabs on his collar, his flying brevet and the medal ribbons beneath it made me feel quite naked, with just a solitary pip on each shoulder and a flying brevet, as I stood rigidly to attention. I knew the brigadier would know what he was talking about as he had commanded a wing of the Independent Force in France.

'Sit down, Mr Blacking,' he said quietly. He went on, 'You have been recommended by your squadron for training on long-range bomber operations, and you have had the purpose of these explained to you during your visit to the Air Ministry. Your records and your medical condition are satisfactory, so you may consider yourself in line for training on the new V/1500s. However, you will have to remember two things. One, that there are very few of these aircraft yet, so naturally the amount of crew training that can be done is limited. Secondly, the policy of long-range bombing has not been finally fixed upon, and may be changed. Consequently, all that we can offer you at the moment is a temporary posting to a Training Depot Squadron. There you will keep up your practice in night flying in readiness for going back to heavy bomber operations.'

Having explained the situation with beautiful and deliberately worded clarity, the brigadier looked hard at me and asked, 'Have you any questions?'

For a moment I considered saying, 'In view of what you tell me, then, I might just as well have stayed with 207 Squadron if my chances of flying V/1500s are so slender,' but I at once thought better of it and contented myself with a formal 'No, thank you, sir.'

'Good,' said the brigadier, who must have pressed a buzzer for at that moment his PSO appeared like a *deus ex machina*. 'Lt-Col Warriss will arrange a posting for you. Good luck — and thank you for the part you have played in the bombing offensive. It has made a considerable contribution to an eventual Allied victory.'

'Thank you, sir,' I mumbled, as the PSO ushered me through the door into his office. I had been made to feel I had played a part, however small, in the Allied war effort. My thoughts flew back to Ligescourt and the other boys on the squadron and I was thinking of them when I heard Major Duncan say, 'A messenger will take you back to Room 279, Mr Blacking.'

This time a cheerful little figure escorted me, down in the lift and along the corridors. I'd begun to feel like one of those sealed tubes shot from one side of a department store to another, carrying invoices and money, change and receipts.

'I can offer you a choice of four night-flying aerodromes,' said Lt-Col Warriss when I was sitting in front of him again, his lined face now like a familiar map to me. 'Ternhill . . .' — the other three names didn't mean anything to me; they might be anywhere in the wilds. At least I'd know where I was going to; and was that nice little bundle of cuddle still working in the Post Office at nearby Market Drayton, I wondered?

I appeared to be giving judicious consideration to all four possibilities. Then I said, as if announcing a balanced verdict, 'I think I'd like to go to Ternhill, sir.'

'All right. Ternhill it is. Captain Starton will arrange travel papers for you. Good luck, Mr Blacking, but don't be disappointed if you never see a V/1500. You know how things can change — these are long-range plans, for 1919, but a lot can happen by then. Perhaps the war will end; who knows?'

Once more I was in the outer office, the typist tapping out documents for me — a travel warrant, a movement order. In a few moments they would have forgotten all about me, busy in their administrative affairs, running the Air Force.

Captain Starton received the papers, signed them and folded them into a buff envelope which he handed to me.

'Thank you,' I said.

He looked immaculate and superior, and I was just wondering how he would have got on on our squadron when the messenger appeared. 'Escort this officer to the front entrance,' he instructed her, then, to my pleasure, he added. 'Good luck, Mr Blacking.'

I thanked him, then as we were going along the corridor the messenger, the cheerful little woman again, chirped up, 'Got a Blighty posting, sir?'

'Well, I suppose so,' I said. 'For the time being, anyway.'

It seemed to take much less long to get out of Bolo House than to get in. I thanked my guide, handed in my pass and went through the swing door into the sunshine and bustle of the Strand. To get to Ternhill meant taking a train from Paddington. First, however, to collect my baggage from the hotel. My mind felt clear and refreshed as I walked away from Bolo House, as if I had been somehow purged by my visit to the Air Ministry, having been through the interview, medical examination and posting routine at the HQ of the air war. Now my course was clear: go to Ternhill, keep in night flying practice and hope for a posting on to V/1500s. If not, back to France and on to 0/400s again. At least, in the meantime, Shropshire would make a pleasant change from Picardy.

When I got back to the hotel the same pale, plain, unpretentious lady who had appeared when I arrived there the evening before reappeared when I rang the bell at reception, still in her black dress. She seemed to be quite unmoved or unaffected by anyone who came or went, or maybe she didn't like Service people; perhaps she had lost a husband, a lover or a brother in Flanders in the terrible slaughter during four years of warfare. I paid my account, thanked her and picked up my baggage. Hopefully, I could get a cab outside the hotel.

It was a beautiful crisp autumn day, and although mid-October, still quite warm. Perhaps the same conditions prevailed at Ligescourt, helping our bomber operations but also aiding the enemy's defences. The cab driver merely nodded and put his flag down when I said, 'Paddington station, please.' En route, along the Strand, through Trafalgar Square with its view down Whitehall to Westminster — the governing heart of our war enterprise — up Regent Street and along Oxford Street to Marble Arch, Hyde Park and the Bayswater Road, everything looked pretty normal apart from entrances; and at Paddington, the scene of smoke, steam and bustle must have been much the same as the high glass roof had witnessed every day for the past fifty years.

'Change at Wellington,' the booking clerk informed me when he exchanged my travel warrant for a ticket.

This meant a Shrewsbury train, and a tedious journey through Warwickshire and the West Midlands. Ah well, at least there was no doubt about my destination. I established the time for departure and the platform, then bought myself a copy of *The Times*. When there was plenty of time to read, I thought, one should read *The Times;* at least I would get to know how the war was going, on the Western Front, at sea and in Palestine.

I had barely stowed my baggage on the rack and settled myself in a corner, however, when a lady entered the compartment. She was preceded by her scent, which I found quite seductive, and — being an officer and a gentleman — I got up to help her with her suitcase.

'Thank you so much,' she said, with a dazzling smile and a hint of breathlessness which I found rather exciting: 'I just couldn't find a porter.'

There was an interval of embarrassed silence, at least on my part. Secretly I felt that there might be advantages in being posted to Home Establishment after all. To cover my embarrassment I opened *The Times* to its centre pages, making a crackling noise that seemed to rend the silence. Fortunately the train had started, with much hissing and a convulsive jerk, and I was able to pay studious attention to the grimy landscape of West London through wafts of smoke and steam passing the carriage windows as we got under way into the countryside.

I then returned to *The Times* and was beginning to read a leading article on Mr Lloyd George's problems and policies in the conduct of Britain's war effort, when I heard my lady travelling companion say, 'Are you back from the Front, may I ask?'

'Yes,' I replied, briefly but not rudely. I had heard of Mata Hari.

'On leave?' she persisted charmingly.

'No, on posting,' I said. I was determined not to reveal where I had come from or where I was going to.

There was a further silence, while the countryside through which we clattered at increasing speed grew greener and more open. Didn't she have a book or a paper to read, or should I offer her my copy of *The Times*?

Suddenly the door was pushed open and the ticket inspector came in. He looked at hers without comment, merely a 'Thank you, madam.' When he checked mine he said, 'Change at Wellington, Sir,' before slamming the door shut again.

Well, at least she knew now roughly where I was going; but either through innate tactfulness or some inscrutable female logic she didn't take advantage of this unexpected information.

Instead she asked, 'You're in the Royal Flying Corps, aren't you?'

'Ye-es,' I said hesitantly, 'only it's the Royal Air Force now — a quite separate Service.'

She smiled but made no response. Looking at her briefly over the top of *The Times* — so often used as a kind of social escarpment — I noticed how regular her features were, how clear her skin was. She didn't seem to have been seriously affected by any wartime privation. As she was wearing gloves, I couldn't tell whether she was married or not. There was a further, quite long, silence as the lovely sweep of English countryside unrolled its autumn vistas through the carriage windows.'

Then as if *à propos* of nothing, she said, 'My brother was killed on flying operations — only recently. He hadn't been in France long.'

'I'm sorry.' I put down the paper and looked at her with a sudden surge of sympathy. How many hundreds of sisters, mothers and fathers had not been bereaved in the same sad way in this fifth year of this terrible war? 'Was he on a scout squadron?' — their casualties had been particularly heavy when flying low-level strafing sorties to try to stem the Hun offensive.

'No,' she said, 'he was an observer — on day bombers.'

I looked out of the window for a moment at the rolling, peaceful landscape, untouched by war. I thought of how many of my fellow-members of the RAF had looked their last on a war-torn French landscape as they went spinning down to their doom, and I considered what I might say to this charming woman who had lost a brother in the war in the air.

'Those boys had a hard time of it,' I told her gently, 'especially when they encountered German fighters. But they used to form defensive circles, which the Huns found hard to break, and could give a good account of themselves.'

She received this information in silence. Perhaps, in her mind's eye, she was picturing one of the battles over the Western Front. Her silence continued for a long time; I did not wish to break it by any irrelevant remark or intrusion into her thoughts.

Suddenly she asked, 'You're a flyer yourself, aren't you?'

'Yes,' I said. There seemed to be nothing to add; I didn't wish to volunteer any information about my own activities. But I was quite unprepared for her next remark.

'My brother used to mention in his letters home a friend he'd made in training and whom he'd met again afterwards in France, although they were on different squadrons. Apparently this friend invited Oscar to visit his squadron. He told us about this in one of his last letters.'

'Oscar?' I said. 'Did you say your brother's name was Oscar?'

'Yes, Oscar Darke; I'm his sister Kathleen.'

Oscar Darke. I was so stunned by the coincidence of this meeting that I could think of nothing to say. My mind flashed back to those training days with Oscar, and the mishap we'd had, then to my meeting with him in France and the change I'd observed in him, and finally to when I'd been told he was missing.

'Did you know him?' I heard his sister say.

Just then the train rushed into a tunnel, the suffocating noise obliterating our conversation for what seemed like minutes, but could only have been a few seconds. In that time I tried to decide: should I tell this attractive woman, in our unexpected tête-à-tête, that I knew her lost brother and accept whatever consequences might flow from this disclosure? Or should I tell her a white lie, saying that I never knew Oscar? It is extraordinary how much flashes through one's mind in an instant.

We emerged into an open landscape, the pale afternoon sunshine making long shadows across it. She seemed to have forgotten her question, and as the train slowed down and the outer houses of a small town began to appear she made preparations to get off there, pulling up her gloves and gathering her handbag to her side. I got up to lift her suitcase down from the rack.

'That's very kind of you,' she said.

A porter's voice called out as we drew into the station; doors were opened and steam rose; I preceded her on to the platform and helped her down.

'Thank you,' she said again, 'and good luck to you.'

'It has been a pleasure to meet you, Miss Darke.'

Within seconds she had disappeared among the figures milling around the station and I was back in the compartment, which now seemed very empty, as if a light had gone out in it. Should I have told her about my friendship with Oscar and, as a result, made her acquaintance? What would have flowed from that? Perhaps, if our journey together had been longer, it would have come out that I knew her brother. These thoughts troubled me for the rest of the way, when I changed at Wellington and got on the branch line to Ternhill. The weather had changed; it had become cloudy from the west. I couldn't help recalling Matthew Arnold's opening lines from the poem we read at school:

> Coldly, sadly descends
> The autumn evening.

11

Back to Ternhill

'Transport?' echoed the venerable porter after the branch line train had chuff-chuffed out on its way to Market Drayton and left only silence and a whiff of smoke behind. 'Why, 'ee can see it from here.'

Sure enough I could: a vague outline of wooden huts, of hangars and shapes of aircraft could be seen from the platform, seemingly little changed from what I remembered; but it was still a mile away, a long trudge with a suitcase and a flying jacket.

'Could I use your telephone?' I asked.

The ancient railwayman led the way grudgingly into his office and picked up the 'phone, giving its handle a vigorous whirring. I noticed the black-leaded grate with the embers of a fire just glowing, a little kettle on the hob, neat stacks of tickets behind the booking counter and a well-thumbed timetable.

'Give me the air force station, dear,' I heard him say. 'An officer here wants to speak to them. 'Ere 'e is.'

With that he handed the instrument over to me and I heard a girl's voice say, 'Just one minute, sir.'

The 'phone went on ringing for a long time, it seemed, but I waited patiently. Then a voice came on the line, 'Royal Air Force station Ternhill.'

'Can I speak to the Duty Officer?' I said.

'Hold on, sir,' the voice responded.

There was another interminable pause, then a crisp announcement: 'Flight Lieutenant Hannett, Duty Officer, speaking.'

'Oh,' I said, almost taken by surprise after the long silence. 'This is

Second Lieutenant Blacking, ex-207 Squadron. I've been posted here by the Air Ministry. Is there any chance of some transport from the station?'

'Yes, I think so,' the DO replied. 'I'll do what I can. But you'll have to wait.'

There was a click and he rang off. I thanked the porter and walked out of his office. All I could do now was to pace up and down the platform until the tender arrived, reflecting on the events of the day and pondering my new situation. After about ten minutes of this cogitation I heard the sound of a car engine. Although it wasn't quite dark the driver had his lights on: he hopped out and saluted in a rather unmilitary fashion, touching his forage cap like a forelock.

'Mr Blacking, sir?' he said.

I returned his salute and picked up my bag and flying jacket, slinging them in the back and taking the seat beside him. In a second we were off, down a Shropshire lane, and after a few minutes the aerodrome buildings hove into view.

'Where d'ye wish tae be?' said my driver. 'By the way, sir, I'm Jock.'

He had a toothy grin, a weather-beaten complexion and a twinkle in his eye; he looked as if nothing would ever perturb him.

'Well, I really want to find the Duty Officer, Flight Lieutenant Hannett,' I replied as we swung round the roads of the camp, between its wooden huts. 'Perhaps we'd better make for the Officers' Mess. Is that where we'll find him?'

'Aye, I reckon so,' said Jock laconically.

He pulled up in front of a wooden hut which was set back a bit and I noticed had a hint of a garden in front of it. I lifted my baggage out of the back of the tender, said, 'Thank you, Jock,' and as he disappeared into the dusk went up the steps into the Mess.

There was nobody about, so I left my baggage in the hall and set out to find my way around. I located an office, which was empty, a cloakroom and a locked door; moving on down a short corridor with windows on either side, I encountered what looked like a dining-room. Beyond it was an ante-room, with wicker chairs and a few old copies of *Punch* and the *Illustrated London News* lying around; then I caught sight of some bottles and glasses glinting, which proved to be a small bar, and the flickering flames of a blazing fire.

In front of this cheerful sight on an autumn evening stood a figure with a sallow complexion and large moustache and a broad, gap-toothed grin (like Chaucer's Wife of Bath).

'Hello,' the figure said, extending a hand, 'I'm Hannett. Welcome to Ternhill — or, as some say, Tern-Hill.' He pronounced the two versions with careful distinction. 'Same place, anyway. Care for a drink, eh?'

His hand, having grasped mine, pointed to the bar. 'I'm afraid it's too late for some grub — we didn't know you were comin'. But we can certainly refresh you. Have a good journey?'

'Yes, thank you,' I said. 'I didn't know I was coming myself until I was interviewed at the Air Ministry this morning.'

'Ah, Bolo House, palace of intrigue,' observed Hannett, who seemed to me to be about the oldest Flight Lieutenant I had ever seen. 'Well, I won't ask you what you're doin' here; must be some State Secret. What'll you drink, old boy?'

'I'll have a beer,' I said non-committally. It had been a long day, with some important experiences, and I was beginning to feel a trifle frayed; besides, Ternhill hadn't yet quite come into focus. Nevertheless I was warming to it under the influence of Flight Lieutenant Hannett.

'A beer for Mr Blacking,' he called out to the barman, and went on, as if reading my thoughts, 'The reason why there's no one in the Mess tonight is that when there's no night flying, as there isn't tonight, they all buzz off into Market Drayton or one of the local villages or — you know where,' tapping the side of his nose and giving me a confidential wink. 'After all, *c'est la guerre*, you know. Cheers, old boy.'

I got the impression that Flight Lieutenant Hannett did most of his Duty Officer duties in the Officers' Mess; but no doubt he slipped out from time to time on his rounds of inspection.

'Cheerio,' I responded.

'I'll fix you up with a room and in the morning you'll need to see the CO, Major Villiers. He's a great character.'

I began to feel I might enjoy my second posting to Ternhill. As I sipped my beer Hannett continued to chat away, in a kind of this-is-what-you-need-to-know monologue; he didn't require any prompting:

'We're a training station, you know, mainly for night flying — either to refresh the experienced flyers or indoctrinate the inexperienced. I expect you may get some instructing to do; we're rather short staffed. I'm sorry, old boy, that wasn't very well put. I didn't mean to be uncomplimentary.'

'That's all right,' I said. 'I understand.'

'The point is,' he went on hastily, 'that there aren't enough pilots with sufficient experience who can be spared from operations: it's all-out offensive now against the Hun. I think he may crack soon.'

There was silence for a moment. I suspect we were both thinking of the pilots, observers and gunners on the Western Front and the air offensive going on day after day: the dogfights as patrols met and clashed, the bombing at night and in daylight, the low-level strafing, the reconnaissance. In the silence a piece of coal crashed down in the grate, sending up a shower of sparks: I thought of an aircraft spinning down, smoke streaming from it, its crew doomed.

'What kind of aeroplanes do you fly here?' I asked, more to keep the conversation going than because I really wanted to know — I'd find out from the CO in the morning.

'Oh, an assortment, old boy. Mainly Fees and Handleys.'

I noticed that his tankard was empty. 'Can I get you another one?' I said.

'No, thank you, old boy — must keep sober for my duties. The CO doesn't care for DDOs.'

'DDOs?' I echoed.

'Drunken Duty Officers,' Hannett explained with a guffaw. 'Come on, old boy, I'll show you to your room.'

As we went down a corridor to another wing of the Mess building he explained, 'We keep a room here for odd visitors and people in transit. I'll put you in here and tomorrow you'll be fixed up with permanent accommodation.'

I thanked him and he disappeared on his duties, or maybe back to the bar.

Then I looked around. Well, it wasn't the Ritz, it was just the bare essentials — an iron-framed single bed, a bedside locker, a folding wooden chair, a strip of red-patterned carpet and a hook behind the door. It seemed to me to have all the comforts of a monkish cell. Still, it was only meant for occasional visitors and I didn't wish for anything more elaborate: it was clean and quiet. I'd had a long day and quietness and privacy occurred only seldom in Service life, in my experience. That evening I welcomed them.

As I drifted off to sleep I thought of my visit to Bolo House, of the interviews I'd had and the medical examination, and of the prospect of flying V/1500s and bombing Berlin. Perhaps I'd win one of the new awards, a Distinguished Flying Cross, if I managed to survive one or two trips.

Then I thought of my meeting with Oscar Darke's charming sister on the train. Should I have told her I knew him, and if I had, what might that disclosure have led to? Still, it was too late now; I'd never see her again. Or should I try to get his home address and write to her? That would be something I could do while at Ternhill. It would give me something to look forward to — the possibility of seeing her again, after I'd explained who I was and told her of my connection with Oscar. I could visualize her, sitting in the corner of the compartment, smiling at me, her perfume wafting towards me, as mysterious and subtle as her smile . . .

Suddenly the door burst open and a man's voice said, 'Tea, sir; lovely morning.'

Before I could answer he'd picked up my shoes and gone. Where was I? Not on the train — that had been only a dream. The sunlight was bursting through the window behind me. I pulled back the meagre curtain and looked out; it was a bright autumn morning, my first day back at Ternhill.

There was no sign of Flight Lieutenant Hannett at breakfast. I had found my way there in some embarrassment, not knowing where the dining-room was and not wishing to show my ignorance of the Mess geography by asking the way to it. But I needn't have worried: there were only three or four officers there and none of them took any notice. Two of them were reading newspapers and I spotted a headline about Further Allied Successes on the Western Front.

I'd just finished my sausage and egg and was dipping into the marmalade to put on some bread and butter when I felt a tap on my shoulder and a voice said, 'Mornin' Blacking. Trust you slept well.'

Hannett's cheery grin, as he rustled up the ends of his moustache with his forefinger, subsided into the chair beside me, where he continued in a confidential tone, 'I've told the CO you're here. He'd like to see you at 8.30: I'll take you across. Bring your baggage with you and I'll show you your permanent billet.'

'Thank you,' I said.

'Good lad.' He patted me on the shoulder and disappeared: he had either breakfasted earlier or didn't have any.

I sipped a second cup of tea and thought about my meeting with Major Villiers. Better spruce myself up a bit. 'A great character,' Hannett had called him, but it pays to make a good initial impression. One shouldn't make assumptions or take liberties.

There was plenty of time, as it happened, and I was standing at the

Mess doorway looking out over Ternhill's wooden huts and green acreage when Hannett drew up in his open car. 'Hop in, old boy,' he said. 'I'll take you to the CO first.'

I put my bag and flying jacket in the back and we surged off. It was a beautiful morning for mid-October, a bit of mistiness around but the sky clear and serene. I felt quite content to be doing some flying here for a while, until my posting came through.

HQ was a wooden hut, like all the other buildings, and Hannett led me along a corridor to the right from the front entrance. At the end was a door marked firmly 'Commanding Officer'; the door to the left of it was open. He tapped lightly on it and looked in.

'Second Lieutenant Blacking here, Polly, to see the CO.'

Polly was a demure-looking dark-haired girl with a fringe and cheerful dimples, the CO's PA. Clearly Flight Lieutenant Hannett found her rather attractive. She flashed a collective smile at us, tapped on the CO's door and half disappeared inside. I noticed one slim little hand still holding on to the edge of the door; then she reappeared and said, 'Major Villiers will see you, Mr Blacking.'

'I'll wait and take you to your billet,' put in Hannett, clearly not averse to chatting up Polly in the meanwhile.

'Ah, Mr Blacking,' the Major greeted me. 'Welcome to Ternhill. Tell me what brings you here — we haven't yet received any official notification from the Air Ministry.'

'Well, sir,' I explained. 'I've been posted from my squadron — No 207 — to convert on to V/1500s, but I gather there's a bit of a hold-up with aircraft, so I've been sent here to keep in night-flying practice.'

'That makes sense,' said the Major, a cheerful-looking, red-haired pipe-smoker. He leant back in his chair, looked at me keenly and went on, 'We're No 13 TDS — Training Depot Squadron, as you probably know. As such, we have quite a floating population: officers like yourself, waiting to be posted elsewhere, new pilots sent here to get night experience, and old hands putting enough hours in to qualify for their flying pay.

'I suggest that you familiarize yourself with the local area by day, initially in a Fee, then in a Handley; then get in some hours by night. Our chief instructor, Captain Chamier, will probably ask you to do some instructing and there will also be extra duties like O/C Control Tower for night flying.

'Are you fixed up for accommodation and is there anything you want to ask me?'

'Yes, sir,' I said in answer to his first question. 'Flight Lieutenant Hannett has been looking after me. No, sir; I don't think there's anything else.'

'Good. Well I hope you'll enjoy your stay here, however long or short it is. We expect people just to get on with their job and use their own initiative.'

'Thank you, sir.' I saluted and went through the door, noticing as I did so that the windows in the CO's office gave him a clear view of the airfield: nothing much would escape his eye.

Clearly Hannett had not passed the time unpleasantly with Polly. He gave her a large wink as we set off down the corridor and looked pleased with himself.

As we climbed into his car I said, 'You don't need to do all this for me, you know. Your duties finished at eight o'clock.'

'That's all right,' he responded cheerfully. 'I've nothing else to do and I know what it's like when you come to a strange place. First your billet, then . . .?'

'I have to see the Chief Instructor, Captain Chamier.'

'All right, I'll take you to his office, then leave you in his care.'

My room was on one side of a hut divided by a central corridor: there were about a dozen rooms in all. I felt I could make a home there for a week or so, until my posting came through.

Captain Chamier, when the genial Hannett deposited me at his office and departed, I found to be a big, bluff, cheerful fellow. He hadn't known I was coming but readily accepted my story of how I got to Ternhill — my experiences with No 207 Squadron, the posting to Home Establishment and my interviews at the Air Ministry. Clearly they were used to odd pilots drifting in. On a chart on the wall behind him were names arranged according to experience — new pilots, old pilots, refresher courses, and so on — with horizontal coloured lines showing how much flying each had done. Through the window I could see a Handley being towed out, its wings still folded.

'So, you want to do some flying here, Blacking, especially at night?'

I nodded. 'Yes sir, that's the purpose of my posting — to keep my hand in until I'm called for a V/1500 course.'

He tapped his fingers with a pencil, looked hard at me, then said, 'Right. Well, the first thing to do is to get you in the air by day. How long since you've flown a Fee?'

'About six months,' I said, 'before I converted on to Handleys.'

'Well, they're quite an easy aeroplane, as you know. I suggest you spend the morning looking over one, to refresh your memory, then take it up this afternoon to get the feel of it again and see the local area.

'But let me give you a word of warning. In flying terms, we're very close to the Welsh mountains here. Keep away from them unless you can see 'em. In any conditions of poor visibility, or low cloud, keep to the east of here: the west is a danger area. We don't want casualties in training, as far as we can avoid them, though there are bound to be accidents owing to lack of experience.

'One thing more. There's no formal course of training here because pilots come to us for different reasons, from differing backgrounds, so their requirements vary. But we do aim to keep up good standards.'

'Any questions, or are you happy?'

'No, sir,' I said after a moment's thought. He seemed to have covered everything.

'All right; I will tell the Flight that you will be looking over a Fee this morning and will fly one this afternoon. There should be no problem about weather today.'

He glanced out of the window. It was a golden day with a clear sky and that stillness unique to autumn.

'Good luck, Blacking. I may call on you for other duties when you've got the feel of things: some instructing, and i/c Control Tower at night, perhaps.'

I liked Chamier: his manner was as open as his appearance. He made me feel I wanted to do well at Ternhill, however long or short a time I was there, even though there was no specific course to be followed.

I made my way over to where two or three of the aeroplanes were standing out in the open, the Handleys towering over the Fees with the great spread of their wings, their twin engines and long fuselage. There couldn't have been a greater contrast with the Fees, with their short boot-shaped fuselage, pusher engine and girder-like booms connecting the tailplane structure to the wings. Certainly not a beautiful aircraft but a workmanlike one and, as I recalled from when I'd flown them before, a docile type.

I chose one of the Fees which was not being worked on, which in fact looked ready to fly, and seeing no-one around climbed into the pilot's cockpit. This was done by stepping on the tyre and then on the lower mainplane, then heaving myself in. Once up there I looked forward over the gunner's cockpit. There was an unrestricted field of view, especially when in a flying attitude, and this was one feature which made the Fee such a good fighting aeroplane, although its role was now restricted to night bombing.

I'd just got my head down into the 'office' and started to feel the movement of the controls and to look at the instruments, which were pretty standard, when I heard a voice say, 'Can I help you, sir?'

Suddenly I realized that I'd committed the unforgiveable sin of climbing into a parked aircraft without asking the engineering officer's or flight sergeant's permission. The reason for this was that some delicate maintenance might be going on, or the machine might be armed, with ready-cocked machine-guns or fused bombs — one had to assume this always. I looked out and saw a cheerful, weather-tanned face looking up at mine.

'Hello, Mr Blacking, sir,' its owner said, 'it's you, is it?'

This being a physical and philosophical fact I couldn't dispute, I responded sharply, 'Yes, indeed,' then, recognizing my interrogator, added,

'Why, hello, Corporal Sheed. I didn't expect to find you here.'

'Sergeant Sheed,' he corrected me. 'Been promoted since we last met — Stonehenge, wasn't it, when you flew Fees? Then you went on to Handleys. What are you doing here, sir? Surely not more training?'

'No,' I explained. 'Been posted here to keep up my night flying prior to converting to V/1500s. Captain Chamier told me to go and look at a Fee then fly one this afternoon. I'm sorry, I should have asked your permission before climbing into one.'

'That's all right, Mr Blacking; you have a look round. I was just a bit anxious in case some stranger had found his way in. When you come to fly this afternoon have a word with me and I'll fix you up with a good aircraft; some of 'em are getting a bit long in the tooth.'

'Rightho, sergeant, thanks; I'll get an early lunch and come over.'

Left to my cockpit study as he went off, I felt delighted to have met him again and glad that he'd been promoted. He was always so cheerful and reliable, a thoroughly efficient fitter and a likeable character.

I'm afraid I didn't linger long over lunch, which was a kind of hash, with a treacle sponge and custard for sweet. Neither Hannett nor the CO nor Captain Chamier was in the Mess, so I could only nod to the others at the lunch table, who were strangers to me. I deliberately hadn't gone to the bar beforehand because I was flying.

It was shortly after one o'clock when I got back to the Flight and found Sergeant Sheed. The autumn afternoon was calm, sunny and almost cloudless, though there were some wisps high up away to the west; perhaps a change was on the way.

'Ah, Mr Blacking, Sir. I've got just the aeroplane for you, a good one, but she needs an air test — had a plug change because there was a drop in revs. Would you like to see how she goes now, sir? You could combine that with a taste of refresher flying.'

'Certainly,' I said, 'I'll see how she performs.'

I already had my flying jacket on, having picked it up from my room after lunch, and when I pulled on my helmet he asked, 'What squadron badge is that, sir?' He was looking at the piece of black felt depicting the black cat with his tail up, his red glass beads for eyes and his red collar.

'207's,' I said, 'and I couldn't fly without it.'

Sergeant Sheed nodded, then gave me a reminder; 'Don't forget the starter magneto, sir; give the handle a whirl and she should fire. It saves us having to heave the propellor around.'

As soon as he was clear I looked down for the little dynamo with the handle on it, looked up again for his thumbs-up in response to mine, then spun the handle. At first the 160 hp Beardmore engine merely coughed, though there was a suggestion of a turn by the blades, but the second time the start was successful: the propeller revolved, slowly at first, then faster and faster. I had set the throttle too far forward and pulled it back to idling revs. As soon as the engine was running smoothly I waved to Sergeant Sheed to take the chocks away. He held them up for me to see; I opened up and the Fee rolled forward. I was on my way.

As I trundled past the Control Tower, giving the Beardmore short bursts to get used to the feeling of taxying a single-engined aircraft again after becoming so used to Handleys, I noticed that there was no-one inside it: perhaps it was only used for night-flying. It was merely a wooden hut strategically placed with a good view of the airfield, not nearly so elaborate as the one we had at Ligescourt. As there was hardly any wind I chose the longest run. I revved up the engine as far as it would go; it sounded all right, so I throttled back and had a good look round the local sky to see that it was clear, then turned on to my take-off run and opened up. I'd forgotten the extraordinary sensation provided by the Fee's long oleos as she gathered speed: first the rumbling sound, then its gradual cessation as the aircraft got airborne and the undercarriage legs dropped down to their full stalky length.

I hardly bothered to look at my airspeed indicator. It was one of those days when everything was in tune; the aircraft and I were one, the weather perfect. It seemed strange to be flying by myself again, having become so used to a crew. I was 'master of my time', as Shakespeare puts it in *Macbeth* before that ill-fated banquet; what should I do?

The first thing was to take the Fee up as high as she would go, perhaps to 10,000 feet, then to spend the rest of my flight in a gradual descent. This would give me a bird's eye view of the surrounding Shropshire countryside and also remind me of any prominent local landmarks. I'd taken off towards the west, so soon began to see vague outlines of the Welsh mountains, and remembering the CI's warning I made a gradual turn towards the east while still climbing.

It began to get a little chilly, however. We were now well into the autumn and temperatures were lower. I just achieved 10,000 feet, tried the mag switches and got no appreciable drop in power, then throttled back until the Beardmore was purring and began a lazy descent. I was enjoying this — the pure, cleansing recreation that only flying can provide.

Why was this, I wondered, as the Fee lost height in wide circles while I varied my turns from left to right, above the Shropshire countryside laid out in neat patterns down below. Sitting in that pulpit-like eminence I could 'view the landscape o'er', as the hymn says.

The reasons for the therapeutic value of flying were, I reflected, that one was in another, more spacious dimension, no longer earthbound; and that one's mind was concentrated upon the job in hand — whether just flying the aeroplane, keeping an eye on the immediate environment, or watching the weather.

I had just done another gentle turn and was thinking about locating my position — that was Market Drayton down there, wasn't it? I wondered what that bundle of cuddle in the Post Office had been up to last night, when the engine spluttered, picked up again for a second, spluttered momentarily again, then died into an awful silence.

I was suddenly gliding, at about 4,000 feet. What had gone wrong? What was I to do?

The mag switches were on; I turned them back again after testing them. The throttle was partly open, so I should have power. Fuel: I had three tanks, two pressure and one gravity. I found the fuel selector and turned it to the next position; there was a sudden burst of power as the petrol surged through the pipeline into the carburettor and the throttle was still open. I pulled it back then pushed it forward again gradually. All seemed normal and I flew along under power again, maintaining a straight-and-level attitude until I recovered my composure, trying to sort out what had gone wrong.

I gradually realized that, in my enthusiasm to get into the air, I hadn't checked carefully enough which fuel tank I'd selected: I must have taken off and climbed on the gravity-feed tank, the smallest of the three, and it had just run out. While I'd been philosophizing to myself about flying, I'd be taught a sharp lesson in the practicalities of the art — how you should always do a correct cockpit drill before take-off and constantly keep an eye on your fuel in the air.

Ah, well, one lived and learned. I steadied myself and started to look again for the airfield. That little shock had done me good: it had been a kind of catharsis, like the effect of Greek drama, which we used to be told about at school.

Gradually Ternhill came into perspective: a larger, flatter green area than the surrounding fields, with patterns of wooden huts in lines and groups. I decided on my landing run and settled on the approach, getting the speed steady at 65 mph with a trickle of throttle. Once over the grass I checked back; she floated, the wheels touched and then I got the reverse effect of those long oleos — a rumble as they absorbed the shock, then telescoped to take up the strain. The tailskid soon brought us to a halt, and I had to look round to see where I should taxy back to, not yet being familiar with the airfield. Then I caught sight of an AM, waving his arms above his head in a crossover motion as a signal, so I taxyed towards him and switched off.

As I climbed out on to the wing and dropped on to the grass via the port tyre the AM said, 'The Chief Instructor wants to see you, sir.'

I nodded in a nonchalant kind of way, but privately thought: goodness, what have I done wrong? Did he hear my engine cut out? Then, thus reminding myself of it, I told the AM, 'The engine seems to be all right. No magneto trouble — the new plugs seem to be doing their job.'

I trudged across the grass to the CI's office, carrying my helmet. The air smelt fresh and sweet with an autumnal crispness to it.

'Ah, Blacking, come in,' Captain Chamier greeted me when I tapped on his office door. 'How did it go?'

'Fine,' I said. 'I enjoyed it.' I wasn't going to tell him about the fuel tank business.

'Good. I want you to do a job for me tomorrow. Will you demonstrate a Handley to a couple of pilots being posted here temporarily?'

'Of course, glad to. But may I first fly one around this afternoon to get more acquainted with the local area and do one or two landings here? I'd like to feel competent to demonstrate one of your Handleys.'

'Oh, I think so, Blacking. See the sergeant you met this morning — Sergeant Sheed — and ask him to get a Handley ready for you.'

As I was leaving the office he added, 'By the way, the sergeant may ask you if he or one of the AMs could come up with you. If he does, let him — we encourage that sort of thing. Also, if one of them flies with you, you can bet your boots that the aircraft will be in top condition.'

I walked back across the grass to find Sergeant Sheed and ask him for a Handley that afternoon.

'Right, sir,' he said, his face crinkled with cheerfulness. 'Half-past-three, say, it will be ready for you. By the way, sir, do you mind if I come up with you?'

'You're a trusting soul, sergeant. Yes, of course you can; we shall be up for thirty or forty minutes.'

I wasn't, of course, taken by surprise at his request in view of what Captain Chamier had said. I wasn't displeased, either, at the thought of having some company in such a big aeroplane. As I walked across to the Mess for a break until the machine was ready I reflected with pleasure on the day's experiences — flying a Fee again and the prospect of a local reconnaissance in a Handley.

I'd just got in to the Mess building when a now-familiar voice hailed me: 'Hello, Blacking, how did you get on? Care for a drink?'

Flight Lieutenant Hannett was on his familiar track to the bar. He appeared to be particularly spruced-up; perhaps he was going out somewhere. My hunch was correct. We had barely got to the bar counter when he asked, 'Care for a run into Market Drayton this afternoon?'

'I'm sorry,' I said. 'I'm flying again, in a Handley this time. So if you see one going over, you'll know who's driving it. In view of that,' I added, 'I'll only have a half-pint now. Let me buy one for you. Cheers.'

'Cheerio, old boy. You've certainly started with a bang at Ternhill — two flights in your first day.'

'It won't last,' I put in. 'This afternoon's extra sortie is only because the CI has asked me to demonstrate the Handley to some new fellows tomorrow.'

'Well remember, young Blacking,' Hannett assumed a confidential air, stroking back his moustache with his right forefinger. 'If I see a Handley low flying over Market Drayton I'll take its number.'

'And I'll wave to you,' I retorted.

I left him at the bar, picked up my flying jacket and helmet then made my way slowly back across the grass. It was a beautiful afternoon, but there were mare's-tail wisps of cloud in the west; it looked as though a front was on its way in, and the weather would become cloudy and wet — not unexpectedly, as October's days were numbered. I thought of that line of poetry I'd read — I couldn't remember where:

When drear November gathers in the skies.

Another month gone; another winter about to set in: when would the war end?

'She's all ready, sir,' Sergeant Sheed announced cheerfully when I got to the Handley. There were a couple of AMs there with him, to start the engines.

I had a good look round the aircraft, checking everything I could see; then I climbed up the ladder and squeezed through the tunnel into the cockpit. It was easier to get through with only a flying-jacket on, instead of a Sidcot suit. Once in the right-hand seat, I had that commanding view one got in a Handley, though it was odd to be looking out over an English airfield once again and not to be lined up for an operational flight. I checked the controls carefully, heaving the wheel over to its fullest extent, then back and forth, and exercising the rudder pedals.

'Ready for start, sir?' Sergeant Sheed called up. 'Port engine first.'

The AMs wound away, the Eagle fired, I caught it on the throttle and held the power until it was idling smoothly. The starboard one was more difficult; twice it nearly fired, blue smoke came out of the exhausts, showing that the mixture had got a bit rich. The third time it fired I managed to catch it, much to the relief of the AMs. Sergeant Sheed climbed up the ladder and crawled through the tunnel.

'Mind if one of the AMs comes too, sir, in the gunner's position?' he shouted.

I gave a thumbs-up; what could I say, at that stage? He disappeared down to the ground, pushed one of the AMs up the ladder and into the front cockpit, then climbed up himself. The other AM removed the ladder, put it on the grass at a safe distance and stood ready to see us out.

'Chocks, sir?' yelled Sergeant Sheed.

Again a thumbs-up: all I was being asked to do, I thought, was to fly the thing. The good sergeant seemed to have taken over.

The AM on the ground signalled to me to move forward. I opened-up the throttles and gradually the Handley began to roll. While taxying, I realized that neither of my passengers had helmets or flying clothing; they were going to be cold in the late October air, so I'd better not go too high. I decided to make it a kind of sightseeing tour of the local area, perhaps going over Market Drayton, Audlem and Whitchurch. It seemed strange to be in a Handley without a crew, without bombs or ammunition, and in daylight.

We passed over the control tower: there was someone inside who gave me a green with an Aldis lamp, but the sunlight's brightness made it barely discernible. I taxyed up to the end of the field and ran up each engine in turn: no trouble — Sergeant Sheed and his AMs had seen to that.

I felt very comfortable and confident as I opened-up one engine to bring the Handley round into wind, then both of them to take-off power; I had that feeling of being at one with the machine. I'd given the sky a good look-round, of course, before opening-up. Then as we rushed — or perhaps I should say ambled: the Handley was too sedate an aeroplane to rush — across the grass, I felt this to be an echo of many past flights. Now, however, there was no target to be worried about, no magnetic courses, no lighthouses, no flak, no fighters; only an autumn afternoon in England, as if one were out for a spin in a motor.

Some people had compared the Handley to a comfortable big car; but although the controls were slow to react, I found on this sortie that they responded beautifully as we banked over the Shropshire towns, Sergeant Sheed and the AM hanging over the side to look down: it was a real joy ride. When we got to Whitchurch I did a gentle circle around it, at about 2,000 feet, and kept the Handley in the turn until we were on a south-easterly heading which would take us back to Ternhill.

As we turned I glanced towards the Welsh hills and saw that the clouds over them had thickened and darkened: it looked as though Wales was going to send some of its rain over England, and I could imagine the good citizens of Whitchurch scurrying home under their umbrellas that evening. Eastward, though, the land was still bright (to misquote Mr Clough's poem): late afternoon sunshine illuminated the Shropshire landscape as we headed back to the airfield.

Sergeant Sheed, sitting next to me, seemed highly delighted by his experience; as for the AM, his head was everywhere, as he looked ahead and to the port and starboard sides. With a little training he would have made a good gunner.

What could be more pleasant then flying over a still-green England before winter set in, over an England still untouched after more than four years of war? Looking down on the patchwork of fields and villages, they seemed to have been undisturbed for centuries, though no doubt every family living and working there had been affected in some way or other by the Great War.

Looking down again, in the midst of these philosophical musings, I began to realize that the landscape below was taking on an unfamiliar appearance: I had missed Ternhill and gone too far south. In other words, I was lost. I would have given a lot at that moment to have had Harrison sitting beside me — I realized how much I had come to rely on him.

There were only two things to be done: one was to stay calm; the other, to turn northwards and hope to see some familiar landmark in the Ternhill area, or the railway line going to it. Sergeant Sheed grinned cheerily as I put the Handley into a left-hand bank; he was clearly enjoying his experience, while just as clearly not aware of how I felt at that moment. I would look pretty foolish if, on only my second sortie from Ternhill and the first one out of sight of the airfield, I got lost. I steadied the aircraft on to a northerly course and looked down on the starboard side: I remembered that the railway line ran northwards to Ternhill and hoped to be able to catch sight of it.

Instead I spotted, at about our altitude, a Fee heading in the same direction as ourselves. Perhaps it was one of those belonging to No 13 TDS — maybe even the one I'd flown earlier. This was the first time I'd ever seen a Fee in the air — always the best way to view an aeroplane, in its proper environment — so it was the first opportunity I'd had of observing one of its curious characteristics (apart from its box-girder type of rear fuselage): the way its long undercarriage legs hung down to their full extent. I could thus appreciate how much 'give' there was in them when one landed and they took the shock, making that familiar rumbling noise as they telescoped upwards.

I was contemplating this Fee (which we were gradually overhauling) with some fascination when Sergeant Sheed tapped me on the shoulder and pointing excitedly, yelled, 'Ternhill, sir!'

I pulled the Handley over to port, away from the Fee, and then into a starboard bank so that I could look down. Sure enough, there was the airfield and its buildings, a welcome sight. I gave the good sergeant a thumbs-up sign and did my best to assume a nonchalant air, as if I'd never felt lost. It wouldn't do for an experienced bomber squadron pilot (admittedly without a navigator) to have to admit that he'd been guided home on a local daylight cross-country flight by a groundcrew sergeant. I decided to swallow my pride and gratefully accept the value of another pair of eyes in the cockpit.

I swung the Handley into a port turn again (the AM in the front cockpit would be getting value for his money, I thought) and went into a wide circuit round the field and camp area to look out for any other aircraft. Where was that Fee? It was always difficult to pick out a machine at low level against a green landscape. Perhaps he wasn't one of ours after all. Ah, there he was, about 500 feet below us now, turning in on his final approach.

I decided, in order to keep the airfield and any other machines in view, to do a right-hand circuit — so again changing the direction of our turn. (The AM would now either be feeling quite sick, or still enjoying his flight.) I suddenly realized that it had been a long time since I'd done a daylight landing in a Handley, so I concentrated hard on getting my angle of glide correct, and as we whistled over the airfield boundary I only needed to give a trickle of throttles before pulling them back and using both hands on the wheel. We floated for a bit, as there was hardly any wind, then the wheels and tailskid seemed to touch together and we rumbled bumpily over the grass as the Handley lost speed.

Sergeant Sheed pointed again, this time towards the dispersal. I looked round to see if any other aircraft was taxying or taking off, but all seemed clear so I opened-up the Eagles and we moved slowly across to our parking point. When I switched them off Sergeant Sheed said, 'Thank you, sir,' and disappeared through the tunnel. I heard him say, 'Come on, lad,' to the bemused AM, who disappeared from the front cockpit, and was left with the sound of the engines crackling as the hot metal of the exhausts cooled, and with my own thoughts. It had been a pleasant flight, despite nearly getting lost, and I was ready to demonstrate the Handley on the following day.

I went down the ladder and said, 'Thank you, sergeant. In the morning I'm due to be doing a demonstration flight, so perhaps I could take this machine.'

'Yes, sir, she'll be ready.'

As I walked back to the Mess I noticed that the cloud had increased, though it was still high. There was a bright fire burning in the ante-room. No one was about and I picked up a copy of the *Illustrated London News:* its leading article on the Western Front situation indicated that the Allied leaders were discussing Armistice proposals. If the RAF were to use V/1500s to bomb Berlin in the final efforts to defeat the Germans, then those of us posted to fly them would need to start training soon, otherwise it would be too late. However, any day now my posting might come through. Meanwhile, I'd better make the best of things at Ternhill.

Tea was brought in while I was still glancing through the magazines: bread and butter, with jam in large tins. I enjoyed it after my day's flying, which had seemed to cleanse and refresh me. I was ready now to make a further contribution to the war effort. But there was nothing more to do now until the morning. I knew Hannett wouldn't be back until late from Market Drayton, so I went along to my room and threw myself on the bed.

When I awoke it was quite dark and I became aware of flurries of wind, a whistling round the eaves, and of rain pattering against the windows. The weather had changed, as I thought it would; a frontal system, of which I'd seen signs in the afternoon sky, had moved in from the direction of Wales. I lay there for a while, wondering what the time was and what to do. I felt I was living in a kind of timeless zone, but reality re-asserted itself and I discovered from my watch that it was seven o'clock — time to smarten myself up, to go and have a drink and get some dinner.

When I got into the bar it had only one occupant: Captain Chamier, who was sipping a whisky and soda.

'Evening, Blacking,' he said. 'Have a drink? How did it go this afternoon?'

'All right, sir,' I said. 'It seemed strange to fly a Handley in daylight again.'

'Well, you'll get another opportunity in the morning, provided the weather is suitable. Drink?' he repeated.

'I'll have a Scotch, thank you, sir. What time do you want me to report to meet these officers?'

'Well, they're coming in this evening and will need time to sort themselves out. I think we'll say ten o'clock.'

He took a final swig at his glass.

'Another one, sir?'

'No, thank you. Must be off. Got a spot of local business to transact.' He winked knowingly at the barman. 'Good night, Blacking. See you in the morning.'

In the sudden silence a burning coal dropped in the grate, sending up a puff of smoke and a shower of sparks.

'I'll have another one,' I said to the barman, and took it in to dinner with me.

That night it rained and blew hard. Eventually, lulled by the stormy sounds and gusts of wind, I dropped off. I dreamt that I was in a Fee on a daylight bombing mission, with a grinning Sergeant Sheed in the front cockpit as gunner/observer. There was a whole squadron of us, being buffeted by the wind and rain. Great clouds towered up around us, in mountainous peaks and deep cavernous valleys; then up came the Hun fighters — Pfalzes and Albatrosses — and we formed a defensive circle to fend them off. Sergeant Sheed fired away and I fired too, but we were hit; the engine stopped and smoke began to pour from it. There was nothing for me to do but to spiral down, to hope that the fire — if there was one — would blow itself out and that I could make a successful forced landing. We came down in a meadow near a little wood and started to run for it, but were surrounded by Boche soldiers. Sergeant Sheed was taken off one way and I was taken off another way. I found myself in a small cell where, exhausted by my experiences, I fell asleep until I was awakened by a knocking at the door. I was struggling to remember what the German was for 'come in' — 'eingangen', wasn't it or something like that? — when a voice said:

'Tea, sir, seven o'clock. Still raining. It's a nasty morning, sir.'

As so often after bizarre dreams, it was a salutary shock to come back again to the commonplaces of everyday life.

I felt reassured by the touch and sight of ordinary things as I went along to breakfast; but when I sat down the sense of unreality suddenly returned as I looked across the table. Surely that wasn't — ? No, it couldn't be — or was I back at Ligescourt?

'Tex!' I yelled, springing up and going round to shake his hand. 'Surely it can't be you?'

'Sure is,' said the American with a broad grin, 'and you remember Captain Musgrove,' indicating the officer sitting beside him.

'Of course I do. I made my first flight with you on 207,' I reminded him as we shook hands. 'What brings you here, gentlemen, and how's the squadron? Don't let me interrupt your breakfast — you can tell me when you've finished.'

Were these the two pilots to whom I was to demonstrate a Handley? I wondered as I resumed my seat. If so, perhaps there'd been an administrative misunderstanding or else I'd been the victim of a deliberate leg-pull. Tex and Captain Musgrove were far more experienced on 0/400s than I was. However, I wasn't left long in doubt. Barely had I finished my egg and sausage, had a spoonful of plum jam on my bread and butter, and started on a second cup of tea when they moved over to adjoining chairs.

'When did you get here?' I asked, taking the initiative.

'Late last night,' explained Tex. 'We've been posted to Home Establishment like you, to fly Bloody Paralysers to Berlin. Now, where are they? Not here, I think.'

'No,' I said. 'All we can do here is keep our hand in on 0/400s at night and wait for a posting. What news from Ligescourt? How's Harrison?'

'Still surviving,' Musgrove put in. 'That young Reddaye, who took over your crew, is doing quite well — after they'd been badly shot up on his first operation. We've had several other new pilots since then, which is why we're here.'

'I'm due to meet two pilots who need a Handley demonstration, at ten o'clock in the Chief Instructor's office,' I said. 'If it's yourselves, let's play it straight: Captain Chamier will introduce us to each other.'

'Oh,' said Tex, 'I like that. We'll see you there.'

With a pat on my shoulder they pushed their chairs back and left. Life at Ternhill was going to be a good bit more lively with them there, I thought as I sipped my tea. There were compensations, even in wartime, like these chance renewals of former friendships, compensating for those friendships which were suddenly cut off for ever.

I glanced through the corridor window as I went back to my room to get my cap and greatcoat. The fine autumn weather which we'd had until yesterday had gone; in its place was traditional English rain — the kind that looks as if it's never going to stop. I was standing at the doorway of the Mess contemplating the grey, low could that blanketed Ternhill like a sodden shroud when I heard a cheerful voice behind me.

'Want a lift over, young Blacking?' it said.

Hannett's generous offer couldn't have been more timely.

'No flying today, old boy, I think,' he commented, as we roared across to the HQ building. 'I'll see you in the bar at lunchtime,' he added, as he dropped me off.

Captain Chamier was on the telephone. I could hear his voice as I went along the corridor towards his office. The call seemed to be an important one, long distance and not a very good line.

'Yes, sir,' he was saying. 'Yes. No, three of them so far — two more arrived last night . . . Well, I haven't seen them yet, sir . . . Oh, a change of policy, is it? Yes, well we'll keep them busy here until postings come though. Pardon, sir? Oh, bloody awful, bloody awful . . . No, nothing doing at all at the moment . . . Rightho sir. You'll be back tomorrow then? . . . Rightho, I will. Cheerio, sir.'

He put the 'phone down with a bang. In the ensuing silence I knocked on the half-open door of his office.

'Come in!' he yelled, his mind obviously still preoccupied with the information he'd just received.

'Ah, Blacking, come in. I've just had a message about you and the two other Handley pilots who arrived last night. I'll tell you what it is when they report here — should be here any minute. That was the CO on the 'phone; he's at the Air Ministry. How did you get on yesterday?'

I'd almost forgotten about my Handley flight, what with my dream and the arrival of Captain Musgrove and Tex.

'All right, sir,' I said, non-committally, hardly wishing to admit I nearly got lost, any more than I'd wished to admit my Fee misadventure with the fuel tanks.

'Good,' he said crisply. 'Well, we'll get you on night flying as soon as the weather clears.' An impatient gust blew a pattering of rain across his office window. Even the charts on the wall started to wear a despondent look. 'Whether tonight or not I don't know —'

There was a knock at the door and Captain Musgrove's face appeared round it.

'Ah, come in, gentlemen. Let me introduce you — Captain Musgrove, Lieutenant Beech, this is Second Lieutenant Blacking. He's also here to keep up his 0/400 flying, until posted on to V/1500s. He can give you a Handley demonstration when the weather clears.'

We shook hands gravely, none of us revealing any knowledge of the other.

'In the meantime, gentlemen, Mr Blacking can show you round and help you get settled in. But I have some discouraging news for you. My CO has just been on the telephone and it seems that the V/1500 scheme has been scrapped. You are to stay here until posted back to your squadron. I'm sorry, gentlemen.'

Musgrove and Tex looked at each other. They were too experienced to be surprised at sudden swings and switches in military policy.

'I guess we'll have to make the best of it, sir,' commented Tex. 'The Air Ministry must know what it's doing.'

'Perhaps,' said Captain Chamier, leaning back and tapping a pencil between his finger tips. 'Any questions, gentlemen?'

There were none, and in a second we were back in the corridor, Tex grinning hugely.

'C'mon, Mr Blacking,' he said, 'just you show us around — we're strangers here.'

'I'm a stranger here myself,' I retorted. 'I haven't been here much longer than yourselves, but I can assure you there isn't much to see: an assortment of aircraft, mainly Fees and Handleys, a control tower and some hutted buildings, and there's no point in walking around them in the rain. As an alternative —.' An idea had just struck me. 'Just a moment.'

I went back to the CI's office, knocked on the door and put my head round it. 'Sir, if there's no flying today, is there any reason why we shouldn't go into Market Drayton this morning?'

Captain Chamier looked up from his papers and gave me a quizzical glance, obviously wondering what was behind my request. After a moment he said: 'I don't see why not. There's a tender going down, so you could go with that as you haven't any transport, but you'll have to come back with it, after about an hour.'

Well, it was one way of passing a wet wartime morning in Shropshire, though Tex and Musgrove must have wondered why I was so anxious to buy some stamps. When I got to the counter, however, the nice little bundle of cuddle behind it hardly recognized me — and I wasn't really sorry. She seemed to have changed and I wondered what I'd ever seen in her. Perhaps she'd been spoiled by too much attention. She looked to me rather plump and blonde and ordinary, or perhaps this was by subconscious comparison with Jeanne's sinuous dark charms. At any rate, I bought my stamps in anonymous fashion and hurried out to the street, where Tex and Musgrove were waiting.

'You look as if you'd seen a ghost,' said Tex.

'Maybe he has,' added Musgrove, drily. 'Let us retreat into the White Hart where we can at least drink some coffee and keep out of the rain until the tender takes us back to Ternhill.'

It was still raining when we returned to the station, where the airfield lay under a pall of grey cloud, blanking out any hopes of flying that afternoon. Naturally we gravitated towards the Mess bar, the only antidote in such a situation, a cheerful corner in a world of gloom, with a fire blazing in the grate.

'Now tell me about the squadron,' I said when I'd set them up with drinks.

'Much the same,' observed Musgrove. 'We're still hitting the Hun's supplies and damaging his morale.'

'There's quite some talk of an Armistice, though,' put in Tex. 'Everywhere the Boche seems to be in retreat.'

'Could it all be over before Christmas?' I asked.

'I guess it could,' Tex opined. 'Things are pretty bad on the Hun's home front. If he's pushed sufficiently by the Allies in the West he'll collapse altogether.'

For some reason a shiver ran down my spine. Here I was in good company, hearing cheerful news, looking at the bright flames in the fireplace, but I couldn't help feeling chill.

'I think,' I said. 'I'll have a scotch — or rum. I don't usually drink spirits at lunchtime, but for some reason I'm cold. I need warming up.'

'I'll get it,' put in Musgrove. He ordered me a large rum and two more beers for Tex and himself. 'Maybe you've got a chill — the English autumn doesn't agree with you any more. Here, drink this.'

He put the rum into my hand and I took a swig of it. The fumes made me shiver, but the liquid gave me a comforting glow inside, at least temporarily. I was beginning to feel quite wretched. It seemed as though there were icy fingers on my spine. I took a second swig of my rum, but by now I'd lost interest in Musgrove and Tex and indeed in the cheerful surroundings of the Mess bar; all I wanted to do was to go to my room and get into bed.

I excused myself and left them with as much dignity as I could muster. I hoped no-one would see me in the corridor, which seemed to me like part of a ship, heaving slightly and with the rain lashing the windows.

It's surprising how quickly, when necessary, one can get undressed and into bed — though I took care to leave my clothes tidy, in case anyone should come in to see me. Although the bedclothes were cold at first, it was comforting to wrap them round me and just lie there in the silence. I soon felt very hot, and had pains in my back and head; then, perhaps under the influence of the rum, I dozed off into a fuzzy kind of sleep. As I drifted away, objects in the room started to come nearer and then receded; even the walls seemed to contract and then expand. I was in a dream world, one where everything I'd known and experienced was mixed up in a totally bizarre manner — my schooldays, the Western front, bombing operations, the Air Ministry: I was in an open cockpit with the slipstream streaming past and in the other seat was Jeanne, with a large box camera, taking photographs. Suddenly a German fighter appeared alongside us, the pilot wearing a *picklehaube* and a monocle. He looked very like Kaiser Wilhelm II and gave us a mock salute with his fingers. He was going to shoot us down and I pulled back on the wheel to escape his gaze: we must get above him, fly slower than he, get behind him. We seemed to be hanging in space, rocking from side to side, occasionally banking and turning, then we came to earth with a bump and everything was quiet. I seemed to be by myself, lying on the ground; everything around was white — perhaps it had been snowing. The Great War had gone into another winter. But I felt I couldn't care any more: everything was unutterably peaceful.

Then I heard voices. Were they English or German? Had I come down on the wrong side of the lines? Gradually I began to distinguish what they were saying.

'I think he's over the worst now,' one of them said. 'His temperature's back to normal — the fever's gone.'

The other, a female one, went on, 'His delirium's gone, too. What's to be done with him, doctor?'

'Usual thing,' the man's voice said. 'Keep him there, give him some nourishment when he can take it — liquid at first.'

The voices moved on and I gradually became aware of a world of whiteness, a strong antiseptic smell, a much larger room than mine in the Mess. Where was I? The effort to think was too great and I closed my eyes again. I drifted off into a dream in which I seemed to be floating above fleecy white clouds, a vast cumulo-stratus acreage. Then I sank through them, into the darkness beneath. After a long time I heard a woman's voice. She seemed to be repeating herself, as if calling me:

'Mr Blacking. Mr Blacking. Would you like something to drink?'

I opened my eyes and saw a face, surrounded by whiteness. Only a nurse could look as white and starched as that. She also smelt peculiarly hygienic. As she came into focus I said, surprised at the sound of my own voice, which I didn't seem to have used for a long time:

'Where am I?'

'You're in Prees Heath Military Hospital,' she said. 'You've had 'flu — Spanish 'flu. There's been a bad epidemic. Now, would you like a drink?'

She put up to my lips one of those special hospital cups, covered and with a spout on it, so that nothing is spilled on the bedclothes. The liquid tasted lemony; it was thin, cold and refreshing. I recalled that when someone had last said to me, 'Would you like a drink?' I'd had rum. How long ago was that, and how did I get to this hospital?

'What day is it?' I asked, remembering not to say, 'What time is it?' Time seemed quite irrelevant just now.

'It's November 5th,' the nurse said.

'Good lord,' I countered, with a feeble attempt at humour, 'We ought to be letting off some fireworks then.'

She smiled wanly and laid a cool hand on my forehead. 'Not today — perhaps next year. You'd better rest now.'

I must say I didn't feel capable of doing anything else: I just felt incredibly weak. But I tried to think of what had happened during those lost days. The last dates I remembered were about the end of October or beginning of November, when Tex and Captain Musgrove had come to Ternhill. That's right: I'd left them and gone to bed. Someone must have found me in my room.

I looked up: there was a high ceiling. I looked to the left and then to the right, letting my eyes do the work as I just couldn't be bothered to move my head. There was a bed on either side of me.

That effort was enough for the time being and I closed my eyes again, trying to assess the situation, but I found that making a mental effort was just as hard as making a physical one so I drifted off into an effortless semi-conscious state.

12
Armistice Day

When I came out of that state — it might have been minutes, or even hours, later, I just couldn't tell — I looked with more consciousness to the bed on my right. As I did so, a pair of eyes met mine. They seemed familiar.

'Tex,' I said unbelievingly. 'What are you doing here?' This was the first proper, ordered, logical sentence I'd uttered for a long time.

'I guess the same as you,' was the muffled reply. ''Flu.'

All at once life took on a new and better significance and regained some meaning. At least I wasn't alone in this hospital; I had a friend beside me, and each of us would spur the other on in recovery.

'Where's Musgrove?' I asked, for if Tex and I had both been affected, he could hardly have escaped. Maybe they brought it over with them from France and I was the first to succumb.

'I don't know,' said Tex, 'but no doubt we'll see him again soon, either as a patient or a visitor. This thing strikes so quickly, you go out like a light. How ya feeling?'

'Pretty weak,' I confessed. 'I don't think I'll be flying tonight.'

With that feeble joke I lapsed into sleep again, and when I awoke it was dark. Dimmed lights were burning in the ward, and occasionally the shape of a nurse flitted past. I felt I just wanted to let life flow past me, like that.

'How are you feeling now?' I saw a white coat, and a nurse's starched apron and cap: I was being visited by the MO.

'Better, thank you,' I muttered. What else could I say? My lips felt dry and my voice sounded cracked.

'Good,' said the doctor briskly. 'We'll soon have you up and about again. It's just a question of building up your strength.'

He passed on the next bed and I looked around. Tex was sitting up.

'Hiya,' he said briefly. 'You slept like the Sleeping Beauty. It ought to have done you good.'

Things had begun to come into focus again but I didn't feel like getting up and dashing around. I was quite content to let the world go on without me.

Instead it came to see me. I became aware of a figure in a dressing-gown standing by my bed.

'Hello, young Blacking,' it said. 'How are you now?'

Captain Musgrove's face looked down at mine. He was pale and unshaven, not at all like the smart officer we knew.

'You'd better hurry up and recover if you're going to get back to the squadron,' he went on. 'There's a lot of talk now about an Armistice being signed. The Boche armies are in retreat.'

I groaned. 'I'll do my best,' I said weakly. 'I think I've only just come round.'

'He's on the mend,' Tex's voice came from the next bed. 'Just you wait: the next time that pretty nurse comes by he'll start leaping about the ward, offering to lend a hand.'

'You let me know when you're going,' I retorted, 'I'll be ready to come with you,' expressing a determination I didn't really feel.

But when daylight came again I felt more myelf, was able to sit up and take some nourishment, then to get up and take some unsteady steps along the ward. When I was able to shave myself, I felt that I had broken through a psychological barrier and was on the road to recovery, though I still wondered when my strength was going to come back.

Musgrove was our bearer of the latest news about the peace negotiations, and one afternoon he came in to the ward simply bursting to tell us something, unusually animated for such a usually dour man.

He sat down on Tex's bed and looked at us. 'I hear an armistice is being signed tomorrow.'

'That'll be a big date in world history,' observed Tex.

'What's today?'

'November 10th,' said Musgrove, and went on, 'There's bound to be a huge celebration in London. Why don't we . . . ?'

Tex and I looked at each other; we were all thinking the same thought.

'Right,' said Musgrove. 'I'll find our uniforms and we'll plan a dawn take-off. Make it look as if you're going out of the ward just to answer the call of nature.'

I couldn't sleep at all that night, partly because I couldn't stop thinking about our impending adventure, partly because I was wondering how I would get on in the outside world after so long in a hospital bed. But on balance the exciting thought of going to London proved stronger than my misgivings.

It was still quite dark. The only light in the ward was at the far end, where the night-duty nurse sat at her desk. There were half lights in the corridor, giving an eerie, cold glow.

'Well, what about it?' I heard Tex ask me, *sotto voce*, from the next bed.

Now it came to it, I didn't really feel too good — I think I still had a temperature — but the game was worth the candle. This was an opportunity not to be missed, so I plucked up my courage:

'Right,' I said. He must have known I was fully awake. 'You go first.'

We'd arranged our clothes and shoes in our lockers. Tex deftly extracted his own, concealing them as best he could against his pyjamas, and slipped noiselessly out of the ward.

In a few moments I followed the same procedure, though not with quite the same success: I dropped one of my shoes. For a second or so I froze, then I half got back into bed and made out that I'd just been looking for a handkerchief in my locker. If the night nurse came along to see if I was all right, the game would be up. Two officers in adjoining beds creeping out of the ward at the same time would be too much of a coincidence.

But she didn't get up, and obviously suspected nothing. Perhaps, hopefully, she had dozed off for a bit. I gathered my things together, successfully this time, and crept out like a practised cat burglar.

Tex was waiting in the corridor. 'Come on,' he whispered urgently. 'I thought you were never coming.'

We made our way to one of the bathrooms, had a quick sluice and put our clothes on. I was struggling with one of my socks, sitting on the edge of the bath, when a figure darkened the doorway: it was Musgrove, with our uniforms, having timed his arrival with military precision. I must say that my admiration for this dour and rather saturnine chap, whom I'd never had much to do with on the squadron, went up by about two hundred per cent at that moment.

'Good morning, gentlemen,' he said softly, as if we were about to be briefed at Ligescourt. 'Here are your uniforms. Get into them and let's be off.'

I must say it felt funny, putting mine on again. It seemed several sizes too large: I'd probably been a bit dehydrated, and shrunk, during my time in bed. But I made myself look as presentable as possible.

Musgrove was at the doorway, peering up and down the long corridor: he'd obviously planned the whole operation with care and proved himself an ideal leader. 'Make sure the coast is clear,' he whispered, 'then head for the entrance one at a time. If you see anyone, appear to be duty-bound somewhere: don't panic.

With a confirmatory nod, he'd gone. Tex followed and a second or so later I went too. There was no-one about, and I could hear snores and the occasional groan as I passed the entrances to the wards. I shut the entrance door as quietly as I could behind me and found Musgrove and Tex outside. The former led the way round the side of the hospital to a parked staff car, which he had somehow managed to 'borrow' — another tribute to his organizing genius.

He produced an ignition key and started up, the engine making a great roar, amplified by the high brick walls, which shattered the silence. He didn't waste any time warming-up, simply let off the hand-brake and pressed on the accelerator pedal. The engine responded and we were away, into the drive heading for the gates and the Shropshire lanes. I have never admired a Grand Prix driver more, though I felt sure everyone in the hospital must have heard us and couldn't help looking back nervously to see whether we were being pursued.

But there was no pursuit. In any case we were patients, not prisoners, and feelings of anxiety were quickly succeeded by ones of exhilaration. We realized, as Tex put it, that this was going to be 'one of the great days in the world's history', and we wanted to be as close to the centre of things as possible. After all, what had we to lose? If the war ended today we would soon be demobilized, and how much we had to gain!

We were heading north to Whitchurch in the cold early morning air. Musgrove had carefully worked out his route, but the only thing he couldn't really plan for was the time of a train from there; they were bound to be sparse at that time of day, and when we'd located the station and parked the car we found the shutters down in the booking office.

However, it wasn't long before the clerk appeared, on his bicycle. He was somewhat startled to find so many early morning customers, but the fact that they were young Air Force officers moved him not at all. He opened up with the steady routine derived from years of railway experience, and it was only with difficulty that Musgrove elucidated from him — as if it were a secret not really to be disclosed — that there would be a down train along shortly. It would stop at all stations and if we wanted to go to London Paddington we would have to change at Shrewsbury.

It was an important-sounding little train — only two carriages — that eventually puffed in, pulled by a tank engine, after we had paced up and down the platform numberless times to keep ourselves warm, had admired the local scenery *ad nauseam* and gazed up and down the lines.

'Tha she blows,' yelled Tex when the first puff of smoke appeared, gradually materializing as a Great Western train. Nobody got off; we were the only passengers to get aboard. The guard waved his green flag and with a belch of steam and several jerks we were off.

'We've done it,' said Musgrove triumphantly as we arranged ourselves in the corners of a compartment, 'and damn the consequences.'

'Hear, hear!' I added. 'It's thanks to you we've got away and it's up to us to make the most of if.'

We lapsed into silence, gazing out on the passing countryside. Prees, Wem, Yorton, Hadnall; it seemed to take ages to reach Shrewsbury. We could hardly believe that we'd got there until we found ourselves ensconced in a main line train. Now our adventure would really begin.

With the warmth of the compartment, our early start after a short night's sleep and the regular dit-dit-dit-dah of the train — like a kind of metal Morse code — it wasn't long before I dropped off, and I fancy the others did too.

Tex woke us up. 'Paddington!' he yelled, and I think he was all for making a bee-line for Buckingham Palace there and then; but Musgrove had another, wiser idea.

'Breakfast,' he said firmly, 'after a good wash and brush-up.'

There's nothing like breakfast, as a meal, when it's been got for you and you've time to enjoy it. We didn't stint ourselves: after all, we had to fuel ourselves for the day's operations; goodness knew when we would have time to refuel. So, washed and refreshed, we availed ourselves of the menu at the Great Western Station Hotel: porridge, bacon, egg, sausage and tomato; toast and marmalade, and tea. Then, like giants refreshed, we stepped out to find a cab which would take us to the centre of the day's activities.

It wasn't easy, but eventually one rattled along with its flag up.

'Buckingham Palace,' said Musgrove in his most important-sounding tones.

''Ere, guv,' responded the driver, 'where 'ave you come from — the Moon? You can't get near the bleedin' Palace. Don't you know what today is? It's the end of the war.'

'We know that, driver. Just take us as far as you can,' Musgrove retorted. 'We'll have to walk from there — wherever it is.'

The driver's reply was muffled, fortunately, behind his glass screen and we set off into the swirling London traffic, into the Bayswater Road, then down Park Lane, its noble houses enjoying their superb view over the green acres of Hyde Park, their façades seeming unchanged and impregnable whatever catastrophes — like the Great War just ended — overwhelmed the country.

Swinging right at the end of the lane, then left into Constitution Hill, the driver got as far as he could along it, but the crowds had thickened up so much as we reached the Palace that he was forced to slow down to a walking pace and finally came to a halt.

'Sorry, guv,' he announced through his speaking tube, 'this is as far as we'll get. It's jam-packed down to the Strand.'

'All right,' said Musgrove as we got out. 'We'll have to walk, then. Thanks, cabbie.'

He paid the driver and we set off, the dank trees of Green Park on our left. It was a misty November morning and we were aware of only one sound: the shuffling of thousands of feet, like a great army marching towards the Palace.

Suddenly, above it all, we heard the distant chimes of Big Ben and counted out the ponderous strokes.

'Eleven o'clock,' said Tex, as if to himself. 'I wonder whether the fighting's stopped?'

By the time we got to the junction of Constitution Hill and the Mall there was hardly room to move at all. A great crowd was pressed against the railings of the Palace, waiting for the King and Queen to appear on the balcony. Many people were waving flags and cheering, some scaled the Queen Victoria monument to get a better view, others climbed up the plane trees; Musgrove had his cap knocked off when a girl flung her arms round him and kissed him; Tex, when the word got round that he was an American, was lifted shoulder-high and cheered.

Suddenly, but only for a moment, a hush fell on the great crowd as five figures appeared on the Palace balcony; then the cheering erupted again in a great, spontaneous burst, like a crowd at a football match when a goal is scored. This was a great, speechless celebration, a popular demonstration at the end of the greatest war in history.

The figures on the balcony looked tiny from where we were: I knew two of them were the King and Queen. The knowledgeable around us — there are always people who seem to know everything — said that the others were Princess Mary, the Duke of Connaught and Princess Patricia. I wouldn't have known. They waved, disappeared from view like puppet figures, re-appeared and waved again, each time to thunderous cheers.

When they'd disappeared for the last time there was a sort of anti-climax. People simply didn't know what to do: some stayed where they were, hoping for another glimpse of the Royal family, others started to move off.

'Let's go to Downing Street,' said Musgrove, almost shouting to make himself heard above the surrounding hubbub. 'We might see the Prime Minister.'

We made our way over to St James's Park, just managing to keep together, so thick was the moving mass of people. Apart from the excitement of the occasion, I was beginning to wish I hadn't come.

In the middle of the park, keeping an eye on Musgrove and Tex, I managed to catch that beautiful view from the bridge over the lake; the white domes and pinnacles of Whitehall to the left — like Milton's lines,

> Towers and battlements it sees
> Bosomed high in tufted trees —

and the majestic mass of Buckingham Palace to the right. Then we made our way through the trees to the corner of Storey's Gate and up the Clive steps, to get into Whitehall by King Charles Street, past the great and gloomy government buildings which had presided over Imperial wars on many a far-flung battle front.

The crowds thickened again. It seemed as though several thousand other people had had the same idea: to see the Prime Minister.

Musgrove had a sudden change of plan. As most people would endeavour to get into Downing Street from the Whitehall side, he argued, why should we not try to get into it from the Horse Guards side? So we back-tracked down the steps and along by the park and made our way into the West end of Downing Street, a rather narrow funnel, and there were railings in the way, but it was worth it. Over the heads of the crowd, and people clinging to lamp-posts and railings, we caught a brief glimpse of a white-haired figure: Lloyd George himself, standing on the steps of Number Ten flanked by two London bobbies who made him look small, acknowledging the cheers and applause with a few sweeping waves and a wide grin. Then he disappeared inside the front door.

'Let's go down to Trafalgar Square,' suggested Tex.

Horse Guards Parade was thronged with people, milling about under the damp November sky. We cut across it towards the Mall, then along it into the square. I was beginning to wish I hadn't come, or rather to wish that we could get back quickly, now that we'd seen all we came to see. That splendid breakfast seemed a long time ago; I felt exhausted, not yet being used to staying on my feet for so long.

However, I kept up with Musgrove and Tex, not wishing to show any lack of enthusiasm. They seemed to be in better fettle than I was. Trafalgar Square was thick with people climbing on the base of Nelson's column, falling in the pools under the fountains, waving flags, riding on Landseer's lions. Somehow, in the crush and confusion, I lost sight of my two companions and with the surge of the crowd got carried out of the square through the narrow funnel of Duncannon Street, past St Martin-in-the-Fields and into the Strand.

Although there were hundreds of people milling around and they were all very cheerful, shouting and slapping each other on the back, I suddenly felt very much alone and rather frightened. My temperature seemed to have come back and weakness and exhaustion overcame me. I managed to lean up against a wall outside Charing Cross Station, then for some reason it started to move, I was looking at it from a horizontal position and everything was green and white. I felt myself swinging round a corner and heard low voices, then everything went quiet and still.

'Been celebrating in the Strand, 'ad 'e?' I heard one voice say. 'Lucky for him that ambulance picked him up.'

'All we can do is leave 'im for a while, till 'e sobers up,' another voice said.

They went away and I lay still, glad to be quiet and warm and comfortable. But where was I? The last thing I remembered was going into the Strand from Trafalgar Square. I certainly wasn't celebrating — we'd had nothing since breakfast.

We? Where were Musgrove and Tex? I raised my head, but all I could see was a door and white walls. There may have been a window behind me, but I couldn't make the effort to look. There were certainly no other beds.

It could have been hours later when a figure materialized and looked at me. I could see a white coat and a stethoscope and a voice said, 'How do you feel now?'

'All right,' I said. 'Where am I?'

'This is Millbank Military Hospital,' the voice continued. 'You were picked up in the Strand and an ambulance brought you here. Had you been celebrating too much?'

'No, not at all,' I replied weakly. 'We'd come down from Ternhill for the day — three of us. But we'd all had 'flu. I must have passed out.'

A thermometer was pushed into my mouth and I lay still. The white-coated figure appeared to be looking out of the window. 'Right,' he said, after removing the thermometer and studying it. 'You've had a recurrence of 'flu and your temperature is up again, but as soon as you're fit to travel you must return to your unit.'

With that he was gone, and I was left to consider my situation. There was bound to be a row when I got back to Ternhill. Perhaps Musgrove and Tex had already returned there; if so, they would explain things and my return would pass unnoticed. In any case, demobilization would be in the air. I pondered these things as I lay in my bed at the Millbank Military Hospital, with a guilty feeling that I was causing them unnecessary trouble. However, the experience had been worth it, just to be in London to see the official ending of the Great War.

A young Army corporal, a pleasant chap — a clerk — came to see me to take down details of name, rank, number and unit for me to be documented for RTU (return to unit). No use telling him that I was waiting to fly V/1500s. He'd never heard of them anyway, and I never would fly them now. The war was over now and Berlin would never be bombed.

I reflected on the implications of this as my temperature returned to normal and I gradually felt better and stronger. I had to get back to Ternhill. Would I be demobilized from there or would I have to return to the squadron? I would have to find myself a job, like thousands of other young officers. What would I do? Perhaps I would try banking; I knew there were opportunities abroad — they would give me a chance to see more of the world.

An Army doctor came along. To me he looked quite an elderly chap, though he probably wasn't more than thirty.

'How do you feel now, Mr Blacking?' he said in a kindly way. By then I'd had two nights' rest and felt stronger. 'Your temperature's back to normal,' went on the MO.

'Do you feel strong enough to make your way back to your unit? We need these beds — there are still casualties coming back from the Western Front. They're clearing out the field hospitals there.'

These were my marching orders from Millbank, and I realized that the best contribution I could make to the British war effort at that time was to get back to Ternhill, so I did not demur. One of the nurses brought my uniform and put up the screens round the bed. I dressed carefully: I was probably in better shape now, after this extra rest and rehabilitation, than I had been when we crept out of Prees Heath Hospital on our jaunt to London. The 'flu was behind me now. When I was ready I pulled the screen aside and sat on the bed, not knowing quite what to do; I wasn't familiar with the geography of the hospital.

Eventually the corporal clerk reappeared. 'Will you come to the office, sir, and collect your papers,' he said, half as a question, half as an instruction. 'Please follow me.'

I'd never have found my own way. All the corridors looked just the same to me — white, with green stripes, clinical and endless, including some stairs. I realized I must have been in a ward on the second floor. The corporal led me into a ground-floor office, where he handed me a travel order and a rail warrant, asking me to sign for them. What a neat, efficient, tidy, orderly clerk he was, I thought. No army could really do without people like him.

'It happens that we've got a transport going to Paddington Station to pick up some walking wounded,' he said, 'so if you'll come this way, sir.'

I was speechless with admiration at his efficiency and could only manage a 'Thank you, corporal,' as I got aboard and we swung out into the London streets. How noisy they sounded after the unmechanized peace of the hospital! Round we went into Horseferry Road and Victoria Street, up Grosvenor Place, along by the high wall that protects the Buckingham Palace gardens, round Hyde Park Corner, where our Armistice Day adventures seemed to have begun, and up Park Lane then into the Edgware Road.

When I parted from the genial civilian driver at the great smoky greenhouse of Paddington Station, I felt I'd lost a friend, albeit a temporary one. I was now on my own for the long, lonely journey back to the West Midlands, no charming female companionship this time, no pals to lead me astray.

But in the event, as so often happens in life, things turned out rather better than I had expected. For the first part of my journey I ruminated on the passing countryside, watching the white smoke from the engine as it was wafted past the window, rising and falling over the fields and farms. Then I dozed off in my corner into a sleep which probably did me good; it was deep and dreamless.

I was awakened, fortunately, by a banging of doors. Not realizing where I was for a moment, my instincts warned me and I looked out of the window: Wellington, the sign said, through a cloud of steam which hissed up from beneath the carriage — the station where I had to change.

In a second I was through the door and on the platform. It is extraordinary how fast the human body moves in an emergency: every mental attribute, every muscle is spontaneously co-ordinated by some miraculous process.

The problem was now to find out which platform the Ternhill train left from, and I was lucky to encounter a friendly porter, who directed me. There it was, three carriages only, drawn by a tank engine. I found a first-class compartment in the middle and jumped in.

'Hello,' a voice said from the corner, behind a newspaper. 'Where have you been, stranger?'

'Hello, Hannett,' I responded, surprised and glad to see a friendly face.

'Well, I've been to London to see the Queen.'

'Really.' There was a touch of cynicism in his tone. 'Well, you'll have to explain that to the CO; the others did. There was a bit of a to-do when you three decamped from the hospital. What Musgrove and Beech couldn't explain was what had happened to you, when you didn't come back with them. Where have you been? Went off with some popsy you met in the Strand, eh, I'll be bound.'

'No,' I said patiently, as our train jerked and puffed out of yet another local station on its way to Ternhill. 'I've been in hospital.'

'In hospital? Again? How did you get there?'

'I don't know,' I said lamely. 'I lost the others in Trafalgar Square, in the crush. The next thing I knew I was being carried along this hospital corridor, on a stretcher.'

'What was wrong with you? Drunk again, eh, Blacking?' He gave me a malicious leer, as if enjoying this inquisition, determined to find the real truth.

'Not at all,' I retorted. 'We hadn't had a drink. Recurrence of 'flu, I think, but I'm better now.'

He seemed satisfied, so I changed the subject. 'How are things at Ternhill?'

'Well, the ending of the war has changed everything. Demobilization is now the order of the day: it's all most people think about.'

'Any flying?' I asked.

'Not in an organized sense; mainly officers putting in a few hours weekly to qualify for their flying pay. Anyway, you'll see for yourself — here we are.'

There was no difficulty about getting transport to the airfield; Hannett had his car at the station.

'I think you'd better report to the CO straightaway,' he advised when we arrived there.

Major Villiers listened to my story with patient courtesy. Then he said: 'Mr Blacking, as I told your companions in this escapade, you had no business to abscond from the hospital — whatever the temptation to do so. However, your adventure's over and you yourself paid for it by landing yourself in hospital; fortunately the right place to recover from your 'flu.

'Your colleagues were ordered to report back to their squadron, but I've had no instructions about you, so you will remain here. We're now a demobilization centre, which means you may end your service here. Don't let me down in your last weeks in the RAF.'

'No, sir; thank you.' I saluted and retreated. The Major had been very reasonable.

Fortunately I was able to return to the room I'd had in the Mess, because accommodation was at a premium those days. Ternhill had a shifting population, with officers up to the rank of major drifting in. I wondered what had happened to Musgrove and Tex, and wished I could have gone back to the squadron, to be demobilized from there.

Instead, we were in a never-never land, between the Service and civilian life. There was little organized flying, but there was organized physical training, all officers being required to keep fit. The senior officers in particular resented the sessions, and it wasn't uncommon to see majors disappearing behind the hangars in order to avoid the PT instructors, good fellows though these were. I thought the fit young corporals admirable, but they had an uphill task.

One day, when I was least expecting it, I was called in to see the station adjutant, a thin-faced fellow, Captain Rocke, whom I'd got to know in the Mess, but who was one of those characters for whom social and official acquaintanceships just didn't mix.

'Ah, Mr Blacking,' he said in bank manager-like tones, when I entered his office.

'Good morning, Rocky,' I responded cheerfully. 'Good news or bad? Have I been cashiered?'

He winced, and went on in an icy manner. 'I have your demobilization papers here. Would you please read them and sign where necessary?'

So this was it: a formal and precise termination of my engagement. In return for my signature, I was free to go, out of the world of the squadron, the 0/400s, the bombs, the lighthouses, the flaming onions, the Hun night fighters, the ack-ack, Harrison and Brinden, Musgrove and Tex, and all the other fellows on the squadron, and the joys and terrors of flying. I was to return to the assistance of His Majesty should any of his Dominions or Colonies be threatened, but in the immediate aftermath of the huge blood-letting of the Great War, that contingency seemed unlikely for some years to come. In order to fulfil this heroic obligation (should it ever arise) I was placed in a Reserve class. The pallid Captain Rocke handed me my copy of the paper and slipped another copy into his filing tray with a practised hand.

'Goodbye Mr Blacking,' he said formally. 'Thank you for your service. Good luck.'

'Cheerio, Rocky,' I retorted. 'See you in the next war.'

He didn't look up as I went out of his office. I thought I'd better pay a courtesy call on the CO to say farewell.

'Come in!' he barked when I knocked on his door. Then, in kinder tones: 'Oh, it's you, Blacking. Not in trouble again, I hope?'

'No, sir. I've just had my demob papers. I came to say goodbye.'

'Well, you can go to London any time you like now,' said Major Villiers, 'and you won't need to come back here to explain why you went. What are you going to do?'

'There's a possible opening in banking — abroad.'

His eyebrows lifted.

'Abroad? Where?'

'Hong Kong,' I said.

'Hong Kong, eh? I know it well from pre-war days, You'll enjoy the experience.'

'I hope so, sir.'

'Well, good luck, Blacking. I'm sure you'll remember your last days in the RAF, and the earlier ones, on operations. A pity about the V/1500s.'

'Yes, sir. Apparently they weren't needed.'

'Apparently not. Goodbye, Mr Blacking.'

I saluted and made my exit.

There was no fanfare — just a farewell, as for hundreds of other young officers like myself. In the corridor I almost bumped into the ubiquitous Hannett. He was hurrying along to see the CO.

'Stand by, old boy,' he said as he passed. 'You off now? I can give you a lift to the station.'

I nodded. 'Thanks — see you in the Mess then. My bag's there.'

As we drove away from the airfield, a strong north-westerly wind sent dark, angry-looking clouds scurrying across the sky: just as if the heavens were reflecting the post-Armistice state of Europe, there seemed no stability or certainty, only darkness and a restless confusion.

On the station platform Hannett grasped my hand. 'Can't wait, old boy, must get back — things to attend to. Good luck and God bless.'

'Cheerio, Hannett, you've been a really good friend to me here. Good luck to you too.'

As he roared off I felt an extreme sense of loneliness. The train would take me to London; it had fixed lines on which to travel. What about my life after that, what lines would it follow, after a regulated life in the RFC/RAF?

The train puffed in and I climbed aboard, looking back through the carriage window for a last glance at the Fees and 0/400s, the hangars, the huts and the green grass of the airfield. As the engine pulled us out I lost the view in the steam and smoke that blew across. My view of the world of military flying had been blanked out for ever.

Epilogue 1

Early in February 1919, just before I was (as they said) 'transferred to the unemployed list', I was making my way down to Crystal Palace for demobilization and had got permission to travel via Salisbury in order to visit my parents who were temporarily there. It was a bright, sunny winter's day and I was enjoying my last few hours of being an officer.

Just as we were pulling into Salisbury station I spotted some Handleys in an airfield on the other side of the tracks. They were olive-green, and as we went slowly over the points I looked at the markings on their fuselages: these were, on either side of the RAF roundel, A 1, B 1, etc. — 207 Squadron's markings! I couldn't wait to get out of that train, and after standing some time at the station entrance (where I found it was colder than it had looked through the carriage window), got a cab and told the driver where I wanted to go. He, being a local man, had no difficulty in identifying the airfield where 'the big bombers' were (where had I heard that phrase before?), and deposited me at the gate.

There was a sentry on duty, but when I identified myself as a former member of No 207 Squadron he allowed me through, directing me to 'the office' — a wooden hut. I knocked on the door and asked for Captain Bishop. It would be good to see his cheerful face again If not, was Flight Sergeant Arnett there?

It seemed that neither were, and no-one knew them. The Second Lieutenant who appeared in answer to my enquiry looked very young (though he can't have been much younger than I was) and explained that 207 was now in the Army of Occupation, but was being reduced to cadre basis. Its aircraft had either been handed over to No 100 Squadron or flown back here.

'May I look around them?' I asked. 'I did some of my raids in these aircraft.'

'Certainly,' said the young officer. 'You won't find them here much longer — they're going to be sold for scrap and broken up.'

Like war-weary veterans the 0/400s stood disconsolately around. They had fought their last battles, made their last flights and now were back on English soil for destruction. I suddenly spotted B2, the first aircraft I'd flown on the squadron, and went up to look at her again. She was a bare hulk, no guns, no bombs, her fabric tattered; just flyable, I supposed.

I thought of George Harrison and of Sergeant Pilcher, with whom I'd shared so many experiences, both heroic and terrifying. All around was silence. A bit of canvas flapped in the breeze; a skylark rose up and up into the peaceful Wiltshire sky. I thought of all the squadron's pilots, observers and gunners who had flown these aircraft on operations, and of the engineer officers and AMs who had maintained them. For a while on the Western Front, 207 had been a close-knit unit with a common purpose. Now there was no war, its swords were being turned into ploughshares and its personnel into civilians.

That reminded me: I had a call to make in Salisbury, then I too was to be turned back into a civilian. It had begun to get chilly. I pulled up my collar and grasped my bag; then I thanked the young officer and returned the sentry's salute as I went through the gate.

Do inanimate things like aircraft have any memories of events in which they took part, I wondered as I strode along. Probably not, but we remembered them — a part of our lives we would never forget.

Epilogue 2

I was having breakfast in my flat one sunny morning in Hong Kong when a buff envelope arrived in the morning's post: it contained a letter from the Air Ministry offering me a permanent commission in the RAF.

From outside I could hear the early-morning bustle of the traffic of Kowloon; from inside I could just see the sunlight sparkling on the waters of Victoria Bay and around the numberless islands. The Great War in Europe, over now for nearly a year, seemed very far away and I was happy and settled in my new career in banking. In any case, as I had signed a three-year contract I couldn't accept the Air Ministry offer. Even if I could, life in the RAF would never be the same as it had been in 1918: No 207 and all the others would never be the same squadrons as they had been then; 207's personnel would have changed completely, and Ligescourt would have returned to being farmer's fields. As for Jeanne and her father . . . As for Harrison and Pilcher, the CO, Musgrove and Tex, the 0/400 night operations, Oscar Darke, his sister, Flight Lieutenant Hannett and Ternhill, the Fees at Stonehenge, Denham, Bolo House, the Armistice celebrations, the Spanish 'flu epidemic . . . Memories began to crowd in on me — happy ones, sad ones, heroic ones, tragic ones . . .

I looked at my watch. It was time to go to the bank. I would write to the Air Ministry when I returned, thanking them for their offer.

Bibliography

The War in the Air, Vol VI, H A Jones (OUP, 1937)

First of the Many, Alan Morris (Jarrolds Publishers [London] Ltd, 1968)

The Royal Flying Corps, Geoffrey Norris (Frederick Muller, 1965)

Handley Page Aircraft since 1907, C H Barnes (Putnam & Co, 1976)

The Struggle in the Air 1914-1918, Major Charles C Turner (Edward Arnold, 1919)

A History of the Air Ministry, C G Grey (George Allen & Unwin, 1940)

A Regional History of the Railways of Great Britain, Vol 7 The West Midlands, Rex Christiansen (David & Charles, 1973)

British Aeroplanes 1914-18, J M Bruce (Putnam & Co, 1957)

Farewell to Wings, Cecil Lewis (Temple Press Books, 1964)

To Win a War, John Terraine (Sidgwick & Jackson, 1978)

Aviator Extraordinary, The Sidney Cotton Story as told to Ralph Barker (Chatto & Windus, 1969)

Flying Clothing — The Story of its Development, Louise Greer and Anthony Harold (Airlife Publications, 1979)

Bomber Squadrons of the RAF and their Aircraft, Philip J R Moyes (Macdonald, 1964)